Mediterranean Urbanism

Besim S. Hakim

Mediterranean Urbanism

Historic Urban / Building Rules and Processes

 Springer

Besim S. Hakim
Albuquerque, NM, USA

ISBN 978-94-017-9139-7   ISBN 978-94-017-9140-3 (eBook)
DOI 10.1007/978-94-017-9140-3
Springer Dordrecht Heidelberg New York London

Library of Congress Control Number: 2014946288

Cover image: Close up view of a sector of Oia village, Santorini, that faces south towards the
Mediterranean Sea. 2013. Copyright © Raoul Kieffer (used with permission).

Printed on acid-free paper

Springer is part of Springer Science+Business Media (www.springer.com)

To Mariam

Contents

List of Figures

Acknowledgements

A book, such as this one, cannot be accomplished without the assistance of numerous individuals. I would like to thank the following: Dr. Sara Saba for her generous offer to publish her translation of the law of the *Astynomoi* that appears in Appendix 1 and for her assistance in transcribing Greek terms. Professor Vasso Tourptsoglou-Stephanidou for agreeing to publish her excellent study on Roman-Byzantine Building Regulations that is reproduced in Appendix 3, and Vera Pavlovic Loncarski for agreeing to do so on behalf of the journal *Saopstenja* published by the Institute for the Protection of Cultural Monuments of Serbia in Belgrade. The George William Hopper Law Library of the University of Wyoming College of Law for the text in Appendix 2. Professor Francesca Bocchi for information about her extensive work on historic Italian statutes. Professor Ferid Bin Sulaiman for the gift of a copy of his book that is the transcription of Ibn al-Imam's treatise from the tenth century. Jesus Padilla Gonzalez for his generosity in sharing his numerous studies about the urban and building rules of the *Alarife* institution in the sixteenth century Cordoba during our meeting, in Cordoba, in November 2004. I would like to thank Jose R. Carrillo Diaz-Pines for hosting my short visit to Cordoba and providing me with information on the urbanism of historic Cordoba. Professor Martin Torres Marquez, of the University of Cordoba, for providing links to images of historic Toledo and Cordoba.

I like to thank the following individuals for their hospitality and cooperation during the conference La Ciudad en el Occidente Islamico Medieval, first session: La Medina Andalusi, held at the

Escuela de Estudios Arabes in Granada, Spain, November 2004, in which I presented my work: Dr. Julio Navarro Palazon, Pedro Jimenez Castillo, Antonio Orihuela Uzal, and Javier Garcia-Bellido.

A number of individuals assisted me in providing reliable translations to English of important studies in the following languages: Caterina Basba from Greek, Tiziana Destino from Italian, Giovanni de Venuto from Latin, Dr. Benito Quintana and Dr. Jaime Gelabert from Spanish, Dr. Jenny Quillien from French, and Professor Nikos Salingaros for clarifying text from a Greek manuscript.

I would also like to thank the University of New Mexico Interlibrary Loan Service for help in finding sources. The individuals and libraries that were very helpful in the early 1990s are acknowledged on page 22 of my published study on Julian of Ascalon's treatise (Hakim 2001), which is cited in the references of Chap. 1.

Sources for the illustrations are acknowledged in the caption for each figure. In addition, I am grateful to Raoul Kieffer, owner of the website: http://www.raoul-kieffer.net, for granting me permission to use some of his wonderful photos in this book.

For the encouragement to keep working on this project to meet the publisher's deadline, I thank my eldest daughter Lena Hakim. I also thank my wife, Mariam Bashayan, for providing a working environment to research and write this book and for earlier published studies since the early 1990s. And Dr. Robert K. Doe, Senior Publisher at Springer, for his encouragement and support during the time I was working on the manuscript for this book.

Introduction

I was aware of my interest in traditional "vernacular" urbanism in the early 1960s when I was nearing the completion of my architecture studies at Liverpool University, UK. The opportunity to pursue this interest presented itself in 1975 when I organized a studies abroad program to take ten senior architecture students from Canada to Tunisia, specifically to study the village of Sidi Bou Sa'id located 20 km northeast of the capital Tunis. That village is a great example of traditional Mediterranean architecture and urbanism. The abundant results of the students' work were published in 1978 followed by a revised edition in 2009. While in Tunisia, I also began to undertake research on the "medina," the historic district of Tunis, and managed to gather the necessary information for analysis to include it in my book *Arabic-Islamic Cities: Building and Planning Principles* published in 1986. The information presented in the book applies, with variations relative to local conditions, to the countries of North Africa from Libya to Morocco. It also provides insight to certain regions of sub-Saharan Africa such as northern Nigeria. A study of the nineteenth century rules that shaped the traditional built environment in that region was undertaken and published in 2006.

Having covered the cultures and territories located on the southern coasts of the Mediterranean Sea, my interest shifted toward its northern regions to the predominant European countries of Greece, Italy, and Spain. They were selected for this study for the following reasons: (a) in the case of Greece and Italy, rules for the built environment were authored there since before the Common Era and diffused into various regions of Europe, and in some localities, these rules are found to be still in use well into the nineteenth century; (b) the case of Spain provides insight into the interface between the earlier layer of the built environment from centuries of Islamic culture followed by the Christian era that had to deal with this vast heritage; and (c) those three countries still have standing, and continuously used, traditional patterns of built environments in the form of historic cities and numerous towns and villages.

This effort started after a lecture tour in Greece in the spring of 1992 that prompted me to study the Byzantine codes that affected the built environment. In Greece, I was made aware of the sixth century treatise of Julian of Ascalon, a Greek architect from Ascalon in Palestine. I started my work on Julian's treatise in the mid-1990s and the results were published in 2001. The importance of that treatise and its influential longevity on subsequent codes is impressive. It became a part of the efforts that Emperor Justinian instigated in the early sixth century that resulted in the *Corpus Juris Civilis* that in turn had great influence on subsequent laws in most of continental Europe. The influence is also evident in the historic codes of Greece, Italy, and Spain.

In November 2004, I was invited to make a presentation of my work on Mediterranean codes at a conference in Granada, Spain, titled "La Ciudad en el Occidente Islamico Medieval—La Medina Andalusi." From Granada, I made a visit to Cordoba, Las Alpujarras region south of Granada, and towns along the southern coast that included Salobrena and Frigiliana. While on these trips, I met a number of very helpful individuals who provided information. They are mentioned in the acknowledgements. The bulk of the information that I needed for my research to cover traditional urbanism in the northern regions of the Mediterranean Sea were not available in English. They were in Greek, Latin, Italian, Arabic, and Spanish. This posed a challenge to select those that are relevant to this book's project. The experience that I have acquired undertaking the study of Julian of Ascalon's treatise was invaluable. It taught me how to ascertain relevant material that is necessary and important to translate. Happily some of those had already been translated and available in English. I cannot claim that I have examined all relevant information, but I believe enough was included in the research to make this book possible and its contents representative of the rules and codes that are pertinent to the built environment.

To organize the book so that it would be easy to use and become a valuable reference, stand-alone appendices for each chapter were selected and grouped sequentially at the end of the book. Selection of photos and images for each chapter was based on the criteria that: (a) the oldest available the better, and (b) they were from as varied sources as possible. The figures are numbered sequentially throughout the book with the exception of the figures in Appendix 3 that are independently numbered and grouped at the end of that appendix.

The sources for the Greek chapter date from the second century B.C.E. to the nineteenth century C.E. It starts with the law of the *Astynomoi* that dates back to the second century B.C.E. in the city of Pergamon. The original is lost, but it was revived in the form of an inscription on stone in the second century C.E. when Pergamon was under the Roman rule. The stone was discovered in 1901. A German translation of the law was published in 1954 and an English version in 2012; its text is available in Appendix 1. Zeno's code from the late fifth century and Julian of Ascalon's treatise from the sixth century are discussed, and supporting material is included in Appendices 2 and 3. They are important in representing the Byzantine contribution to codes that addressed the built environment. Following that, an analysis of the Frankish *Assizes of Romania* is presented to determine how much of the Assizes addressed the local level of the built environment. The role of the church in the continuity of Byzantine law is briefly discussed followed by examples of customary laws from the islands in the Aegean Sea. Those customary rules affected building practice to the early years of the nineteenth century.

The Italy chapter is based on sources from the tenth to the fourteenth centuries C.E. The chapter concentrates on the southern regions of the country that includes sources from Calabria and Puglia for the period of tenth to twelfth centuries. This region has abundant traditional towns but scarce studies of their codes. The Greek text of the *Prochiron Legum*, a legacy of the Byzantine period in southern Italy, fills the gap and its influence in the region is evident from its stipulations. Studies of codes from the twelfth to fourteenth centuries do exist for the northern regions of Italy, particularly the extensive work on this topic by the Italian scholar Francesca Bocchi from which I have drawn. The issue of aesthetics and beauty, especially of buildings facing the public realm, is included in some of those codes. It represents top-down intervention and control that offsets the bottom-up process, which was otherwise prevalent.

The Spain chapter covers sources from the fifth to eighteenth centuries C.E. It begins with a review of the rules that specifically address the built environment in the Visigothic code, the *Liber Iudiciorum*. This is followed by a study of the earliest extant treatise from the tenth century of the Islamic period in the Iberian Peninsula that lasted seven centuries. During the late thirtieth century, an important treatise, the *Las Siete Partidas*, in its third redaction, was circulated. It can be considered as a major reference of the law and as a model code. The intent of each rule is clearly indicated and supported by the reasons for its adoption and implementation. It can be described as being a *proscriptive* code that can be responsive to the particular conditions of a locality. After the conquest of major cities from the Muslims, municipal government in each city was established and the institution of *alarife* was a part of it. *Alarife* codes were established in important cities such as Toledo, Cordoba, and Granada. The earliest that was studied by contemporary scholars is from the fifteenth century Toledo. It is fully analyzed in this chapter, followed by the *alarife* code for Cordoba that dates about a century later. Continuity of specific rules is indicated as well as highlighting new additional rules that were absent in the earlier Toledo code. The *alarife* codes embody rules that address the compact built form characteristics of the towns and cities that were inherited from the previous Islamic period, and such rules, in essence, preserved the physical qualities of these towns and cities to the nineteenth century when "modern" planning and building regulations began to replace them.

In Chap. 4/conclusions, it is demonstrated how the bulk of these codes have an underlying similar goal and intentions, their attributes ranging from the proscriptive to the prescriptive, and both these qualities might be present in the same code. I also explain the dynamic, nonlinear qualities of these codes but avoid suggesting specific design features that we can learn from so as to negate the notion that a specific urban morphology and related building typology is an essential feature for any of the codes presented in this book to operate. Nevertheless, it cannot be avoided to note that compactness of the traditional built environment, found in countries and regions around the Mediterranean Sea, was a major consideration that the codes had to address. In that sense, the codes provide the insight on how to deal with compact urban form if it is used in the contemporary era or in the future.

Finally, it should be pointed out that I deliberately avoided imposing a model that is to be used as a prism to view the rules and their characteristics. More than one model may be developed for this purpose and I leave that task to other scholars. The issues and analogies raised in Chap. 4/conclusions should be sufficient for appreciating the nature of the rules and how they impacted the processes of change and growth in the built environment. Chapter 4 may also be referred to while studying the contents of Chaps. 1, 2, and 3 and their related appendices.

Albuquerque, NM, USA   Besim S. Hakim
April 2014

Chapter 1
Greece: Sources from the Second Century B.C.E. to the Nineteenth Century C.E.

Greece and Greek civilization has a very ancient and distinguished history in the area of rules that addressed issues resulting from change and growth in the built environment. This chapter will briefly explore the pre-Byzantine period to demonstrate the type of information that is available from ancient Greece. It will concentrate only on material that is related to laws and rules addressing the built environment. It will be followed by the Byzantine period and the continuity of its influence during the Ottoman occupation of Greece, including the Cyclades islands, from 1430 to 1830 C.E. (Hupchick and Cox 2001).

George M. Calhoun, who passed away in June 1942, had prepared a manuscript on Greek legal science that was subsequently edited for publication by Francis de Zulueta (Calhoun 1944). In it he divides the historical era that spans from 800 to 30 B.C.E. into five periods: (1) primitive monarchy, extending to about 800 B.C.E.; (2) aristocracy, from about 800 to 650 B.C.E.; (3) age of lawgivers, from about 650 to 500 B.C.E.; (4) Athenian democracy, from 503 to 338 B.C.E.; and (5) Hellenistic period from 338 to 30 B.C.E. During the first period, the law was based on customs, i.e., customary law whose principle sources were Homeric poems. The sources for customary law during the second period were Hesiodic poems and Homeric hymns. In the former period, one of the fundamental rights established and protected was ownership, inherent primarily in the household, the family, and vested in the head of the household as trustee and representative. In the latter

---

A part of this chapter are Figs. 1.1–1.11 and Appendices 1–3.

B.S. Hakim, *Mediterranean Urbanism: Historic Urban / Building Rules and Processes*, DOI 10.1007/978-94-017-9140-3_1,
© Springer Science+Business Media Dordrecht 2014

1

period, pronouncements and decisions continued to be based on customs. However, it became more akin to law by the recording of existing customary law. Hesiod influenced this transition by what he had to say about justice and injustice, so as to counter the natural tendency on the part of judges to construe the unwritten law in the interest of the ruling class (Calhoun 1944).

The third period that Calhoun describes is the age of lawgivers; the first written codes were not intended to change age-old customs but to publish it and thereby prevent its misapplication or distortion in particular cases. Thus, the law was no longer intangible and inviolate but has become a product and instrument of human thought and purpose. Dracon of Athens is on record to be the earliest jurist who has left an authentic record in the legal history of Europe. He was chosen in 621 B.C.E. as special commissioner to record the law, and the course of legal development that begins with his legislation can be followed through the work of his successors, Solon and Clisthenes to Athenian democracy (Calhoun 1944, p. 23).

Dracon was by birth a member of the ruling class who alone had knowledge of the customary law. Ancient writers are agreed that Dracon did not introduce new elements but only recorded customary law as he knew it, and his code may have been in part a systematization of laws already sporadically reduced to writing. His codification was followed by a period of factional strife within the ruling class. By 594 B.C.E., the situation had become so acute that the only alternative to revolution was compromise, and in that year Solon was made head of the government, *archon*. As the case with Dracon, Solon's selection as sole legislator is evidence that he was learned in the law. He was regarded by the ancients as the author of important innovations. He was born circa 630 B.C.E. and died in the year 560 at the age of 70.

No original copy of Solon's laws was found, but information is available from the writings of historians Herodotus (484–425 B.C.E) and Plutarch (46–120 C.E.), each having stated that they saw copies of the originals. For example, Solon's laws about farm and land laws and about planting address issues related to human settlements. The following extract is from Plutarch's history of Solon, written in 75 C.E., as translated by John Dryden:

> Since the country has but few rivers, lakes, or large springs, and many used wells which they had dug, there was a law made, that, where there was a public well within a hippicon, that is, four furlongs, all should draw at that;

but when it was farther off, they should try and procure a well of their own; and if they had dug ten fathoms deep and could find no water, they had liberty to fetch a pitcherful of four gallons and a half in a day from their neighbours'; for he thought it prudent to make provision against want, but not to supply laziness. He showed skill in his orders about planting, for any one that would plant another tree was not to set it within five feet of his neighbour's field; but if a fig or an olive not within nine; for their roots spread farther, nor can they be planted near all sorts of trees without damage, for they draw away the nourishment, and in some cases are noxious by their effluvia. He that would dig a pit or a ditch was to dig it at the distance of its own depth from his neighbour's ground; and he that would raise stocks of bees was not to place them within three hundred feet of those which another had already raised. (Solon by Plutarch, 75 C.E.)

The fourth period according to Calhoun is the Athenian democracy, 503–338 B.C.E.; in this period, what is known about Greek legal thought has to do mainly with Athens. This is followed by the fifth period that Calhoun names as the Hellenistic period, 338–30 B.C.E. This is the period from which we have examples of laws that are related to the management and administration of cities. And it is the period in which Greek law and thought were later to be brought into contact with Roman law (Calhoun 1944).

The Law of the *Astynomoi*

During the Hellenistic period, the Attalids, who became the rulers of Pergamon, constructed a new capital there, situated 16 miles from the Aegean Sea on a lofty isolated hill. Their fortress and palace stood on the peak of the hill, while the town occupied the lower slopes. During the later Roman period, the city also occupied the plain below (Pergamum-EB 2007). According to Sara Saba (2012), it was probably under Eumenes II's reign of 38 years (197–159 B.C.E.) that the law of the *Astynomoi* was written and enacted, as well as the construction of nearly all of the main public buildings. There is now adequate information to cite the details of this law as a fine example of ancient Greek law and rules addressing the management of the built environment.

The actual extant text that we have today was inscribed on a stone during the second century C.E. during Hadrian's period, when Pergamon was under Roman rule, three centuries after its original composition during the Attalid period (Saba 2012). The German Archaeological Institute discovered this stone in 1901 within the lower agora of Pergamon. The stone documents the text of the original Attalid period and was not inscribed on the stone by a public body but by an individual as dedication either during or after his term as one of the *Astynomoi* (Pitt 1999). Klaffenbach's commentary on the law, published in 1954, represented a watershed in the history of studies of the *Astynomoi* law (Klaffenbach 1954; Saba 2012). Klaffenbach's opinion is that the law was reinscribed three centuries later because it was still valid in the management and administration of Pergamon. This view is corroborated by various sources that testify that the institution of the *Astynomoi* existed in the second century C.E. The basic tasks of this institution in the Roman period seem to be similar as it was in the Hellenistic period as indicated by Papinian in the Digest 43.10.1 [1–5] whose life span was 142–212 C.E. Here is Papinian's description of the duties of the city overseers, which is the equivalent of the *Astynomoi* institution, as published in the Digest (Alan Watson, translator of the Digest of Justinian 1985):

> *Care of cities*: The city overseers are to take care of the streets of the city, so that they are kept level, so that houses are not damaged by overflows, and so that there are bridges where they are needed. (1) And they are to take care that private walls and enclosure walls of houses facing the street are not in bad repair, so that the owners should clean and refurbish them as necessary. If they do not clean or refurbish them, they are to fine them until they make them safe. (2) They are to take care that nobody digs holes in the streets, encumbers them, or builds anything on them. In the case of contravention, a slave may be beaten by anyone who detects him, a freeman must be denounced to the overseers, and the overseers are to fine him according to law and make good the damage. (3) Each person is to keep the public street outside his own house in repair and clean out the open gutters and ensure that no vehicle is prevented from access. Occupiers of rented accommodation must carry out these repairs themselves if the owner fails to do so and deduct their expenses from the rent. (4) They must see to it that nothing is left outside workshops, except for a fuller leaving out clothing to dry, or a carpenter putting out wheels; and these are not by doing so to prevent a vehicle from passing. (5) They are not to allow anyone to fight in the streets, or to fling dung, or to throw out any dead animals or skins.

The following are some relevant observations by E. J. Owens (1991). Laws addressed three main areas: first, those that defined the relationship between the state and the individual and the responsibility of the latter to the community; second, relations between the individual and his neighbors; and third, the general health and well-being of citizens and the overall maintenance of the city. Encroachment onto public streets was a serious problem. Rules were established for the width of streets. Overhanging balconies, illegal dumping, and digging of drains and cesspits created problems for the pedestrian. At Athens, for example, Hippias (ruler of Athens during 527–510, died 490 B.C.E.) taxed overhanging balconies and doors and shutters that opened outward onto the street (Owens 1991).

Rules also addressed an individual's responsibility to his neighbors. For example, in the law of the *Astynomoi* of Pergamon, there are sections on party walls and related problems of adjoining properties (see Appendix 1, Col. III, lines 112, 116, 121, 123, and 127). Steeply sloping terrain compounded problems as in Pergamon, such as damage to neighboring properties from water. The law specifically allowed property owners at a lower level to build a second wall on the neighbor's property if vacant so as to create a gap for drainage purposes called *peristaseis*, which had to be covered, and the space above it remained as part of the owner of the land (see Appendix 1, Col. III, lines 132, 136, 142, 144, and 149). The drainage of rainwater on such steep slopes was an issue affecting the well-being of citizens and the overall maintenance of the city. Thus, the *Astynomoi* had the legal right to inspect private cisterns and *peristaseis* and to report his findings, in the form of a list of cisterns inspected, and turn this over to the office of the *strategoi*, the *archeion* (Pitt 1999).

I will now show how the public and private spheres intertwined and the underlying principles that are inherent in the law.

The public sphere in the law included streets, public fountains, and latrines. The underlying principles were as follows: (1) There should be respect for the right of way; (2) public fountains and latrines are for public use, and everybody should avoid damaging them; and (3) there are occasions when responsibility is shared between the public and private spheres.

Streets

Lines 23–38: Minimum width of streets. Twenty cubits for main suburban roads that connect one destination to another. Eight cubits for all other streets, unless there are existing pathways for access (a cubit is about 0.46 cm).

Lines 29 to end of Col. I: Maintenance of streets is the responsibility of those abutting them. When necessary, owners of property abutting streets must work together for repairs.

Lines 72–86: Damaging streets are prohibited, such as digging for rubble or stones, removing bricks, or uncovering conduits. Those who do are subject to fines and are ordered to restore things to their previous condition.

Fountains

Lines 172–175: Responsibilities of the *Astynomoi* toward public fountains.

Lines 176–179: Implementation of procedures for maintenance of public fountains.

Lines 180–183: Things that are not allowed in public fountains, such as water animals, wash clothes or vessels, or any other such use of the fountain.

Lines 184–186 and Lines 187–202: Level of fines as determined if the person committing the damage to the fountain is a free person or a slave.

Latrines

Lines 233–235: The *Astynomoi* is responsible for the maintenance of public latrines including their conduits and their covers.

The private sphere in the law included common walls, cisterns, and *peristaseis*. The underlying principles were (1) interdependence between neighbors such as issues relating to common walls and (2) accepting the intrusion of public authorities into the private realm to ensure safety of the public at large, such as the inspection of cisterns and *peristaseis*. According to the law, the *peristaseis* is a ditch dug along the wall of a house and located at a lower level but could be built only if free space (such as a courtyard) was available on the higher level. The ditch was not supposed to be wider than one cubit and had to be covered with stone copings. It would act as a catchment for rainwater running from higher ground down the slope, and then the water would most probably be channeled to a cistern.

Common Walls

Lines 112–115: On equal use of the wall—when a common wall is in need of repair and the neighbors use the wall in the same way, then they shall contribute equally to its repair.

Lines 116–120: On unequal use of the wall (condition A)—if one house abuts the wall, while the neighbor's house is detached from it, then the former is responsible for two-thirds of the cost for repair or construction, and the balance of one-third is the responsibility of the other.

Lines 121–122: On unequal use of the wall (condition B)—when one neighbor has two floors using the wall, while the other has one floor. The responsibility is the same as in condition A.

Lines 127–131: Permission is necessary from the other neighbor if one of the neighbors wants to cut through the wall or build onto it.

Lines 159–162: It is prohibited to damage someone's wall or a common wall by digging trenches adjacent to the wall.

Lines 163–165: If an owner files charges against his neighbor, then the *Astynomoi* shall investigate and make a fair determination.

Cisterns

Note: The use and maintenance of cisterns represent a good example for the interface of the responsibilities of the private and public sectors. Although most cisterns in Pergamon were within the private realm, they had to be accessible for inspection by the *Astynomoi* due to their importance for collecting rainwater that is flowing down the slopes of the city.

Lines 203–208: The *Astynomoi* was responsible for keeping a record of all existing cisterns.

Lines 208–211: Owners of cisterns must keep them waterproof, and no owner of a cistern is allowed to discontinue its use by filling it with earth.

Lines 212–232: Explains the procedures for enforcing the water-proofing and maintenance of cisterns and the procedures, when applicable, for administering fines.

Other issues covered by the law of the *Astynomoi* at Pergamon, from the transcribed stone that was discovered in 1901, can be found in the translated edition by Sara Saba (2012). It is included in its entirety in Appendix 1.

Zeno's Code and Julian of Ascalon's Treatise

From the second century C.E., we move to the next important source, i.e., about 350 years later, during the early Byzantine period. The period from the late fifth to the mid-sixth century is important, covering the reigns of the Emperors Zeno (A.D. 474–491), Anastasius I (A.D. 491–518), Justin I (A.D. 518–527), and Justinian I (A.D. 527–565). The law of Emperor Zeno, who reigned during the years 474 to 491 C.E., is of interest to this study. It concerns private buildings and was enacted between the years 476 and 479 and recorded in the Code of Justinian (C.8.10.12) in Greek. See Appendix 2 for an English rendition. It is a corpus of building codes for the city of Constantinople addressed to the city's prefect Adamantius. However, with a new edict in 531, Justinian extended its initially local application throughout the Byzantine Empire, to be applied when the new law did not oppose existing customary laws of a province. In such instances, the old customary law was to be applied (C. 8. I0.13). Zeno's code is cited, and its application is discussed in Appendix 3 titled: "The Roman-Byzantine Building Regulations" by Vasso Tourptsoglou-Stephanidou (2000). For example, Zeno's laws, particularly those related to the preservation of mountain views and the construction of new balconies facing the public realm, influenced related stipulations in Julian of Ascalon's work that is discussed below.

The next example of important coding within the Byzantine era was composed within the years 531–533 C.E. in Greek by architect Julian of Ascalon in Palestine. It was very influential on later laws that dealt with construction and building issues. A detailed study of this treatise and its applications was published by this author (Hakim 2001). Based on available evidence, Julian's treatise was disseminated as part of the *Book of the Eparch* in Constantinople, 377 years after it was written in Ascalon. In 1345, in Thessaloniki, it was included in book two of the six books of laws of the *Hexabiblos*. Its author, Constantine Armenopoulos, was a fourteenth-century jurist; he is identified with a document signed by him in 1345, indicating his title as judge of Thessaloniki. From then on, it spread wherever the *Hexabiblos* was adopted and used, particularly in Greece, where it survived well into the twentieth century, as well as in many Slavic countries. In brief, Julian of Ascalon's treatise, written during the years 531–533 C.E., was resurrected at least two times, approximately 400 years apart, a span of 812 years after its authorship. Its influence endured a span of about 1,400 years. It is because of its widespread impact and longevity within the eastern Mediterranean that the treatise is important.

Here are highlights from Julian's goals and intentions (Hakim 2001): The goal of Julian's treatise is to deal with *change* in the built environment by ensuring that *minimum damage* occurs to preexisting structures and their owners, through stipulating fairness in the *distribution of rights and responsibilities* among various parties, particularly those who are proximate to each other. This ultimately will ensure the *equitable equilibrium* of the built environment during the process of change and growth. Julian's intentions can be grouped in seven categories:

1. Change in the built environment should be accepted as a natural and healthy phenomenon. In the face of ongoing change, it is necessary to maintain an equitable equilibrium in the built environment.
2. Change, particularly that occurring among proximate neighbors, creates potential for damages to existing dwellings and other uses. Therefore, certain measures are necessary to prevent changes or uses that would (a) result in debasing the social and economic integrity of adjacent or nearby properties, (b) create conditions adversely affecting the moral integrity of the neighbors, and (c) destabilize peace and tranquility between neighbors.

3. In principle, property owners have the freedom to do what they please on their own property. Most uses are allowed, particularly those necessary for a livelihood. Nevertheless, the freedom to act within one's property is constrained by preexisting conditions of neighboring properties, neighbors' rights of servitude, and other rights associated with ownership for certain periods of time.

4. The compact built environment of ancient towns, such as Ascalon, necessitates the implementation of interdependence among citizens, principally among proximate neighbors. As a consequence of interdependence, it becomes necessary to allocate responsibilities among such neighbors, particularly with respect to legal and economic issues.

5. It is desirable to maintain a built environment that will uplift the spirit of its inhabitants. Certain views should be preserved, especially those that give pleasure to the beholder or bear cultural significance. Making use of the bounties of nature within one's property, such as collecting rainwater and planting fruit trees and vineyards, is encouraged.

6. The use of improved building materials and construction techniques is encouraged, as their utilization will reduce the burden of preventive setbacks from property boundaries and thus maximize the potentials of the land.

7. The public realm must not be subjected to damages that result from activities or waste originating in the private realm or from the placement of troughs for animals.

This author developed a framework of five categories to analyze the technical aspects of Julian's treatise: land use (including baths, artisanal workshops, and socially offensive uses), views (both for enjoyment and those considered a nuisance), houses and condominiums (involving acts which debase the value of adjacent properties, walls between neighbors, and condominiums in multistory buildings and those contiguous with porticoes), drainage (of rainwater and wastewater), and planting (of trees, shrubs, and other vegetation). For details of the numerous cases that are included in Julian's treatise, please refer to Hakim (2001).

Five conclusions are discussed in the referenced study. The following is a discussion of the fifth conclusion regarding the nature of the Julian's rules. It concerns the nature of codes and rules that are *prescriptive* versus those that are *proscriptive*. This issue is rarely raised in studies of the history of construction codes or laws promulgated for construction or urban development. Yet, the distinction between prescriptive and proscriptive stipulations has profound implications for their use and the outcome they generate in the built environment. Prescription is the laying down of authoritative rules or directions, usually associated with a central administration that has jurisdiction over the area where the rules will be imposed. It is a top-down mechanism designed by officials who may or may not be familiar with the area in question. Such stipulations, by their very nature, dictate absolute solutions to a problem regardless of the local conditions.

Proscriptive rules, on the other hand, tend to allow freedom of action and initiative within a framework of prohibitions, for example, the freedom to make changes to one's property provided no damage is inflicted on a neighbor. Due to their flexible framework, proscriptive codes tend to evolve over long periods of time and rely on accumulated experience. They are in part associated with customary laws, and the prohibitions they assume tend to overlap with the predominant (largely religious) value and ethical system of the community. Due to the community roots of proscriptive rules, they need to be viewed as a bottom-up system of self-regulation and thus democratic in spirit (Hakim 2001).

Most of the stipulations in Julian's treatise are prescriptive, some more so than others. This is a major difference from earlier Roman laws for the built environment, which were more proscriptive.

It is over fourteen centuries since the time of Julian's treatise. Despite its rigid prescriptive nature, we find that its influence survived well into the first decades of the twentieth century, within the former Byzantine cultural sphere. This longevity is not necessarily due to the adaptability of the treatise to changing conditions in various periods and geographic locations, but rather to the importance attached to the continuity of certain Byzantine traditions that persisted well into the long period of Ottoman rule. Nevertheless, Julian's treatise is more than a regional document; it provides us with numerous lessons about building and urban codes in general, as well as with insights into the nature of those codes.

The Frankish Period and the *Assizes of Romania*

Before explaining the role of the church in the continuity of Byzantine law and presenting examples of local customary rules in selected Greek islands in the Aegean, I would like to review briefly the role and influence, if any, of the *Assizes of Romania* on those customary rules. It is mentioned by some scholars that during the Frankish period in mainland Greece, named Morea, and the Cyclades, named the Duchy of the Archipelago, the Assizes influenced subsequent customary laws (Marmaras 2008). I have explored this feudal code that is composed of 219 articles (Topping 1949) and discovered that none of the articles directly address issues related to the built environment at the settlement or building levels. In general, the Assizes cover the following issues:

> They reflect, for example, a remarkable development of the community of goods between spouses; precariousness and revocability seem to distinguish several types of grants; there is an unusual treatment of the subject of investiture and seizin; the treatment of wardship – conjugal as well as that of minors – is rather detailed; and the miscellaneous provisions relating to procedure and justice suggest a vigorous development of baronial jurisdictions". And the author of the Assizes "...has left us an honest recording of the law he knew, and it is this record of northern French law of the early thirteenth century as implanted and preserved in conquered Morea that justifies our viewing the *Assizes of Romania* as a 'typical' code which reflects a good deal of western feudal practice before it has been changed under the influence of the growing royal administration and of the ideas of Roman law. (Topping 1949)

However, the following topics in the Assizes, identified by article number, do have an indirect effect on the tenure and usage of land and property:

94—How no person can construct a castle in the principality without the permission of the prince.

103—How a ward, after he has been invested with his land, can grant his movable goods.

110—How the land remains to the wife when, her husband having died, she is left with a child.

159—How pastures and hunting lands of the subjects of the prince are common.

182—How a serf who has remained on the land of a vassal for thirty years becomes his serf.

184—What happens when a serf has planted a vine on the land of
another vassal.

214—If a vassal has sown seed in another's land and has not paid
the *zemuro* to the lord of the land... (*zemuro* is the Greek term
meaning the portion of the crop given by the cultivator to the
proprietor of the land).

It should be noted that the knights that accompanied Geoffrey II
de Villehardouin (ca. 1228–1246 C.E.) came from France, from Bur-
gundy, and above all from Champagne. These regions of France are
contiguous to each other and to the county of Beauvais. The latter's
customary codes are known to us from the extensive work titled the
Coutumes de Beauvaisis by Philippe de Beaumanoir, who completed
his compilation in 1283 C.E. This compilation does include issues
addressing the built environment directly, and it is highly probable
that the knights that went to the Levant were familiar with these types
of codes and the issues they covered as documented by Beaumanoir.
I will indicate a few examples: from chapter 24 on customs, article 706
on issues related to walls between adjacent neighbors, article 708 on
how to avoid overlooking into a neighbor's private yard, article 709 on
issues related to the freedom of building higher on one's property and
its implication on neighbors, and article 710 on excavating without
creating any damage to adjacent properties and to the public road. And
from chapter 25 on highways, article 719 on types of roads based on
their widths, articles 720 and 724 on restoring the width of a narrowed
road to its original width and the responsibility is on those who own
property on either side of the road, and article 735 on the expected
behavior while using roads. In Chapter 50 on Communes, article 1518
addresses the allocation of uses in the town, and other articles in this
chapter address management, administration, accounting, and taxes
(Akehurst's 1992 translation of Beaumanoir's *Coutume de Beauvaisis*,
1283 C.E.). Note that article numbers are sequential within chapters 1
through 70 of Beaumanoir's compilation.

Role of the Church in the Continuity of Byzantine Law

Before examining examples of local customary laws that relate to
land and buildings, the following are excerpts from a study by
Pantazopoulos that explain the role of the church during the Ottoman

period in maintaining the continuity of Byzantine law (Pantazopoulos 1967). The Ecumenical Patriarch maintained his position as the supreme leader of Orthodoxy and became the political authority of all tax-bound Christians within the Ottoman Empire. The Patriarch had autonomy and self-sufficiency that the church enjoyed as a religious institution within the limits of Islamic law. "The recognition of rights for life, property, free practice of religion . . . has been customarily in force for economic, religious and political reasons in the area of the Mediterranean and the Near East, since the second millennium B.C.E. These privileges are usually granted in exchange for economic returns" (Pantazopoulos 1967). In principle, what was actually recognized were the following: (a) the right of the free practice of religion, the maintenance of churches, and the freedom to use the native language; (b) the jurisdiction of the Patriarch over all disputes between Christians that are related to religious issues such as marriage, divorce, wills, etc.; and (c) the exemption of the Patriarch and all bishops from taxation, although Christian subjects had to pay the annual tax according to stipulations in Islamic law. These privileges were expressly confirmed by Sultan Mehmed II, the Conqueror of Constantinople, when he officially addressed the first Patriarch, Gennadius Scholarius: "Be the Patriarch in happiness and have our friendship on anything you wish and enjoy all your privileges, as all the Patriarchs before you also had" (Pantazopoulos 1967).

The texts used by the clergy for applying the patriarchal law, including the handling of civil cases, were the *Hexabiblos* compiled by the judge of Thessaloniki Constantine Armenopoulos in 1345 C.E. and the *Nomocanon* of Manuel Malaxos, compiled in the city of Thebes in central Greece in 1561 C.E. Until the mid-eighteenth century, the *Nomocanon* prevailed in practice partly because it was written in the spoken language. However, the church tended to extend its jurisdiction into the area of private law that forced it to turn to the most complete of the two texts, the *Hexabiblos*. For this reason in 1744 C.E., Alexius Spanos, prompted by the Archbishop of Heraclea Gerasimos, published in Venice the *Hexabiblos*, and it supplanted the *Nomocanon*. Its use was very extensive by the clergy that within 90 years, from 1744 to 1834 C.E., it had been published in Venice eight times. With the influence of the clergy, the *Hexabiblos* was officially introduced in the newly independent Greece and was valid to 1946 when the new Civil Code introduced the legal regime that was formed during the Greek revolution with the laws of the memorable Christian emperors. Thus, the *Hexabiblos* became the preeminent Greek legal text, and it continued to be used in Greece for 202 years, i.e., from 1744 to 1946 C.E.

As mentioned above, the *Hexabiblos* incorporated Zeno's laws pertaining to private buildings and most of the stipulations in the treatise of Julian of Ascalon. This is apparent in many examples of customary law in Greece and the Cycladic islands during the Ottoman period that related to building activities. Communities that had their own customary laws in the islands of the Aegean Sea (Mykonos, Syros, Naxos, Amorgos, Kythnos, Paros, and Thira) and elsewhere exerted an effort to limit the judicial jurisdiction of the church as expressed in the clause: the clergy is not to meddle in the differences of the community. This clause or something similar was found in the codified customs of Thira-Anafi (1797), Kythnos (1799), and Naxos (1852) (Pantazopoulos 1967).

Examples of Customary Laws from Islands in the Aegean Sea

I will now present examples of customary rules that were prevalent on the islands of Naxos, Syros, Santorini, and the village of Elymbos on the island of Karpathos during the Ottoman period. These islands were selected due to the availability of relevant information (Figs. 1.1 – 1.11).

The Frankish occupiers were confronted with the local customary laws in the islands they controlled. These customary laws had their origin in Byzantine law, especially the codes that were in the *Ecloga* of Leo III published in March 726 C.E. (Vasiliev 1952). In the early years of the Frankish period, the occupiers were indifferent to the local codes that continued to be followed by the people provided they did not contradict the laws of the *Assizes of Romania* that was eventually introduced by the Franks. For example, when there was a dispute between the people on the island of Syros, such problems were resolved by a process of arbitration conducted by arbitrators. The customary laws that were enforced locally influenced the legal awareness of the people in the Cyclades, and this was apparent toward the end of the Frankish occupation as a number of the islanders served as attendants to the local judges when they settled disputes (Drakakis 1967).

Some of the institutions that impacted the built environment and that were in place before the Ottoman period began in 1430 C.E. are:

Ownership by story: This means that each floor of a building can be owned by a different party, and for the purposes of access to air and light, the roofs of a lower building built below another on a slope can be used as a terrace of the upper floor. This necessity evolved due to the compactness of the settlements on the islands. Such a feature of the built environment evolved as a defensive measure against raids by pirates that were common in those centuries. The outer ring of the settlement was of contiguous houses that had few windows on their outer walls, and together they formed a defensive wall. Settlements in general were built on top of hills or on higher ground. The institution of ownership by story was firmly established by the end of the Frankish occupation and continued into the Turkish period and even after the liberation of Greece (Drakakis 1967).

Ownership of trees planted on land belonging to a third party: This institution has a long history in the Eastern Mediterranean during the Hellenistic period and was recognized in the agricultural law, also known as the Rural Code or Farmer's Law, that was issued about the same time as the *Ecloga* in the early eighth century (Vasiliev 1952). It was later included in the *Hexabiblos* of Armenopoulos. It is also included in the *Assizes of Romania* in articles 184 and 214. This institution is still enforced today in the islands.

Party walls: The rules for the use, ownership, and maintenance of party walls were addressed by many codes in the Near East region. In the case of Greek history, the issue was clearly addressed in the Hellenistic laws of Pergamon and in other towns (see Appendix 1). The Franks were also familiar with such rules in the regions of France where they came from. Beaumanoir includes rules for party walls in paragraph 706 of his compilation titled *Coutumes de Beauvaisis* of 1283 as indicated earlier. Drakakis discusses in detail the issues of party walls during the Ottoman period. Here is a synopsis as translated into English from the Greek:

A great number of disputes and quarrels occurred about whether those buildings on land of their own did or did not have the right to lean on an already existing wall of the adjoining house, particularly when the wall was built on land belonging to a third party. Party walls were acknowledged as such when there was no land separating it from the adjoining site. Custom dictated that any wall separating adjoining properties, regardless of who was the owner on whose land the wall is built, can be shared by allowing permission to lean on it by either party on each side. An example of a court decision dated 19 January, 1777 was that the commissioner decided that Mihelis, who was in the process of building, should be permitted to let his beams rest on the wall built by Marinos, but Mihelis should pay for half the party wall, as is the common custom. Compensation was usually estimated not on the total cost of the party wall, but on the basis of the value of its part that the adjacent party would use, even when the need to use it was at a later date. The compensation would also include the cost of the foundations. Drakakis also mentions a judgment that was issued on 14 December, 1826 that is related to owners of lower and upper levels of a building that involves the permission for the lower level owner to use a wall that is owned by the owner of the upper level. (Drakakis 1967)

The Turks in the eighteenth century provided the people of the island of *Syros* with many freedoms, the most important of which was the transfer of the island's administration during the period 1779–1803 to the *Demogerontia* (Council of Elders). Drakakis gives a picture of the self-administrative structure and its components as:

1. The assembly of the community in which all men who reached the age of 30 years took part and usually held outside in the square of the Catholic church of Aghios Ioannis and which developed into a legislative body.
2. Two to four individuals forming the council served for one year. They were selected from the community's assembly and confirmed by the Turkish authorities.
3. The elders, who were former council members, were also selected by the community's assembly, and they cooperated in various administrative and judicial activities of the community. Due to the granting of these freedoms, Drakakis concludes that Turkish law had no influence on the formation of common law on Syros and the islands of the Cyclades (Drakakis 1967).

For another example, we turn to the island of *Naxos*. The information presented relies on the work by Della-Rocca (Della-Rocca 1968). After the fall of the Venetian Duchy of Naxos, the island constituted a small and unimportant part of the Ottoman Empire, and very few Turks settled on it. The only Turkish presence was a governor and sometimes a Turkish judge and few Turkish police. A local administrative structure developed in the form of the "Commons" and the "Council of the Elders." Until recently, no written evidence was found about the laws that were enforced to the end of the eighteenth century; only unwritten customary codes were operational and transmitted across generations. However, in 1805 C.E., the elders of Naxos collected and put in writing the historic customary codes that were operational on the island. Panayotis Mourouzis, the interpreter of the Turkish fleet, entrusted this collection to scholar/monk Ilarion who classified and corrected the text, and it was then submitted to the elders and other eminent Naxians for validation. On June 15, 1810, this collection of codes was ratified by them and became the Civil Code of Naxos. Della-Rocca mentions that due to the difficulty of accessing copies of this code, he decided to publish it. The title of the code is "Laws for the inhabitants of the island of Naxos" (Della-Rocca 1968). Here are extracts that relate to issues of the built environment, by article number, as listed under the subheading "On building and reconstructing":

69—When a house located on a street risks collapse and might block passage, its owner is obliged to repair it or to pull it down so that there is no risk of sudden collapse that might kill somebody. Or the owner can sell it to a third party with the condition that it will be repaired or pulled down. (It is obvious here that what is referred to as a house is most likely a wall of a building adjoining a public street).

70—The lower and upper levels of a house are owned by different parties, and if the lower level is deemed to collapse and would cause the upper level to also collapse, the owner of the upper level can summon the owner of the lower level to court and force him to repair it or to cede it to himself so that he can repair it. The same conditions apply to contiguous neighbors.

71—The owner of a lower level unit is not allowed to open a door or window as it might damage the walls of the upper unit. However, the owner of the lower unit can open a door or window if it is exactly below a door or window in the wall of the upper unit, provided he makes it narrower on each side by six fingers (about 10 cm). In addition, the owner of the lower unit is liable to pay damages to the owner of the upper unit if within one month the unit above suffers damage due to the new opening in the lower unit. [This rule has precedence in the sixth-century treatise of Julian of Ascalon that is 1277 years earlier. Julian also specifies six fingers on each side but allows two months for any damage to show in the upper unit (Hakim 2001)].

72—A door or window is not allowed to be opened that overlooks a neighbor's private areas, if that neighbor does not wish it.

73—Neighbors on opposite sides of a public street cannot prevent each other from undergoing construction as one of the neighbors pleases, including if he wants to build another story.

74—When construction occurs adjacent to the boundary of a public street, the elders of the community must ensure that no encroachment on the street's right of way occurs. If it does and the party responsible refuses to respect this rule, then he must be punished.

75—On undeveloped steep sites that do not include public access or any other use for the public, a private party has the right to appropriate such a site by removing the weeds and making it useful and by notifying the Chancery to obtain a document to prove that the site is now owned by its reviver. However, if the site does contain a road used by the public or is necessary for public access in any way, then it shall remain as it is, untouched and uncultivated, forever.

The customary codes of Naxos also contain 14 articles on rules related to selling and buying, 2 articles on bartering, and 4 articles on votive offerings and donations.

For example, from the famous island of **Santorini**, whose settlements are located on steep slopes overlooking the sea, the following rules are extracted from the sections on "rights" and on "sites and boundaries" (Danezis, 1939–1940: pp. 197–198). They are organized by this author according to topic, and the original article number is indicated in brackets:

On rights:

1 (Article 1): Rights of ownership of land and the right to build on it can sometimes belong to two separate parties.

2 (Article 11): Rights of opening windows must take into considerations determined by the site. When necessary, the Council of

Elders can ascertain conditions imposed by the site to avoid any potential damage to the neighbors.

3 (Article 1 on Rights): Fifteen years are the span of time related to rights of worldly matters, and thirty years relate to rights of church matters.

4 (Article 2 on Rights): If (A) enjoys something for fifteen years without claims by anybody, and if after that time period (B) wants to claim it, then (B) has no right to it.

5 (Article 3 on Rights): Revenue from real property cannot be claimed after the passage of fifteen years during which time no claim was made.

6 (Article 12): Steep slopes and mountains are considered public property, and nobody has any right to them.

7 (Article 13): However, if (A) is granted permission by the community to plant and create a garden on a steep slope, then (A) cannot prevent anybody else from removing stones from the steep slope. Free passage must also be allowed if people cannot find an alternative access route.

On (troglodytic) dugout houses:

8 (from Article 3): When house (A) is located next to a dugout house (B), then (A) cannot extend his house by disturbing the foundations of house (B).

9 (from Article 5): When house (A) is located below house (B) and house (A) is damaged creating potential danger to house (B) above, then the owner of house (B) can demand that the owner of (A) repair the damage or cede the house to him. The same rules apply to houses that are contiguous to each other and are on the same level.

10 (from Article 6): It is not allowed to plant vines or trees on top of dugout houses or cisterns as the roots may cause damage to the house and the one below it if they are on top of each other.

On public streets:

11 (Article 7): Public streets must not be made narrower by adjacent construction or renovations.

12 (Article 8): Placement of stones or rubble on public streets must be cleared without delay. This rule also applies to cleaning of

    public streets and restoring it to its original condition from debris
resulting from adjacent construction activities.
13 (Article 4): When a house is located on a public street and risks
    to crumble down and thereby blocks the street, then its owner is
    obliged to either repair it or donate the house to the community.
14 (Article 9): When a field or vineyard is located adjacent to a pub-
    lic street, its owner cannot claim additional access from the neigh-
    bors above, below, or at the sides.

On windmills:

15 (Article 10): When windmills are constructed first, then later
    neighbors are not allowed to build or plant trees that would
    obstruct the wind.

    The last example of codes and the generative building process is
from the village of Elymbos on *Karpathos* Island. This island is the
second largest in the Dodecanese that lies between Crete and Rhodes.
The island's Turkish period began in 1538 and continued to 1912
when it was annexed to Italy with the rest of the Dodecanese and later
became part of Greece in 1947. Settlements during the Roman and
Byzantine periods were along the coast, but subsequent generations
moved toward the interior to avoid raids by pirates and established
settlements such as Aperi, Menetes in the south of the island, and
Elymbos in the north. Dimitris Philippides undertook an extensive
study of Elymbos village for his 1973 doctorate study (Philippides
1973), followed by his shorter study on Karpathos published in 1985
(Philippides 1985). The following information is from these two
sources.

    The elders of the community of *Elymbos* came exclusively from
the rich landowning families who evolved during the Turkish period.
They were called *kanakarides*, and they had the predominant voice
at community meetings. They had power on administrative and
legislative/judicial issues that involved the oversight of how the
community's rules and building codes were followed and disputes
were resolved accordingly, even though such rules were not written
down but were known as a part of the local customary law. Each
member of the community who decided to build had to respect the
following three rules: (1) maintain unimpeded view for all buildings
(the view in the case of Elymbos was primarily of the sea), (2) must

not block access to the property of each house, and (3) allow the possibility for horizontal or vertical extension of neighboring buildings. Philippides describes the application of these rules:

> Traditionally, each resident could occupy open land on the edge of the village and proceed to build according to his needs. In such cases no restrictions were necessary. If someone decided, however, to build next to an existing structure, he had to respect his predecessor's rights to access, to an unrestricted view, and to future expansion. In the first case one could not block the direct access to another's house, but it was permitted to divert this access route slightly to fit around the newcomer's property. In the second case one could not block a neighbor's view, as defined by the front elevation of the neighbor's house. As a result, in practice newcomers' houses were built either as part of a linear development that followed the contours of the site, or as steps vertically to the contours. In the step-like arrangement the roof of the house below had to be under the level of the window sills of the house above. In the third case the property boundaries of each house extended down the slope in a vertical projection until the roof of the houses before it was reached. A newcomer was not allowed to build on this territory unless permitted by its owner. These norms were sufficient for most sites within Elymbos village, since the settlement was characterized by a steep terrain. The best preserved example of such planning regulations lies within the Exo Kamara quarter. (Philippides 1973:142)

A cross section through the Exo Kamara quarter is shown and a photo from the northwest of the quarter. It shows the typical cascading built form on the steep slope with most windows having access to the view of the sea (Figs. 1.8 and 1.9).

The custom of *allilouitheia* (mutual help) that was practiced in Elymbos as a part of their customary building process heritage reduced the possibility of conflict and acted as a self-regulating mechanism. Relatives and friends assisted in building or renovating a house, offering their labor in exchange for a party put on by the owner when the work is finished.

Despite these rules, transgressions did take place resulting in friction between people. Neighbors were attentive to what was being built or changed adjacent to their property. The possibility of solving any disputes at the local level facilitated an acceptable outcome. This is in contrast to the chaotic situation that evolved on Karpathos Island after the government of Greece abolished local construction codes in favor of the centralized codes that were introduced during the 1920s. This author has discussed the implication of centralized versus local building codes elsewhere (Hakim 2008).

References

Berger, A. (1953). Encyclopedic dictionary of Roman law. *Transactions of the American Philosophical Society, 43*(part 2), 333–806. Philadelphia: American Philosophical Society.

Blume, F. H. (1952). *Annotated Justinian Code* (Book 8–10) (2nd ed., 2008, T. G. Kearley, Ed.). University of Wyoming, College of Law. http://www.uwyo.edu/lawlib/blume-justinian/ajc-edition-2/. Accessed Sept 2013.

Calhoun, G. M. (1944). *Introduction to Greek legal science* (F. de Zulueta, Ed., Reprinted by Scientia Verlag, Aalen, 1977).

Danezis, M. (n.d.). Customary law of Thera island during the eighteenth century. In *Santorini, 1939–1940: General review of the geological, historical, social, economic, tourism and cultural evolution of the Island*, Athens (pp. 193–199) (in Greek).

de Beaumanoir, P. (1283). *Coutumes de Beauvaisis* (F.R.P. Akehurst, Trans.). Philadelphia: University of Pennsylvania Press, 1992.

Della-Rocca, I. (1968). The law of Naxos island during the years of Turkish Occupation. *Yearbook of the Society of Cycladic Studies, 7*, 426–481 (in Greek).

Doumanis, O., & Oliver, P. (Eds.). (1974). *Shelter in Greece*. Athens.

Drakakis, A. (1967). Syros island under the Turkish Occupation: The justice and the law. *Yearbook of the Society of Cycladic Studies, 6*, 63–494 (in Greek).

Ginis, D. (1966). *An outline of the Post-Byzantine law's history*, Athens (in Greek).

Hakim, B. S. (2001). Julian of Ascalon's treatise of construction and design rules from 6th c. Palestine. *Journal of the Society of Architectural Historians, 60*(1), 4–25.

Hakim, B. S. (2008). Mediterranean urban and building codes: Origins, content, impact, and lessons. *Urban Design International, 13*(1), 21–40.

Hupchick, D. P., & Cox, H. E. (2001). *The Palgrave concise historical atlas of the Balkans*. New York/Hampshire.

Klaffenbach, G. (1954). Die Astynomeninschrift von Pergamon. *Abhandlungen der Deutschen Akademie der Wissenschaften zu Berlin. Klasse fur Sprachen, Literatur und Kunst, 6*, 3–25.

Koukkou, H. (1980). *The communal institutions in the Cyclades during the Turkish Occupation*, Athens (in Greek).

Marmaras, E. (2008). Cycladic settlements of the Aegean Sea: A blending of local and foreign influences. *Planning Perspectives, 23*, 503–520.

Miller, W. (1908). *The Latins in the Levant: A history of Frankish Greece (1204–1566)*. New York.

Owens, E. J. (1991). *The City in the Greek and Roman World*. London: Routledge.

Pantazopoulos, N. J. (1967). *Church and law in the Balkan Peninsula during the Ottoman rule*, Thessaloniki.

Papas, C. (1957). *L'Urbanisme et l'Architecture Populaire dans les Cyclades*, Paris (in French).

Pergamum. (2007). *Encyclopedia Britannica 2007 ultimate reference suite,* Chicago.

Philippides, D. A. (1973). *The vernacular design setting of Elymbos: A rural spatial system in Greece.* PhD dissertation, University of Michigan.

Philippides, D. (Ed.). (1983). *Greek traditional architecture* (Aegean: Cyclades, Vol. 2). Athens: Melissa Publishing House (This volume includes chapters on nine islands: Andros, Mykonos, Naxos, Paros, Santorini, Sifnos, Syros, Keos, and Tinos).

Philippides, D. (1985). *Karapathos.* Athens: Melissa Publishing House.

Pitt, R. K. (1999). Astynomoi, law of the (Pergamon). In *The Encyclopedia of ancient history,* 1999–2013 (pp. 887–888). Wiley.

Saba, S. (2012). *The Astynomoi law from Pergamon: A new commentary.* Mainz: Verlag Antike, e.K.

Solon by Plutarch. (75 C.E.). The internet classic archive at http://classics.mit.edu/Plutarch/solon.html, 1994–2009.

Topping, P. W. (1944/1945). The formation of the Assizes of Romania. *Byzantion, 17,* 304–314.

Topping, P. W. (1949). *Feudal Institutions as revealed in the Assizes of Romania: The Law Code of Frankish Greece—Translation of the text of the Assizes with a commentary on feudal institutions in Greece and in Medieval Europe.* Philadelphia: University of Pennsylvania Press.

Tourptsoglou-Stehanidou, V. (2000). The Roman-Byzantine building regulations. *Saopstenja, 30–31,* 37–63, Belgrade.

Vasiliev, A. A. (1952). *History of the Byzantine Empire* (2 Vols.). Madison: University of Wisconsin Press.

Watson, A. (Ed. & Trans.). (1985, revised ed. 1998). *The Digest of Justinian* (2 Vols.). Philadelphia: University of Pennsylvania Press.

 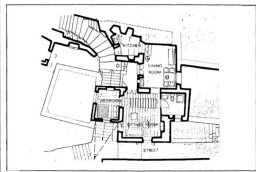

Fig. 1.1 Ano Syros, Syros: Upper and lower level houses belonging to different owners. The plan is of the upper level house showing the bedroom extending over the street and resting on the wall of the opposite neighbor with that neighbor's permission. Access to the upper level house is up the street steps and to the right. The location from which the photo is taken is indicated on the plan (Photo by Y. Skouroyannis, the plan by J. Stephanou (Philippides 1983: 221). Courtesy Melissa Publishing House, Athens)

Fig. 1.2 Naxos Chora: Air photo from the late 1940s by the Ministry of Public Works, Athens. The north direction is toward the top of the photo

Fig. 1.3 Naxos Chora: Compact built form of the Chora. The castle (*Kastro*) walls show on the upper level that was the original defensive line for the settlement (Photo taken from the northwest by Raoul Kieffer in October 2013. Permission granted by Raoul)

Fig. 1.4 Naxos: A street view in Chora showing the street passing under a *Stegasto* (room built over the street) with permission granted by the opposite neighbor because no columns are used to support the room. Access to the upper level houses is by stairs from the street. The first step shows as taking space from the street width. This is allowed by custom as long as the locally agreed minimum width of the street is maintained (Photo by Yannis Skouroyannis (Philippides 1983: 99))

Fig. 1.5 Santorini: Oia village that is located on the northern tip of the island. This photo shows the compact built form that was formed by following the rules presented and discussed in this chapter. The buildings with domes are churches. Many buildings shown are partly built directly into the face of the slope. Access to the buildings is via narrow streets, most of which have steps all along (Photo by Yann Arthus-Bertrand found on this website: http://www.yannarthusbertrand2.org. Date of photo estimated to be in the mid-1990s. Permission granted by Yann)

Fig. 1.6 Santorini: Oia. Cluster of houses and their access paths along the slope that faces the sea (Photo by Raoul Kieffer in October 2013. Permission granted by Raoul)

Fig. 1.7 Santorini: Oia.
Access paths to houses
are sometimes built
under tunnels to
negotiate the
compactness of the
village (Photo by Raoul
Kieffer in October
2013. Permission
granted by Raoul)

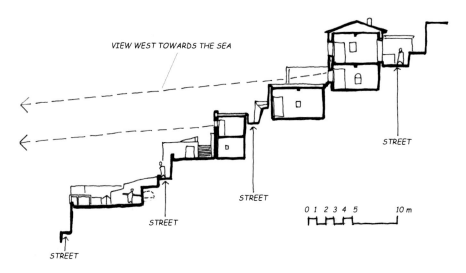

Fig. 1.8 Elymbos, Karpathos: Cross section through the quarter of Exo Kamara. The houses are stepped down along the slope that faces west and the view of the sea. The view is accessible from the windows, the streets, and the access paths (Drawing by the author after the original by Philippides (1973: 167))

Fig. 1.9 Elymbos, Karpathos: View from the northwest of the Exo Kamara quarter. The cross section in Fig. 1.8 is taken from the upper east side of the quarter down the slope toward the west (Photo by M. Vernardos (Philippides 1985:12). Courtesy Melissa Publishing House, Athens)

Fig. 1.10 Paros: This street in Paros shows the following: (1) room covering street that is supported by columns on the left indicating independent ownership of the construction by the owners of the room; (2) steps to an upper level house; (3) the left side of the street is made up of one-story houses; and (4) the mode of moving heavy items is by donkey that was an important determinant for the minimum width of streets (Photo by Constantin Papas during his trip to the region in 1953 (Papas 1957))

Fig. 1.11 Folegandros Street: Shows the following: (1) upper level houses are accessed by stairs, while lower level houses are accessed directly from the street; (2) there are two lines for building up the houses (the first line is the frontage of the houses that show up gray in the photo, and the second line is the space that allows construction of stairs); and (3) the street right of way is maintained by the second construction line for stairs, but occasionally a step or two go beyond this line. This type of intrusion becomes permanent if nobody complains within 15 years to the local community council. Maintaining and keeping the street clean are usually divided up to opposite houses along roughly the middle of the street. These types of conditions and arrangements are found in most settlements on the Greek islands (Photo by anonymous found on this web page: http://www.luxurycruises.gr/islands/big/folegandros_03.jpg)

Chapter 2
Italy: Sources from the Tenth to Fourteenth Centuries C.E.

This chapter will examine the case of Italy that has a very rich tradition of towns that were developed incrementally following simple generative rules. These towns are found on hilltops around the country and more prevalent in the south of the country, in Puglia, Calabria, and Sicily. In the important cities of the north, we also find concern, especially on the part of the municipal governments, for beauty and the establishment of rules that address this concern.

For northern cities in the Tuscany region, I have relied on the work of Wolfgang Braunfels (1953) and of Francesca Bocchi (1990). The latter scholar also covers cities in a number of other regions in central and northern Italy. Their work contains rules that are related to development procedures and rules that address matters for maintaining and improving the aesthetic beauty of a town or parts thereof. This chapter will be in two sections: the first will be about the southern regions from the tenth to the twelfth centuries, and the second will cover towns in central and northern regions during the twelfth to the fourteenth centuries.

Calabria and Puglia in the Tenth to Twelfth Centuries

To study the rules that affected the development of villages and towns in the southern regions, especially in Calabria and Puglia (Figs. 2.7–2.10), I have relied on an obscure text by the name of *Prochiron Legum* that

---

A part of this chapter are Figs. 2.1–2.10 and Appendices 4–6.

B.S. Hakim, *Mediterranean Urbanism: Historic Urban / Building Rules and Processes*, DOI 10.1007/978-94-017-9140-3_2,
© Springer Science+Business Media Dordrecht 2014

was found in the Vatican library and labeled as Vatican "Greek Codex 845." This codex comprises 40 chapters, and the chapter of immediate relevance to this study is 33 on "New Work." It contains 59 articles. Chapter 33 is reproduced in Appendix 4. I have kept the sequence and numbers of the original articles as they were originally compiled. The English translation of the original Greek is based on Edwin H. Freshfield's work (Freshfield 1931). Those 59 articles are not grouped according to a rational commensurate with urban development. To examine their content, I have regrouped them under two categories: (1) rights of ownership and responsibilities and (2) rules for land use, buildings, and access. Each of these two categories has six sections, under which the relevant articles are examined.

The "Vatican Greek Codex 845" known as the *Prochiron Legum* was first revealed by Capasso in 1867, followed by Brandileone and Puntoni's book that was published in 1895 and another study by Brandileone during the same year. Thirty-six years later, Edwin Freshfield published a monograph in 1931 that studies in detail chapter 33 of the *Prochiron Legum* (Freshfield 1931). It is during the dominion of southern Italy by the Byzantine Empire and during the reign of Basil II (976–1025) that the first edition of this codex was written. Its author is unknown. In an index to parallel passages, Freshfield clearly demonstrates the sources of chapter 33 of the codex to chapter 38 of the *Procheiros Nomos* which dates to 872 C.E. (Schminck "Prochiron," *The Oxford Dictionary of Byzantium*, 1991) abbreviated henceforth as OBD. It was assembled during the reign of Emperor Basil I (867–886 C.E.) in Constantinople. The origins of the rules can be traced back to Emperor Justinian's Book 2 of the Institutes and Book 8 of the Digest. In Freshfield's introduction, he specifically refers to the compilation of rules by architect Julian of Ascalon (Hakim 2001) during the period in which Justinian's Civil Code was being prepared. Reference to Justinian's rules appears later in the *Procheiros Nomos*, which was the main source for our codex the *Prochiros Legum*, written to be compatible with the local customs of the period in the Calabria region of Italy. More details of the history and background of the *Prochiros Legum* are included in Appendix 4.

We are interested to convey how the rules were compatible with the nature of the generative process of the built environment. The following criteria indicate the dynamic nature of the rules: (i) Change in the built environment is accepted as a natural and healthy phenomenon, (ii) in the face of change the rules attempt to maintain an equitable equilibrium in the built environment, (iii) the rules recognize earlier usage that is sometimes determined by a specific time period, (iv) the rules mitigate damage that sometimes occurs due to change, (v) the rules address a type of servitude that does not hinder the ability to build compactly, (vi) the rules recognize the necessity of interdependence between proximate neighbors, and (vii) the rules protect the public realm from damages.

The following six categories of rules relate to the *rights of ownership and responsibilities*:

- On *property ownership* (articles 33–37 and 53). Those clearly demonstrate how time, in years, is used to determine rights of ownership in the face of fraudulent attempts to acquire such ownership. These are rules that address the dynamics of change due to fraud. Periods of 10, 20, 30, and 40 years are used to determine rightful ownership, as explained in the specific articles (see Appendix 4).

- On *boundaries* (45, 49, and 50). It specifies a maximum period of 30 years for litigating a boundary (49); specific distances are indicated for various activities and uses near a neighbor's property, such as digging, building a wall, building a house, a pit, and a well, or planting of trees (45); and how a judge may solve a boundary problem (50). These rules address change due to the nature of activity near a boundary. For a specific recorded case that occurred in Salerno in the year 1044 C.E. regarding a boundary dispute, see Ramseyer (2009).

- On *streets* (9, 14, 44, and 51). Article (9) assumes a minimum of 12 feet, about 3.7 meters, between houses across a street. Based on that stipulation, the rule indicates what is allowed or disallowed for window openings, and their type, toward the street. Article (51) stipulates private responsibility toward the public to allow people access if an adjacent street is destroyed by an earthquake or by the inundation from a river. Article (44) stipulates the fine for plowing a public street.

- On *agreements* (24, 25). Agreements must be made according to law or according to established custom, and any agreement by one party to limit the fair use of another's property is not valid. This rule confirms the freedom of the use of one's property provided damage is not inflicted on neighbors.

– On *damage* (54, 59). Selling defective building materials, such as timber, that would endanger the construction of a building is a major liability for the seller, so is the damage occurring to an occupant. The party causing such damage is at fault and is liable to pay compensation. Although these two articles in the codex limit their range, the issue of damage and how to mitigate it is found in many rules, sometimes clearly stated and as an underlying assumption in other rules.

– On *punishment* (55–57). Different forms of punishment are indicated, and they are related to a person's presence or absence and when the punishment commences. The location and time aspects are considered. We find flexibility related to locality and time.

The following six categories of rules relate to **land use, buildings, and access**:

– On *new work* (1–3, 11–13). Chapter 33 of the *Prochiros Legum* is in fact titled "New Work." The first article defines a new work as follows: a person creates a new work when he rebuilds a wall or pulls it down and alters its original aspect. Clearly, this demonstrates the generative aspect of these rules. Article (13) relates to the sequence of incremental development: "Anyone who can legally raise his house can do so provided he does not impose a 'burden' on his neighbor's house. Similarly he must not impose a servitude more burdensome than is appropriate." Article (12) also demonstrates the generative nature of these rules: "Anyone desiring to build or heighten a tumbled down house must not obstruct his neighbor's light or otherwise damage him, and he can be compelled to retain the former style and plan of the original scheme of the house." This rule demonstrates changing circumstances that compels an owner to rebuild provided he does not create conditions that are damaging to the neighbor(s) such as obstructing the light and any other possible damages.

– On *neighbors* (19–21, 39, 52). These rules address issues due to the generative nature of the built environment, particularly as they relate to proximate neighbors, such as opening windows that cause damage by invasion of privacy to the neighbor and roots of trees that cause damage. Another example is the deposit of manure on a neighbor's wall without the existence of a servitude agreement that allows it. Article (52) addresses the accretion of soil due to changing flows of a river that might deposit soil on private land. The article also explains who can claim ownership of such soil deposits.

– On *jointly owned party walls* (7,10, 16–18, 29). These rules specifically address party walls between adjacent neighbors. They are all an outcome of the nature of the building process over periods of time. Article (10) specifically instructs that if both parties are joint owners of a wall, then one party cannot rebuild it without the consent of the other owner. Article (18) embodies within it the concept of the right of prevention of a potential damage from a neighbor's inclined wall. Articles (16) and (29) address what is allowed or disallowed on a party wall, such as building an oven on the wall and allowing the wall to support the stairs. Article (17) addresses vertical neighbors, i.e., neighbors who are located one over the other. A chimney that emits smoke that is considered a nuisance to the upper neighbor is not allowed unless there is a servitude that allows it. The upper neighbor is disallowed to throw garbage or dung that will harm the lower neighbor, and sources of offensive odor from either neighbor have to be prevented.

– On *servitudes* (4, 15, 26–28, 30–32, 38, 43, 46–48, 58). The concept originates in Roman law: "A servitude, an easement, *Servitutes* were classified among *iura in re aliena* (=rights over another's property) since their substance consisted in a right of a person, other than the owner, primarily the proprietor of a neighborly immovable, to make a certain use of another's land. This right was vested in the beneficiary not as a personal one, but as a right attached to the immovable (land or building) itself, regardless of the person who actually happened to own it" (Berger 1953, page 702). Berger provides further detailed explanation and definitions on various types of servitudes. Byzantine law incorporated many of these concepts, and these concepts and related rules spread to territories that were subject to Byzantine rule or influence. In the case of the *Prochiros Legum*, the 14 articles, listed above, address servitudes directly. These rules impact many aspects of the generative nature of traditional built environments, and its legal status, in many cases, is determined by time, usually number of years (articles 32, 28, 48, 43). The rules also cover issues relating to rights for opening windows on streets and when it is allowed to increase the height of a building (30); placing joists, or beam, into an adjacent wall (31); prevention for emitting smoke that harms a neighbor (27); right for water access through another's land (47); access to a water spring (58,15); and allowing to build a shed on another's farm when there is servitude for pasture and providing water to cattle (38). Article (26) discusses the obligation, or lack thereof, of an owner of a house, with or without a servitude, who wants to sell it to an adjacent property owner.

– On *water issues* (22, 23, 40–42). Article (22) on who is responsible for the repair of a rain gutter that continues to the next building and (23) on who is responsible for cleaning and repairing water conduits that serve gardens, plantations, or vineyards. Article (40) on access to water in an adjacent property determined by the passage of time of 3 years. If 3 years passes without objection, then access can be maintained. If objection is raised within the 3 years, then the neighbor who built the water conduit from the water source cannot claim its expenses. In article (41), when change of ownership of property occurs, it will not change the right of the passage of water that existed before the change of ownership. Article (42) addresses the rights of servitude of a lower land to receive water from the upper land.

– On *views* (5, 6, 8). Access to views of the sea was considered a legitimate right governed by the following rules: if there is 12 feet between buildings and the neighbor on the leeward side already has good views of the sea while standing, or even sitting in his house, or from his kitchen, steps, or terrace, then the view cannot be diminished by actions of the owner of a seaward building forcing the owner of the leeward located building to turn and obtain a side view of the sea. This limitation does not apply if there is at least 100 feet between the two buildings. However, if there is a servitude concerning views between two buildings, then the conditions of the servitude will override the general rule (5, 6). A right of view does not apply to a tree(s) or a garden. This was not the case in the sixth-century Ascalon in Palestine, as the view of a garden and trees was also considered important. A new construction that might obstruct such a view must be placed at a minimum distance of 50 feet (Hakim 2001).

The following are a few examples of the effect of Byzantine rules in the city of **Bari**. A document from the year 998 in Bari explains how an owner of a newly built house opened a door on the courtyard of the neighbor. The latter protested and obtained an order for the door to be closed with stones and lime so as to forbid access to the courtyard (Blasi et al. 1981). This is a clear example of the rights of earlier usage, i.e., an owner (A) whose house is built earlier possesses certain rights over an adjacent owner (B) who built later, an indication of the generative process in action. An earlier case documents a long running dispute over a new doorway that came to an end in 988 when Falco (name of the person who opened a doorway) agreed with his neighbors that he had had no right to make it and would block it up (Skinner 1998).

A common cause of conflict in the Bari documents of this period was the indiscriminate disposal of human waste and other rubbish into courtyards and alleys that were used by more than one household. Another cause for conflict was the careless siting of gutters. A case from the year 1034 documents that during building of his house (A) raised the wall between his property and the house of (B), causing water to fall on their house. (A) claimed that he owned the wall, and (B) produced a document showing that the wall had been lower (an agreement by (A), or the previous owner of his house, to keep the wall low). (A) then agreed to provide a gutter (Skinner 1998). This case demonstrates that an existing servitude must be respected and that a servitude is linked to the structure rather than to its owner as explained in the definition above in the section on servitudes. Another case in Bari from the year 1119 demonstrates how accretion of adjacent properties by the same family group results eventually to entire blocks owned by the same family (Skinner 1998).

Central and Northern Regions in the Twelfth to Fourteenth Centuries

According to Bocchi (1990), all Italian cities that formed self-governing communes, from the twelfth century onward, devised rules for orderly development. In the period of greatest urban growth, between the twelfth and fourteenth centuries, they pursued this objective so successfully as to meet a city's needs down to the nineteenth or even, in many instances, the early years of the twentieth century. As legislative activity advanced, numerous manuals were written in many Italian towns and cities addressing rules for the built environment. These rules addressed such matters as the protection of public land; the control of water, health, and hygiene; the protection of the built environment by the preservation of buildings; the prevention of pollution; the disposal of refuse; and the promotion of orderly growth. For a list of such manuals, see Appendix 5.

In discussing civic spirit and the visual arts, Daniel Waley (Waley 1969) cites the following quote from the year 1309 Siena statutes (see Appendix 6):

> among those matters to which the men who undertake the city's government should turn their attention its beauty is the most important. One of the chief beauties of a pleasant city is the possession of a meadow or open place for the delight and joy of both citizens and strangers.

Both Wolfgang Braunfels (1953) and recently Fabrizio Nevola (2009) translated specific rules from the Siena statutes of the years 1262 and 1309 that address issues for enhancing the order and beauty of the city's Piazza del Campo.

When the commune of Milan was established at about 1100 C.E., it soon was confronted with the usual problems of a large town. One of the earliest manuals that was assembled to address the problems associated with growth and changes in the built environment and other issues faced by society was the *Liber consuetudinum Mediolani anni MCCXVI* that was compiled in the year 1216. Professor Francisco Berlan published the original Latin version in 1866. It has 33 chapters. In 1288 Bonvesin da la Riva (1250–1313) wrote a treatise titled *De magnalibus Mediolani* that praises his city Milan. No doubt the statutes of 1216 must have contributed to aspects of the built environment of the city that the author praises (Dean 2000). Examples of rules from Milan and elsewhere are grouped in eight categories as follows:

On *management of the built environment*. The concept of spatial zoning was practiced especially when demand for housing was high due to heavy immigration or population growth and during favorable economic conditions. This would not necessarily be in the city center but also within the walls if there was room, or immediately outside them, particularly if the commune had transformed these areas from country to town by providing ditches, sewers, and defenses to enclose them. All urban communes of Italy passed through this phase of transformation, with varying intensity, during the twelfth and thirteenth centuries. The process began—as was evident in Carpi, which is about 140 km southeast of Milan, with the development of zones in which the blocks of housing are evident, even today, by their elongated parcels of land with very short street frontages (Bocchi 1986). These were laid out by landowners who, when the circuit of the walls was enlarged, found that their gardens, vineyards, and fields had become areas of high demand for building.

The Milanese statutes of the thirteenth century aim to make Milan a well-ordered city, in which the health of the citizens would be protected, by identifying dumps outside the city for the waste products of dirty trades such as tanning, dyeing, and butchery and by controlling the sewage from houses which fouled the air. Having forbidden the old system of discharging waste into side passages that connected to the street and having asserted control over the disposal of rainwater, the Milanese authorities reserved the right to approve arrangements for the private disposal of sewage. Each case was considered individually, and permission had to be sought for every new installation, which had to discharge its sewage below the ground (Bocchi 1989). These rules mark a turning point in the sanitation system not only of Milan but also of all other cities, because they implied on the one hand the construction of underground sewers to carry rainwater into the city ditches and on the other hand the installation of domestic cesspits, under the supervision of the commune's engineers.

On *encroachment on public land* such as on streets and who is responsible to clean and maintain them. City authorities were very strict for not allowing private individuals to encroach on streets or on other properties. According to Bocchi, in the periods before urban independence, local governments did not have the strength to protect such infringements (Bocchi 1987). This was due not only to the weakness of the governing authority but in some cases to a lack of clear distinction between public and private lands. When streets were surrounded by houses on both sides, the principle followed in most Italian cities was that maintenance was the responsibility of the owners of the surrounding houses. Bocchi does not mention whether this principle applied to all streets or only to cul-de-sacs, small courtyards, or squares surrounded by buildings or when the surrounding buildings are owned by the same family. In such cases, the street or square providing access was considered a part of the family property, and they were responsible to administer it (Heers 1984).

On *usage of space between two houses*. In the *Liber consuetudinum Mediolani anni MCCXVI* that was compiled in 1216 and has 33 chapters, we find in articles 6 through 11 of chapter 22 "on servitudes, water channels and other matters" the following: one foot must be established as the minimum distance between the wall of a house and the boundary of the property, allowing rainwater to drip from the eaves and allowing windows to be set on that side. Given the nature of the generative process over time, it was sometimes not possible to determine which neighbor owned the one foot space between houses. This was resolved according to customary practice. It belonged to the house, which, by custom and usage over time, had the right to collect rainwater and the right to light. If however the owner had only the right to light, then the one foot space belonged to the other neighbor.

On *allowing houses to abut onto each other.* This was also practiced, so long as there were no window openings on the party wall and rainwater was not discharged over the neighboring property. Such building practices reflect the divisions into lots that were made when the demand for housing was at its height, at times due to heavy immigration or to population growth and during a favorable economic climate. These rules helped give street frontages continuity.

On *usage of air space onto or over streets* by balconies, corbels, and eaves. The regulation introduced in every city in the thirteenth and fourteenth centuries, each in its own way, embodied two different concerns: the safety of passersby and the prohibition of above-average large projections. These would have stolen light from the buildings on the other side of the street, have failed to respect the minimum distance between one property and another, and have created unstable structures which would have had in the end to be shored up by supports, so that they became a kind of illegal portico. Parma was one of the first cities known to have regulated balconies and porticoes in the same way as Bologna. In 1211, the maximum length of the projection was specified according to local custom.

Eaves or porticoes which exceeded this length had to be either demolished or reduced to the permitted dimensions. Unfortunately, these are not specified in the statutes, because they were evidently well known to everyone to whom the laws were addressed. Eaves were not to project so far as to reduce the distance from the house opposite to less than one *braccio* and a half, which is about 80 cm (*Statuta Communis Parmae 1255*). Bridges joining houses on opposite sides of the street, which often belonged to the same owner, were tolerated up to the thirteenth century as the product of custom strengthened by time. Subsequently, restrictions were imposed on this practice due to the fear that such structures might become vantage points for ambushing the enemy during civil disturbances or defensive positions from which noxious materials could be dropped or weapons discharged (*Gli statuti veronesi del 1276*).

On **obstruction of roads by traffic**. Almost all communes forbade peasants who were bringing foodstuffs, hay, straw, firewood, and building materials into the town to ride on the carts themselves. The object was to compel them to lead their beasts by the halter and make them advance at a walking pace. At Verona, once the market-places had been clearly delineated, it was stipulated that no wagons might stop on the public streets or bridges, even for the purpose of selling their wares (*Gli statuti veronesi del 1276*). The traffic problem had already been so clearly recognized as to give rise to a kind of road tax levied upon the owners of wagons whose iron-rimmed wheels were eroding the paving stones. They were ordered to pay a duty, the proceeds of which were earmarked for the maintenance of the streets (*Gli Statuti del Comune di Treviso, 1283–84*, and *Gli statuti veronesi del 1276*).

On **protection of wells and fountains**. A reading of the statutes indicates that the concerns of the administrators were of various kinds. First, they were anxious that the fountain should be used solely for the purpose of collecting drinking water and that in no way should this be polluted. But the law was equally concerned with the protection of the whole conduit from which the water flowed and of all those persons who came to use the fountain. For this purpose, the Perugian statute makers created a kind of reserve with a radius of three paces around the steps (Perugia, 1342: *Statuti di Perugia dell' anno MCCCXLII*) and decreed that five or six stone vases should be placed on those steps. Persons coming to draw water were to wash their jugs and other receptacles in these vases and especially their outsides, which might dirty the water as it was being collected. To prevent contamination of the water and to provide a service, 13 copper cups lined with tin were to be attached by an iron chain to the pipe from which the water came, to allow people to drink and also to fill their receptacles. Only the specified items were to be used at the fountain, to prevent damage to the structure itself and pollution of the water. Water was not to be collected in barrels which might be impregnated with oil or must or be otherwise unclean. These prohibitions seem to reflect the fact that the main square was also the marketplace. The water of the fountain was not to be given to animals to drink: indeed, they were not even allowed to approach the steps. People were not to go to the fountain to wash themselves, to do their laundry, or to clean food, nor could anyone draw water to make lime, work leather, or prepare parchment. Heavy fines were charged for anyone who soiled the fountain itself or dirtied the water, and they were heavier still for anyone who damaged it.

The responsibility for the working of the fountain lay with the supreme executive authority of the state, the *podesta*. After carrying out a general inspection with the *capitano del popolo*, with the priors of the guilds, and with two deputies from every quarter, he was obliged every month "to inspect the course and bed of the aqueduct and of the piping of the fountain in the main square". It was stipulated that there would be an inquiry as to how well he had performed these constitutional duties. He was to receive support from the guild priors, who would place at his disposal the finances of the commune and all the resources needed for routine and special maintenance work, "that we may have plenty of water and that it may flow into the aforesaid fountain" (Perugia, 1342: *Statuti di Perugia dell' anno MCCCXLII*). Trevor Dean (2000) also describes the Perugia fountain.

On *character and beauty of the built environment*. As mentioned earlier bigger cities also developed rules to preserve their character. There was an awareness that the beauty of the city had to be preserved as evidenced by the measures for the Piazza del Campo in Siena (Balestracci and Piccinni 1977) see Figs. 2.3 and 4.3. This is also evident in the statute of Ascoli of 1377 (*Statuti di Ascoli Piceno dell' anno MCCCLXXXVII*). Bologna's famous arcades that characterized it as an arcaded city were apparently developed over time in response to the wishes of most of its citizens. The commune came to consider the arcades as a public amenity and increasingly demanded it. Each sector of the arcade had to be located within its building lot and must be kept clear of obstacles for the free passage of the public. Eventually Bologna built 37 km. of arcades for which it is famous (Bocchi 1995).

In Appendix 6, there are examples of rules that were developed to protect or enhance the character and beauty of cities, such as in Siena, Florence, and Bologna (Figs. 2.1, 2.2, 2.3, 2.4, 2.5, and 2.6).

References

Balestracci, D., & Piccinni, G. (1977). *Siena nel Trecento: Assetto urbano e strutture edilizie*. Florence.

Berger, A. (1953). Encyclopedic dictionary of Roman law. *Transactions of the American Philosophical Society*, 43(part 2). Philadelphia.

Blasi, D., et al. (1981). *La Puglia tra Medioevo ed eta moderna: citta e campagna*. Milano: Electa.

Bocchi, F. (1986). La storia, in Carpi. In *Atlante Storico delle Città Italiane* (Vol. 1, pp. 7–31). Bologna.

Bocchi, F. (1987). *Attraverso le citta italiane nel medioevo*. Bologna: Grafis.

Bocchi, F. (1989). Il disegno della città negli atti pubblici dal XII al XIV secolo. In C. Bertelli (a cura di), *Il Millennio ambrosiano. La nuova città dal Comune alla Signoria* (pp. 208–236). Milano.

Bocchi, F. (1990). Regulation of the urban environment by the Italian communes from the twelfth to the fourteenth century. *Bulletin of the John Rylands Library*, 72(3), 63–78.

Bocchi, F. (Ed.). (1995). *Bologna, Il Duecento, L'Atlante storico di Bologna* (Vol. 2). Bologna: Grafis.

Brandileone, F. (1895). Studio sul Prochiron Legum. *Bullettino Dell'Istituto Storico Italiano*, 16, 93–126. Roma.

Brandileone, F., & Puntoni, V. (1895). *Prochiron Legum: Pubblicato Secondo il Codice Vaticano Greco 845*. Roma: Istituto Storico Italiano, Fonti per la Storia d'Italia.

Braunfels, W. (1953). *Mittelalterliche Stadtbaukunst in der Toskana*. Berlin: Verlag Gebr.

Dean, T. (2000). *The towns of Italy in the later Middle Ages*. Manchester: Manchester University Press.

Freshfield, E. H. (1930). The official manuals of Roman law of the eighth and ninth centuries. *The Cambridge Law Journal*, 4(1), 34–50.

Freshfield, E. H. (1931). *A provincial manual of later Roman law: The Calabrian Procheiron – On servitudes and bye-laws incidental to the tenure of real property*. Cambridge: Cambridge University Press.

Heers, J. (1984). *Espaces publics, espaces prives dans la ville: Le Liber Terminorum de Bologne 1294*. Paris: CNRS.

Hakim, B. S. (2001). Julian of Ascalon's treatise of construction and design rules from 6th-c. Palestine. *Journal of the Society of Architectural Historians, 60*(1), 4–25.

Kazhdan, A. P. (1991). *The Oxford dictionary of Byzantium.* New York: Oxford University Press (abbreviated in the text as ODB).

Kreutz, B. M. (1991). *Before the Normans: Southern Italy in the ninth and tenth centuries.* Philadelphia: University of Pennsylvania Press.

Nevola, F. (2009). Ordering the piazza del Campo of Siena (1309). Translated from Italian. In K. L. Jansen, J. Drell, & F. Andrews (Eds.), *Medieval Italy: Texts in translation* (pp. 261–264). Philadelphia: University of Pennsylvania Press.

Ramseyer, V. (2009). Property rights and the legal system in Salerno (1044). Translated from the Latin. In K. L. Jansen, J. Drell, & F. Andrews (Eds.), *Medieval Italy: Texts in translation* (pp. 165–166). Philadelphia: University of Pennsylvania Press.

Skinner, P. (1998). Room for Tension: Urban life in Apulia in the eleventh and twelfth centuries. *Papers of the British School at Rome, 66,* 159–176.

Skinner, P. (2009). Bishop Daibert's order on the height of Towers in Pisa (1090). Translated from Latin. In K. L. Jansen, J. Drell, & F. Andrews (Eds.), *Medieval Italy: Texts in translation* (pp. 230–233). Philadelphia: University of Pennsylvania Press.

Waley, D. (1969). *The Italian city-republics.* London/New York: Longman.

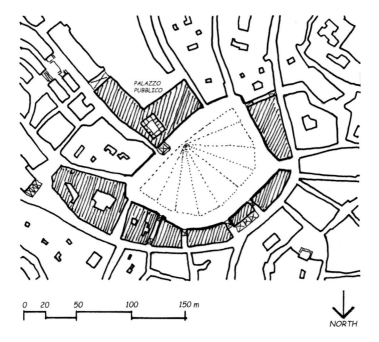

Fig. 2.1 Siena: Plan of the Piazza del Campo and surrounding buildings. The dimension of the piazza along the northeast/southwest axis is about 139 m, and along the northwest/southeast axis about 98 m (Drawn by the author after Braunfels 1953, page 67. The scale bar and north direction were calibrated using Google Earth)

Fig. 2.2 Siena: Bird's-eye view of the Piazza del Campo looking toward the south (Photo by Grassi about the mid-1940s, as published in *Italy: History, Art, Landscape*, 1954, 3rd edition 1959, Edizioni Mercurio, Florence)

Fig. 2.3 Siena: Palazzo Pubblico and the Mangia tower (Photo by Grassi about the mid-1940s, as published in *Italy: History, Art, Landscape*, 1954, 3rd edition 1959, Edizioni Mercurio, Florence)

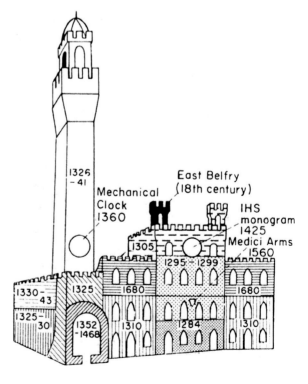

Fig. 2.4 Siena: Stages of growth of the Palazzo Pubblico (From *The Oregon Experiment* by Christopher Alexander, et al., 1975, page 69. The drawing is attributed, in the book's acknowledgments, to Phyllis Carr)

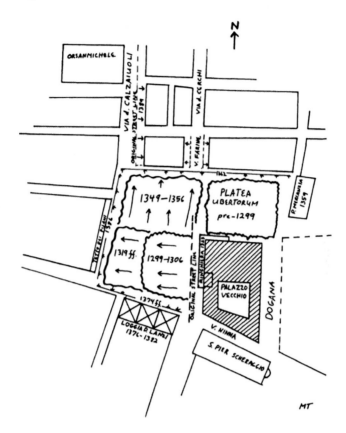

Fig. 2.5 Florence: This drawing by Martin Trachtenberg of the Piazza della Signoria was published on page 25 of his study titled "What Brunelleschi saw: . . ." *Journal of the Society of Architectural Historians*, vol. 47, March 1988, pp. 14–44. It is based on the Frey-Rubinstein chronology that the author cites on page 14. The author demonstrates how the Piazza della Signoria evolved over a period of 90 years (1299–1389) during which time the primary façade of the Palazzo Vecchio was adjusted from a north facing orientation to face west in response to developments of the Piazza. He also clearly shows how the generative process unfolded due to the events and decisions that enlarged the Piazza and affected the shape it took after a century of time (Permission to publish this drawing is granted by its author professor Martin Trachtenberg)

Fig. 2.6 Bologna: Arcades that were developed over time in response to the wishes of its citizens (This photo is located at the Piazza Santo Stefano looking toward Via S. Stefano. It is attributed to bebi on the website www.viaggiscoop.it)

Fig. 2.7 Rivello: Located in the province of Potenza. This is a typical hill town in southern Italy. It shows the compact clustering of the buildings and their adaptation to the natural features of the hilly terrain. This town is about 110 km north of Cosenza where the author of the *Prochiron Legum* lived or nearby in that area. The rules and customary practices that are mentioned in that treatise would have applied to this town (Photo by Raoul Kieffer in November 2006. Permission granted by Raoul)

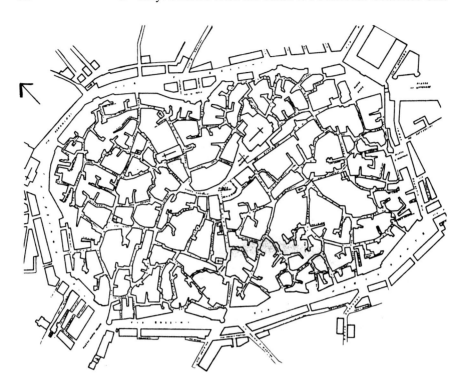

Fig. 2.8 Martina Franca, Puglia. This map of the town from the 1950s shows the complex street system with numerous cul-de-sacs reminiscent of Islamic urbanism. This compact town, which has its origins in the early tenth century, would have followed the rules of the *Prochiron Legum* that were available during its growth and subsequent formation. Other towns in the Puglia region have a similar pattern of streets. Bernard Rudofsky published the map in his book *Streets for People*, 1969, without giving credit to its origin, which probably was the municipality of the town. The north direction and approximate dimensions were calibrated with Google Earth. The width and length of the town plan are about 335 × 560 m. Latest air photos available on Google Earth

Fig. 2.9 Potignano, Puglia. This view of a street in the historic sector of the town shows how the rule works for what is allowed to project into the street. A line of about 50–75 cm from the facades of the buildings allows intrusion into the street by steps at the street level and balconies at the upper levels. In essence, one can imagine two planes: the first are the facades of the buildings, and the second is the line for allowing protrusions at ground and upper levels. The common term in Islamic towns for the space between the facades of the buildings and this line is *al-fina* (Photo taken by Raoul Kieffer in September 2008. Permission granted by Raoul)

Fig. 2.10 Ostuni, Puglia. A view taken from under a room that bridges the street toward a sequence of buttressing arches that are built with the agreement of owners on both sides of the street. These arches strengthen the walls on both sides. The headroom is determined by what is locally viewed as the necessary height to allow the passage of a loaded beast of burden (Photo by Raoul Kieffer in October 2009. Permission granted by Raoul)

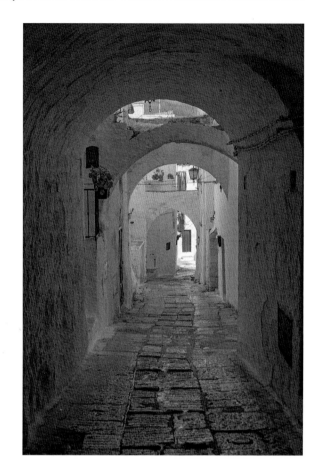

Chapter 3
Spain: Sources from the Fifth to the Eighteenth Centuries C.E.

This chapter will cover sources that include rules affecting the built environment within the time frame of the Visigothic kingdom (456–711 C.E.), followed by a specific tenth century treatise from the Islamic period (711–1492 C.E.). Examples from the model code of the thirteenth century, known as *Las Siete partidas* will be explored, followed by examples of codes that were developed in the fourteenth century in Toledo after the conquest of that city from Muslim rule, and in Cordoba from the early sixteenth century. The rules from Toledo and Cordoba were developed and managed by the *Alarife* institution.

Visigothic Code the *Liber iudiciorum*

By the year 456 C.E. Visigothic rule extended throughout the peninsula of Iberia, but only in 475 that Rome recognized Visigothic sovereignty. Roman rule lasted from about 19 B.C.E. to 475 C.E. (Atkinson 1960). The juridical Romanization of Spain occurred between the years 74 and 250 C.E., and it should be pointed out that Roman practice respected local traditions, such as the Celtic-Iberian customary law (Ruiz 1986). The Visigothic kings encouraged the unification of the sophisticated Roman legal system with their own Germanic tribal customs. There is information that this royal policy started around 450 C.E. and the evidence is available from

---

A part of this chapter are Figs. 3.1–3.9 and Appendices 7–10.

B.S. Hakim, *Mediterranean Urbanism: Historic Urban / Building Rules and Processes*, DOI 10.1007/978-94-017-9140-3_3,
© Springer Science+Business Media Dordrecht 2014

king Euric's Code that was written around 475 C.E. within the period
of his reign (466–484). It brought together elements of Roman law
and Germanic customs. In the seventh century four Visigothic kings
developed their legal work, with the active participation of the
church, that led to the compilation of the highly Romanized code
the *Liber iudiciorum*. It became the sole guide for the administration
of justice in Visigothic Spain starting from the reign of king
Receswinth (653–672). This code is considered to be the greatest
legacy of the Visigoths in Spain. The coming of Islam in 711 C.E.
brought Visigothic rule in Spain to an end. However, it should be
noted that the Christian population that came under Muslim rule
retained their religion and continued to be judged by the *Liber
iudiciorum* (Ruiz 1986). Much later in the eleventh century it was
translated into Castilian and was known as the *Fuero juzgo* and
became the local charter of many towns in the south (Ruiz 1986).

The *Liber iudiciorum* is also known as the *Forum Judicum* and
popularly known as *The Visigothic Code*. It consists of laws originating from four sources: (1) ancient Gothic customs, (2) Roman jurisprudence, (3) acts of the ecclesiastical councils, and (4) edicts of
the kings. It was translated from the original Latin into English by
S. P. Scott and published in Boston in 1910. Scott wrote a lengthy
preface for his translation (Scott 1910). The code consists of 12 books
that contain titles and those in turn contain articles. The codes from
Books 8 and 10 relate to issues of agriculture and ownership of land.
The underlying principle was to ensure that no damage is done. The
details relating to the infringement of the rights of property shows that
abuses previously existed. The numerous stipulations addressing the
protection of agriculture indicates its importance. Severe penalties
in the law against all who deface, remove, or in any way interfere
with established landmarks (Scott 1910). Thus Title 3 from Book 8
is titled as: *Concerning injuries to trees, gardens, or growing crops of
any description*. It includes 17 articles that are specific rules, such as
#2: Where anyone destroys the garden of another; #6: Where fences
are cut down or burned; #7: Where fence posts are cut; #11: Where
animals damage growing crops.

The importance of animals to the livelihood of their owners is
addressed in Title 4 of Book 8 as: *Concerning injuries to animals
and other property*. Rights of public highways is addressed in Article
24 of Book 8: Concerning injuries resulting from the obstruction of
highways, followed by # 25: Of the space that is to be preserved along

public highways- "No one shall rashly violate our laws by enclosing a highway leading to any of our cities or provinces, but a full half *arepennis* shall be left on each side of the same; in order that sufficient space may be available for all travellers." [Full half of *arepennis* is between 1/12 and 1/14 of an acre (Scott 1910)]. This rule clearly demonstrates the sanctity of the right-of-way of streets and its legal designation as a public entity and the responsibility of the governing authority to manage it.

Title 1 of Book 10 has 19 articles and is titled: *Concerning partition and lands conveyed by contract*. Examples are Article 1: A partition once made shall remain forever in force. Article 5: Where anyone violates a contract establishing a partition and seizes a portion of the property, followed by #6: Where an heir plants a vineyard, or erects a house, on land belonging to his co-heirs. And the last Article 19: Where a contract is not complied with according to its terms. The importance of written, and very probably notarized, contracts is very evident from these rules.

The effect of the passage of time on facts is very evident in Title 2 of Book 10 titled: *Concerning the limitations of fifty and thirty years*. Examples are Article 1: After the lapse of fifty years, neither Goths nor Romans can assert a claim to property. And Article 3: No suit at law shall be brought thirty years after the cause of action has arisen. The importance that is accorded to property ownership by the methods of designation is the subject of Title 3 of Book 10 titled: *Concerning boundaries and landmarks*. The five articles in this title clarify these considerations. Article 1: How boundaries and landmarks shall be preserved; #2: Concerning the destruction and removal of landmarks; #3: What is to be done when a dispute arises concerning boundaries, and #4: Where one person makes a claim to land included within the boundaries of another; and #5: Where any change was made in the boundaries of land during the time of the Romans, no claim based upon other boundaries shall prevail.

Islamic Period: Treatises of Ibn al-Imam and Ibn al-Attar from the Tenth Century C.E.

We now turn to the Muslim period in Spain that started in 711 C.E. The treatise that is analyzed here is the oldest extant manuscript, specifically addressing rules for the built environment,

that has survived to this day. Its author was a Muslim jurist
by the name of Isa bin Musa bin Ahmed bin al-Imam al-Tutaili
(940–996 C.E.). Tutaila is the Arabic name for Tudela, located
85 km north west of Zaragoza. His treatise draws on works from the
eighth, ninth and tenth centuries, primarily from the Maliki School of
Law. These sources are from authors who lived in Medina, Cairo,
Cordoba and Kairouan (Hakim 2008). Ibn al-Imam lived during a
stable and culturally productive period known as the Caliphate period
(929–1009 C.E.) that also witnessed construction activities. Cordoba
took a central stage in this period (el-Hajji 1987). Abdul-Rahman III
(912–961 C.E.) who came to power at age 21, proved to be the
greatest ruler in Muslim Spain (Atkinson 1960) when it reached its
best period (al-Tutaili - c 2003). This was consolidated by the rule of
al-Hakkam II (961–976 C.E.). It is estimated that Ibn al-Imam wrote
his treatise sometime during the period of al-Hakkam II's rule
(al-Tutaili - b 1999).

It is also in Cordoba that we are introduced to another individual who
is the same age as Ibn al-Imam. He is Muhamad bin Ahmad al-Umawi
known as Ibn al-Attar (941–1009 C.E.). A specialist in writing and
executing notaries on numerous issues. His manuscript was verified
recently and published in Madrid (Chalmeta and Corriente 1983).

Ibn al-Imam's treatise contains 49 cases that I have regrouped into
seven categories each of which includes related cases. This categoriz-
ation is necessary to convey clearly what its author wants to communicate and still be legible to contemporary readers in related fields.
Each case is prefaced by the word *al-qada'* which means the legal
solution to the case. The essence of what the treatise wants to achieve
is embedded in its title: *al-qada bil-marfaq fi al-mabani wa nefi
al-darar* (legal solutions for servitudes of buildings and negating
damage). Thus the two most important concepts are servitudes and
damage. This author had discussed the latter concept and explained
its origin in prophet Muhammad's saying *la-Darar wa la-Dirar*
(no infringement whether profitable or not), that can also be explained
thus: "One should exercise one's full rights in what is rightfully his
providing the decision/action will not generate harm to others. Likewise others should exercise their full rights in what is rightfully theirs
providing their decision/action will not harm others" (Hakim 1986,
19–22). The concept of servitude is defined by (al-Tuwaijri 1982),
who is the author of the extensive study on rights of servitudes in

Islamic law, as (the right that is bestowed on one property to benefit another whose ownerships belong to separate parties, or to benefit an individual without rent, loan, donation, or a will). There are different kinds of servitudes: excess of water for drinking, passage of water from upper to lower ground, access to property within another's property, building upper on lower levels that belong to separate parties, and between adjunct neighbors on the same level.

The following are the seven categories. They are listed with their original case numbers in Appendix 7. (1) Land and building uses (contains Ibn al-Imam's introduction and twelve cases that cover servitudes between houses, access, usage on other's properties, and avoiding damage from ovens and shops); (2) Streets (seven cases that cover street rights-of-ways, damage to streets, and issues related to private roads); (3) Walls (eight cases that cover party walls, projections from walls, and unstable leaning walls); (4) Overlooking/ Privacy (four cases that cover privacy issues from windows and doors, and overlooking from minarets); (5)- Drainage and Hygiene (four cases that cover rainwater evacuation, garbage removal, toilet cleaning, and garbage on vacant plots); (6) Plants and trees (nine cases that relate to various aspects of trees and dealing with damage from plants and trees); (7) Birds, bees and animals (five cases that cover pigeon houses, bees, damage from animals, damage to plants, and sale of animals).

This author has uncovered the following principles underlying Ibn al-Imam and Ibn al-Rami's treatises. The latter was written in Tunis 350 years later. It is more detailed than the former and contains numerous cases that its author was involved in as a master-mason/ expert. The following is taken from pages 19–22 of (Hakim 1986). The principles are: Harm, Interdependence, Privacy, Rights of earlier usage, Rights of building higher within one's air space, Respect for the property of others, Rights of pre-emption, Width of public streets, No obstruction of streets, Excess water should not be barred from others, Usage of exterior *fina* belongs to the building that abuts it, Sources of unpleasant odor and uses that generate noise should not be located to adjacent or near mosques. The following were values and accepted behaviour that had a self-regulating effect: Keeping things clean, Sense of public awareness, Beauty without arrogance, Trust and peace among neighbors, and Defects should be announced when selling a property. These are all detailed in the source cited above.

As for Ibn al-Attar's (941–1009 C.E.) colossal compilation of model notary documents in his book *Kitab al-Watha'iq wa al-Sijillat*, which is translated into Spanish as (Formulario Notarial Hispano-Arabe). In it he provides model notaries that would have covered any possible circumstance in Cordoban society and beyond in Al-Andalus. To ensure that his examples are understood as generic in nature he refers to individuals as (so and so) and to things as (such and such). There are four examples that specifically address the built environment. I have listed those in Appendix 8 and briefly explained what issues they cover.

These two contemporaries from Tudela and Cordoba in the tenth century provides us with clear examples of issues in the built environment for which rules were developed and the means of documenting agreements between parties by the use of notarial documents and their registration in the courts.

The Model Code *Las Siete Partidas* from the Thirteenth Century

Ferdinand III (1217–1252) had military victories, especially the conquest of Cordoba in 1236 and Seville in 1248 that brought most of Andalusia under his rule. To these cities he established their local *fuero* or municipal charter the *Liber iudiciorum,* the Visigothic code that was translated into Castilian with the name *Fuero juzgo* that became the local charter of numerous towns in the south (Ruiz 1986). Ferdinand III's son, Alfonso X, followed his father's program and the most important legal work finished by his jurists was the *Fuero real* or *Fuero de las leyes*. It was written between 1252 and 1255 and was granted to many cities. It replaced the *Fuero juzgo* to provide uniformity of law throughout the kingdom and remained in force long after 1272.

Traditionally legal historians emphasized that Alfonso's most important legislation was the code that was known in the latter part of the thirteenth century and thereafter as the *Siete partidas*. It was intended as a uniform code for the whole kingdom. Further revisions of the *Siete partidas* throughout the next 100 years emphasized theoretical aspects. Its thoroughness as a law treatise made the *Partidas*, and especially its third redaction, dating from the late thirteenth century an undisputed set of references and was a widely used source for decisions of Castilian jurists and legislators (Ruiz 1986). They were completed between 1256 and 1265 (Burns 2001). Joseph O'Callaghan's essay in (Burns 2001) titled "Alfonso X and the *Partidas*" provides sources for the work. The anonymous jurists who developed the work drew on vast sources. Most frequently mentioned are "los sabios antiguos" (the wise men of old) which likely means Justinian's *Corpus iuris civilis.* Also used were works of canon law. The compilers also cited the *Fuero antiguo de Espana*, referring to the customary law of the kingdom. They were also familiar with the *Fuero juzgo*, the municipal *fueros*, the *Fuero real*, and the *Especulo.* Prominent among "the wise men of old of Spain" was Isidore of Seville. Few studies exist that demonstrate the influence of Islamic law on the *Partidas.* A study by Marcel Boisard (1980) indicates such influences, as well as a study by N.M.I. Goolam (1999). O' Callaghan quotes Robert A. MacDonald's concise description of the *Siete Partidas*:

> The *Siete partidas* represents an encyclopedic and systematic integration of definition, prescription, explanation, and amplification of materials from many sources – classical and contemporary, canonical and secular, Roman and Castilian, legal and literary – in different languages.

Another earlier description of the *Partidas* is by Ernest Nys (1851– 1920), a Belgian lawyer and a professor of Public International Law at the University of Brussels, in his 1917 edited work on *Francisci de Victoria de Indis et de ivre belli relectiones.*

> The Siete Partidas deals with ecclesiastical law, politics, legislation, procedure and penal law; the law of war is the subject of extremely detailed regulations; much is borrowed from the *Etymologiae* of Saint Isidore of Seville . . . and in many respects the influence of Muslim law is very apparent.

Volume 1 of the 2001 English edition of the *Partidas* (Burns 2001) includes the 1st *Partida.* Its Title 1/ Law 1 is on 'What Laws These Are'. The 2nd Title that follows is about Usage, Custom, and *Fuero.* Volume 3 that includes the 3rd *Partida,* is comprised of 32 Titles, each of which includes numerous laws (titles can be considered as chapters, while the laws as articles). The sub-title of the 3rd *Partida* is "Procedure and Property". Of significance, to issues of the built environment, are the following Titles: 19 is about Notaries, 28 on Ownership, 30 on Possession, 31 on Servitudes, and 32 on Buildings. The 7th *Partida* includes title 15 on injury, or damage, which is also an important consideration affecting activities in the built environment. Injury, or damage, and servitudes constitute the two essential concepts that affect and regulate change. This was evident about 270 years earlier in Ibn al-Imam's treatise whose title, *Legal solutions for servitudes of buildings and negating damage*, embodies these concepts. Two other titles also need to be noted here: Title 2 of the 1st *Partida* on usage, custom and *fuero*, and title 31 from the 2nd *Partida* on schools and especially on their locations that address land use issues. The following are details from the contents indicated here that are relevant to the built environment.

The 1st *Partida*'s Title 1/Law 1 on **What Laws These Are**: "These laws are ordinances to enable men to live well and regularly according to the pleasure of God. . . They also show how men should live with one another in right and justice". Law 2: Of Natural Law and That of Nations: "*Jus naturale*, in Latin, means natural law in Castilian, the law which men and also other animals which have sense possess naturally in themselves. Moreover, *jus gentium*, in Latin, means the common law of all nations, which is suitable for men and not for animals". Burns, the editor, indicates that these definitions of the natural and civil law are taken almost verbatim from the Institutes of Justinian.

The 2nd Title that follows is about **Usage, Custom, and Fuero**. It contains 9 Laws. This is an important Title because customary law was followed in the processes of change and growth in the built environment and was incorporated as part of local law in many towns and cities. Law 1 defines what Usage is: "Use is something which originates from those things which man says, does, and pursues continually for a long time without hindrance". Law 3 explains how Usage gains force with time and the reasons it loses it. Law 4 defines what Custom is and how many kinds there are: "Custom is an unwritten law or privilege, which men have made use of for a long period of time, aiding themselves by means of it in matters and on occasions to which it is applicable. There are three kinds of customs. The first is that which relates to something in particular, as a certain place or person. The second is general, affecting many persons as well as places. The third has reference to other distinct acts which men perform and with which they are content, and in which they manifest resolution". The third kind of custom is directly relevant to building practice and also has precedence in Islamic law as it was applied during the Islamic period. For a general analysis of the *Urf* (custom) see Hakim (1994). Law 7 on what a Fuero is: "A fuero is a thing in which are included two others that we have mentioned, namely, usage and custom, because both of them must be combined in a fuero to make it secure; for, if a fuero is – as it should be – a good usage and a good custom, it has as great force as law . . .".

The 3rd *Partida* has Title 28 on **Ownership**. Law 1 defines what ownership is, and how many kinds there are: "Ownership is the power which a man has over his own property to do with it, and in it whatever he desires to do, without violation of the law of God or those of the country. There are three kinds of ownership". One relates to the authority of the king and refers to its details in the 2nd and 4th *Partidas*. "The second kind of ownership is the power which a man has over his movable or immovable property in this world, during his lifetime, and which after his death passes to his heirs, or to whomsoever he may transfer it while he lives. The third kind of ownership is the control of which a man has over the rents and profits of certain property during his lifetime, . . .". The second kind of ownership is very important as it relates to building within one's property. In principle as long as no injury, or damage, is done to the neighbor or the neighborhood then the owner is free to do what he pleases in his property. Title 32 on Buildings includes many laws that create constraints. Servitude obligations discussed in Title 31 provides additional rules. Law 9 explains property that is considered common that everyone has a right to its use. These include fountains and squares where markets are held, places where councils meet, sandy beaches, public roads, mountains and pastures and all places similar to these. Law 15 indicates that walls and gates of cities and towns are holy. Title 28 also includes laws about ownership of animals and bees, such as law 22 on how ownership of bees, swarms, and honey-combs is obtained. It harks back to case number 49 of Ibn al-Imam's treatise. Title 28 also addresses outcomes from natural events such as law 26 on to whom alluvial deposits made by rivers on land shall belong. Law 27 on how islands made by rivers should be divided.

Law 31 on where a river changes its course, who should be the owner of the land it traverses. Law 38 on who is the owner of a building of stone, or of wood, constructed by one of materials belonging to another. Law 43 discusses the planting of trees and its roots extending into the neighbor's property where its nourishment is from his land, who then owns the tree? This law has similar circumstances as those discussed in case 39 of Ibn al-Imam's treatise.

The factor of the *lapse of time* has consequences on ownership, whereby one can gain the property of another or lose his own. Title 29 addresses related issues. This is also related to law 5 of the 2nd title on who can establish a custom and how this is done: If the greater number of people practice doing anything for 10 or 20 years, by way of custom, must be considered and observed as a custom, provided it is not contrary to the law of God, or antagonistic to government or against natural law. Law 7 of title 29 is on ownership of squares, roads, pastures, commons, which are the property of the people, is not lost by lapse of time, except flocks, money, ships or any other chattels like these, even though they belong to the council of any city or town, its ownership can be obtained after the passage of 40 years. Other conditions are indicated in this law. Law 19 is about a party who conveys property and knows that he has no right to do so, he who receives it cannot acquire its ownership in less than 30 years.

Title 30 of the 3rd *Partida* explains the rules that must be followed in how many ways a man can gain *possession and occupancy of property*. Law 2 is about natural and civil possession. Natural possession is when a man is present in his property, such as a house or castle or land. Civil possession is when a man has to be away from his property, and although he is not there, he is so in his will and mind, and such a possession is as valid as if he had remained on the property. Law 14 is in how many ways a man loses possession of property. Law 15 is about the steps that should be taken regarding a house that is about to fall down and the neighbors are afraid of the damage that may result on their property. If the owner of such a house will not respond to the neighbor's demands to repair or demolish it, then the judge can place the building in the possession of the neighbors. The owner of the building will lose the occupancy of his building if he persists to refuse to repair or demolish it. This circumstance is similar to Case 20 in Ibn al-Imam's treatise. There the case specifically addresses the fear of a neighbor's inclined wall that may fall and cause damage on a proximate neighbor's property.

Title 31 of the 3rd *Partida* is on **rights of servitudes** which some buildings and lands have over others. Law 1 defines what a servitude is and how many kinds there are. There are two kinds; *Urbana* which one house has over another, and *Rustica* which one tract of land has in another. Both types provide rights or use that a man is entitled to in the buildings or lands of others to employ it for the benefit of his own. Various detailed definitions of the Roman laws on servitudes, translated from Latin, are available in (Berger 1953). Law 2 is about the types of *urbana* servitudes: (1) where one house supports another story or a room by placing a column upon which the upper neighbor can support his beams; (2) the right to use a neighbor's wall by placing beams into his wall for support; (3) open a window in the neighbor's wall to allow light to come through; (4) to receive rain water from the neighbor's roof; (5) a servitude on the neighbor's house that would not allow its owner to increase the height of the building beyond its height at the time the servitude was imposed so as not to obstruct the view, or the light, or to prevent overlooking; (6) to provide access to one's house, that is locked in by another, via the yard of the other house. And other similar conditions that a servitude might resolve. Law 3 is about the types of *rustica* servitutdes: a path or road through the land of another for the purpose of access. The width should be determined to be the minimum to allow access, 8 f. where the path is straight, and 17 f. if the path is not straight to allow carts to maneuver the curve of the path. The foot was measured then at 28 cm. Eight feet would be 2.24 m, and 17 would be 4.76 m. These equivalents were taken from the web site: http://www. historiaviva.org on measuring units in Spain towards the end of the fifteenth century. Law 4 on the servitude in the property of another for the purpose of conducting water through it.

It should be noted that servitudes remain binding on a new owner that Law 8 addresses, namely that a man does not lose the servitude which he enjoys in the property of another by the sale of a house, or by its ownership passing to another party, except where a servitude was imposed upon a property for a specified time, or during the life time of a particular individual. Otherwise servitudes that are imposed for all time are tied to the property and not to the person. Thus Law

12 states that a servitude cannot be sold separately from the property to which it is attached. Law 13 states that no servitude shall be imposed on sacred, holy, or religious property, nor upon common properties in a city or town such as market squares, commons, and similar properties. Law 14 indicates on the ways servitudes can be imposed upon a property in three ways: (1) by those to whom the property belongs by voluntarily imposing servitudes upon it in consideration of affection, or of money received; (2) granted by will, such as giving permission to the neighbor to insert beams into his wall and other types of servitudes granted by will; and (3) obtain servitudes for a specific period of time. Law 15, explains the lapse of time on obtaining a servitude, e.g. the use of water from a spring in the land of another person and has been doing so for 10 years and the owner of the land that has the spring has not objected during these years, or if he is absent for 20 years or more, such a servitude can then be considered as acquired due to the lapse of time. Any other type of servitude that has been in use for a very long time that people cannot remember when such servitudes began being used. In such cases the servitude is considered as being acquired. Law 16 indicates that the use of servitudes can be lost for lack of their use. The details are explained in the law, but essentially 10 years in the case of those attached or related to buildings, and 20 years in the case of those related to lands. The laws and rules of servitudes are very important mechanisms that allowed compactness in the built environment of medieval cities and towns and that was also the case during the Islamic period discussed earlier.

Another important concept, and its various considerations, was that of avoiding **injury, or damage**, to others by various types of construction activities that relate to change and growth in the built environment. Title 15 of the 7th *Partida* addresses these issues. Law 1 defines what an injury is and how many kinds there are: "Injury is the diminution or depreciation in value, or the destruction which a man sustains in person and property, through the fault of another". There are three kinds: (1) when a property deteriorates because something is mixed with it, or some other injury done to it; (2) when diminished in quantity because of injury it sustains; and (3) when a property is entirely lost or destroyed because of the consequences of the injury. Law 3 asks of what persons and before whom reparation for damage can be demanded? Briefly, the answer is that the party who caused the damage must make reparation for it to the party who sustained it. Law 7 stipulates that damage from dangerous animals is the responsibility of its owners during there transit from one place to another. Law 10 is about a party who in windy weather kindles a fire near straw, wood or growing grain, or in any similar place, is responsible for any damage resulting from it. Law 11 further extends this type of damage to bake-ovens, kiln of lime or plaster, or of bricks. Law 12 is about someone who demolishes his neighbor's house – that is located next to another property on fire – to prevent the fire from spreading to his property, is not responsible for any damage resulting from his action. Law 26 is for inn-keepers who have signs hanging near their doors must ensure that the sign is well secured so as not to fall and cause damage to customers. Type of reparation for damages is indicated. Law 28 is extensive and addresses those with evil intentions who cut down trees, vines, or trellises and what their punishment should be. It is clear from this law that trees, trellises and vines were considered important elements because people benefit from their fruit, and receive great comfort and pleasure from them. This law also addresses a situation were someone has a tree on his property whose branches overhang his neighbor's house and cause damage, he must prune the tree and its branches. The same applies when branches of a fig tree, (the law specifically mentions the type of tree), overhangs a public street and impedes traffic, then anyone can cut those branches and not be liable for punishment. These situations are included in case numbers 40 and 44 of Ibn al-Imam's treatise. They are also addressed in Julian of Ascalon's sixth century treatise (Hakim 2001). Preventing injury is another overarching rule that is of paramount importance in compact built environments. It acts as a self-regulating mechanism in light of the principle that owners of property are free to undertake what they wish within their property's boundary. This principle is cited above under Law 1 of Title 28 on the kind of ownership there are.

Title 32 of the 3rd *Partida* is about **buildings** and type of issues that are related to their construction, changes to edifices, and when necessary their demolition. Although many of the laws in this title refer to new buildings, in fact this designation encompasses additions and changes to existing structures. Law 1 defines what a new building is, and who can forbid its erection. "A new building is every structure that is erected with a foundation in the earth, or one that is newly begun on an old foundation, or wall, or an addition by means of which the form and fashion of the old one is changed", and "Every man can prohibit or prevent such building who thinks that he is wronged by it". Robert I. Burns, the editor of the English edition of the *Partidas* adds a valuable footnote to the latter part of this definition: "This is founded on the time honored maxim; *Ita utere tuo ut alterum non laedas*" (which is translated from the Latin by google.com as: 'Do not damage the other in order to make use of yours'). Law 1 continues by indicating three ways in which the prohibition is made. Law 3 addresses the public realm by stipulating that every man can forbid a house, or other structure to be erected in the public squares, or on the commons of a town or on a street. The law grants responsibility to any citizen the right to intervene as a civic duty, except a minor under 14 years of age or a woman. The latter cannot make such a prohibition, although they can do so when any new structure is erected on his or her property. Law 5 provides the rights of the beneficiary of a servitude to forbid the erection of a new structure: "where a party who is entitled to a servitude in a house or any other building, considers himself injured by the erection of a new structure which may be an impediment to the enjoyment of said servitude". This stipulation does not apply when a servitude exists against one tract of land in favor of another, such as a road, a path, or a water course. In such instances the recourse to prevent any potential damage is to appeal to the judge. Law 7 also excludes the right to forbid when the activity is for repairing or cleaning pipes, roofs, and other similar things that property owners need to do for maintaining their houses. While undertaking such maintenance and repairs the owner of a house might need to place construction materials and pipes on the adjacent property for the time needed to complete the work. The owner of such adjacent property must allow this, provided the owner of the house under repair cleans the adjacent property and restore it to the same condition as it was formerly.

Law 10 is about new or old structures that are in danger of falling down should be repaired or demolished. In such a case the judge must visit the site with expert "master-workmen" to determine the validity of the situation. If the owner of such a building in danger refuses to repair or demolish, then the parties that raised the complaint can be placed in possession of said building(s). This is similar to case 20 of Ibn al-Imam's treatise that addresses the inclined wall that is in danger of collapse. However, it should be noted that Law 10 excludes conditions where the building was destroyed by an earthquake, or by lightning, or by a hurricane, or by a water-course or by similar natural disasters, then its owner will not be liable to pay for damages to his adjacent neighbors. Law 13 addresses the situation when water from gutters injure adjacent neighbors(s) roofs or walls, they must be adjusted or removed to prevent such damage. Law 13 repeats an important principle that "although a man has the power to do with his own property whatever he wishes, nevertheless, he should act in such a way as not to cause injury or wrong the other" The editor of the *Partidas* refers to his footnote to Law 1 which is cited above. This is an important principle, which was also adhered to during the Islamic period, is one of conditions that allows a generative process to function and succeed in the built environment of historic towns. Law 14 addresses the consequences of the passage of time when men sustain injury from the lands of others which they are compelled to endure and cannot complain to their owners. First due to a natural cause in the situation of the force of water from an upper property does damage to a property situated at a lower level. Second the lapse of 10 years, without complaints to damage, by the resident of the property damaged nullifies his right to ask for compensation, and 20 years when the owner of the property damaged is absent and does not complain during that time. Third where the damage results from a servitude. The latter part of Law 15 stipulates the importance of sharing responsibility of maintenance thus: "Where, however, the place where the water is obstructed is a canal belonging to several persons, every one on the boundary of said land is required to assist in restoring the channel, so that the water may flow as it was accustomed to do and they can make use of it". This principle for maintenance has precedence in Islamic law. It can be traced to Sahnoun from Kairouan (777–854). A similar case was documented by Ibn al-Rami from Tunis in his treatise (d. 1334). See Hakim (1986, pp. 52–53).

Law 18 addresses the duplication of buildings with specific uses such as mills and ovens. The principle underlying this law is that duplication should be discouraged if, in the case of mills, less water will be available to the earlier mill and thus affecting its functioning and the potential of less profit to the mill's owner. The latter's consideration of profit applies to the impact of a new oven being proposed in close proximity to an existing one. Law 20 titled: The castles and the walls of towns and other fortified places, along with their sidewalks, fountains, and gutters should be kept up and repaired. The responsibility for this maintenance is a part of the duty of the king, i.e. the public sector. The law stipulates that if funds in the treasury is not sufficient to complete this work, then it is permissible to collect funds from all the residents of the community, each one in proportion to his means, until a sufficient sum is collected for the completion of the work. This principle has precedence in Islamic law: Qadi Iyad (d.1149), born in Ceuta, who later in his career served as the judge of Granada has stipulated this principle. Al-Wansharisi (d. 1508) in volume 5 of his 13-volume treatise stipulates the conditions for asking people to contribute (Hakim and Ahmed 2006). Law 22 stipulates that no house, or any other building, should be erected near the walls of cities or castles. A space of 15 f. (4.20 m) should be left between the building and the wall of a town or castle for defensive purposes. Law 23 forbids the encroachment of construction by building on public squares, streets, or commons of towns. Any building that contravenes this rule should be demolished, unless the Council of the community agrees to keep it for its own use for the benefit of the town. Law 24 stipulates that houses, towers, or other buildings should not be erected near a church, except structures that pertain to "works of piety and mercy". Law 25 decrees that he who wishes to rebuild a house or tower on his premises can do so, leaving space towards the street in conformity with the existing conditions in the neighborhood. He can also raise the height of his building provided he does not create a situation that overlooks the neighbors. This law clearly demonstrates the concern for invading the privacy of the neighbors. This has precedence in Islamic law and is viewed as injurious to the neighbor who will be overlooked due to the increase in height of the neighbor's structure. Finally, law 26 is about a party who repairs a house or a building, that he owns in common with other parties, is entitled to recover his expenses or to obtain the shares of the others. This should be done within 4 months from the day the work was finished, otherwise the other parties will forfeit the shares that they had in the repaired property, and he who undertook the repairs from his own money is entitled to those shares. This stipulation is similar to the rules discussed in case 2 of Ibn al-Imam's treatise.

Land use preferences for certain uses is evident in Title 31 of the 2nd *Partida*. Here **schools and their proper location** within the town or city is addressed. Law 2's title is a question: "In what place a school should be established, and how the masters and pupils should be secure". Part of the answer given is: "The town where it is desired to establish a school should have pure air and beautiful environs, in order that the masters who teach the sciences and the pupils who learn them, may live in health, and rest and take pleasure in the evening when their eyes have become weary with study". This is further elaborated in Law 5's title: "In what places schools of masters and pupils should be located". The answer: "General schools should be located in a place apart from the town, and near one another, in order that the pupils who have a desire to learn rapidly may be able to take two or more lessons if they desire to do so, and can enquire of one another concerning matters of which they are in doubt". The concept of a school campus is implied here where different class levels is encouraged to be close to each other, so that students can interact with each other, enhancing the learning experience. Law 11 stipulates that every general school must have booksellers who rent their books to the students. Clearly the laws of the *Partidas* include provisions for learning environments and thus convey the importance of education in the minds of the law makers.

The final topic from the *Partidas* to include in this chapter is about **Notaries.** Title 19 of the 3rd *Partida* addresses this topic with this heading: "Concerning notaries, how many kinds there are, and what benefit is derived from their office when they perform their duties faithfully". Law 1 indicates two categories: notaries working for the king, and others who are notaries for the public. The latter draw up bills of sale, purchases, contracts, and agreements that men enter into among themselves in cities and towns. Burns, the editor of the English version of the *Partida,* adds a footnote that "the notary was a personage of great influence and importance in an age of general illiteracy, when a layman who could read and write was considered a prodigy of learning" (Burns 2001). Law 2 specifies the eligibility requirements for the notaries, and an important requirement is that they be residents of the places where they work, so that they will be acquainted with the people for whom they draw up documents. Law 9 specifies the requirement that notaries should keep a book, as a register, to record the details of the documents that they produce. This is particularly important, as stated in Law 10, when a party states they lost their document. The notary can then re-produce another document from the information of his register to replace the lost document. Law 14 is on how notaries of cities and towns should be protected and honored. Law 15 on the compensation of notaries for the service they render in drawing up documents. Law 16 on what punishment notaries should receive if they commit forgery while in office. The notaries in the *Partidas* confirms the importance of this institution as it was also practiced during the Islamic period. The study by Chalmeta and Corriente (1983) provides extensive details of Ibn al-Attar's tenth century treatise that includes numerous generic examples of documents that reflected societal issues prevalent in Cordoba.

The general considerations and observations that are evident from a study of the various titles of the *Partidas*, indicated above, are the following:

- Servitudes, in its various forms, were an important mechanism that provided access from and to buildings and land in the urban environments of historic towns and cities. This was also true in the earlier Islamic period.
- Injury, or damage, and its negation and avoidance were to be observed by all parties that undertook change in the built environment, particularly between proximate neighbors.
- Usage and custom of a locality had to be respected.
- The lapse of time, as a factor, affected decisions that impacted servitudes, injury, possession, and other issues.
- Land use considerations were evident as the case for where to locate schools, and the rules for city walls, squares, streets, and of town commons as well as rules for the sanctity of churches.
- Notaries and their registers were essential professions that ensured the legal documentation of ownership and to any related changes to such ownership over time, as well as other societal events and activities. This was also true in the previous Islamic period as in the example of Ibn al-Attar's work (Chalmeta and Corriente 1983).

Alarife Rules for Building Activities in Toledo During the Fifteenth Century

Before examining the rules that were found in a collection named *Ordenanzas Antiguas* the following brief account is of Toledo's history: The city is situated in the autonomous community of Castile-La Mancha, south-central Spain on a rugged promontory surrounded on three sides by the Tagus river. It lies 67 km southwest of Madrid. The city has ancient Roman history, but later, during the Visigothic period of 255 years (456–711), it was the residence of the Visigothic court in the sixth century. During the Islamic period of 373 years (712–1085) it was named *Tulaytulah,* and was then the home of an important Mozarab community (Arabic speaking Christians). The city was taken by King Alfonso VI of Leon and Castile (1072–1109) in 1085, and became the most important political and social center of Castile. It was the context of the fusion of Christian, Muslim, and Jewish cultures, which manifested itself in the famous School of Translators (*Escuela de Traductores*) that was established by King Alfonso X the Wise in the thirteenth century. The city's importance declined after Philip II made Madrid his capital in 1560 (Toledo 2007).

Ricardo Izquierdo Benito (henceforth referred to as Benito) published an important study in 1986 (Izquierdo Benito 1986) titled "Normas sobre edificaciones en Toledo en el siglo XV" (Building norms [or rules] in Toledo in the fifteenth century). This section of this chapter is an analysis of this study including the ordinance's articles that were transcribed by Benito and included in his study. The collection of codes named *Ordenanzas Antiguas* are located in the Archivo Municipal de Toledo. Part of the collection that Benito studied is a volume of scrolls, well preserved, but not dated. It was sanctioned, and possibly transcribed, during the reign of the Catholic Kings, identified as such by the royal stamp. Benito refers to this particular collection as the *Ordenanzas de Toledo* (abbreviated as *OT*). It is a collection of rules that is associated with the institution of *Alarife* (a word that is derived from the Arabic meaning an expert). It usually refers to a master-mason, or it could also refer to an expert carpenter, plasterer, plumber or gravel worker (Benito 1986, footnote 11).

Jean-Pierre Molenat (2000) analysed the *OT* and suggests an earlier date to its official approval in July 1400. He points out the importance to distinguish between the text's origin and its diffusion. He indicates the late thirteenth century or fourteenth century as its origin, and suggests its underlying principles, including the contents of a number of the code articles, to Islamic law, and further suggests the possibility of its diffusion by the Mozarab community in Toledo during that period. I have re-organized the articles of the *OT* into a framework of principles, issues, and rules that affect decisions. This framework is used in this chapter to organize the presentation of the contents of the *OT*. The original sequence of *OT's* articles are included in Appendix 9. The framework is:

(1) Who are the *alarifes*?; (2) Assignment and work of the *alarifes*; (3) Avoiding and negating damage; (4) Servitudes; (5) Rights of earlier usage; (6) Privacy of neighbor must be respected; (7) Maintenance of streets and keeping them clean; (8) Streets and houses; (9) Rules related to houses; (10) Relationship between upper and lower construction; (11) Purchase/sale, pawing, tenants, and heirs.

*Article 1 – **Who are the alarifes**,* what virtues they should possess and who assigns them. They shall be experts in their trade, educated men who are assigned by the King. They shall possess the following attributes: loyal, of good reputation, and not greedy; knowledge of geometry and understanding of engineering and its subtleties; the ability to judge disputes fairly by being humble and articulate with those that they must judge and able to create peace among them; they shall execute their judgment by order of the *alcalde* (judge – from the Arabic *al-qadi*) with clear understanding of the case before them; and above all they shall fear God and the King.

*Article 2 – **The assignments and work of the alarife:*** the first task of the *alarife*, after their appointment, is to inspect the defensive wall of the town for anything that may affect the integrity of the wall, by removing from the wall anything that may cause it damage, such as wall stirrups, that may be used to climb over the wall, or large opening (s) for the drains or aqueducts that are big enough for a man to get through, and ensure that a space of ten *pasadas* (strides) is kept between the wall and nearby houses. The second task, after being appointed, is to make sure that the King's residence is in good condition and does not require any repairs, and the third task is to ensure that the market and its tents are in good order, as well as the stables as a service to the King and for ensuring that no harm occurs. Other articles that include an explanation of the responsibilities of the *alarife* are mentioned in articles 25, 27, 30, 33, 35, 36, 37, 40 and 41 of the *OT*.

Avoiding and negating damage, is an essential principle that underlie most of the articles (rules) that are in the *OT*. *Article 18 is about public or private baths*: all baths that are in towns, cities or villages belong to the King, except those that the King transfers its ownership to an individual as an act of mercy. Anybody who builds a bath on public land, or on his own, must ensure that it is built in a manner that will not harm the neighbors, particularly the ashes from its chimney and the potential moisture from its pipes. However the element of time is a consideration established by the principle of the rights of earlier usage, so that if a nearby house is built after the bath was built, its owner cannot make demands and ask for compensation from the bath's owner, unless the latter agrees as a courtesy or good will. *Article 19 is about ovens*: Just as the previous article, the King owns all ovens, regardless of their location, except those that the King donates its ownership to an individual as an act of mercy. Any person who builds an oven on public land, or on his own land, shall avoid any potential damage to the neighbors from the oven's fire, however, as in the previous article 18, the factor of time and the rights of earlier usage must be considered, so that if a nearby house is built near an existing oven, the owner of the oven is not liable for damage but he must in any case be careful to avoid any damage.

Article 20 is about dove houses or dovecotes: in principle they are not allowed within the town because of the damage they cause to the roofs of buildings and their tiles, unless the *sennor* of the town (possibly referring to the mayor) allows it. Conditions for their construction is indicated. *Article 21* is about the damage that dovecotes cause to towers and *sobrados* of the neighbor(s). *Article 22 is about houses that exceed the height of adjacent ones*: discusses what should be observed between such structures, including issues related to party walls and who is responsible for damages caused such as rainwater from the higher structures onto the lower one. An interesting rule about two heirs that inherit a threshing floor is *Article 15* that specifies a wall may be built to divide the threshing floor between them provided the wall does not exceed half the height of a man (around 86 cm) to allow the wind to reach both sides. In this way damage to both parties is avoided. *Article 24* is about the damage from water channels that may affect a neighbor. The *alarife* will instruct the owner of the channel on how to make changes to the channel to alleviate the damage to the neighbor. *Article 27 is about an old wall that is feared to collapse or has collapsed.* After a complaint is received by the *alarife* from a neighbor, the former's duty is to examine the situation and with consultation with the local judge, *alcalde*, a decision is reached to resolve this problem. This also involves an estimate, with two other associates of the *alarife*, for the cost of repair that the owner of the wall has to pay. *Article 31* addresses three issues, the damage from smoke that a chimney may cause to the neighbor(s), the intrusion into the privacy of the neighbor from a window that an adjacent neighbor might create, and third is about the misuse of an adjacent empty lot by its neighbor. The first issue, regardless if the chimney is older than a neighbor's house, obliges the owner of the chimney to avoid the problem caused by the smoke. It does not say how. The second issue about opening a window is discussed in more detail based on the principle that overlooking a neighbor's private realm is considered not appropriate and must be avoided. Solutions are suggested. The third issue discusses a channel over an adjacent empty lot, how to deal with leakage after the lot is built up, and the use of such a plot to deposit dung on it. The neighbor can continue doing so if there is no complaint from the lot's owner, until the latter wants to make use of his lot. *Article 33* is about the noise transmitted through the walls from one neighbor to another, such as due to hammering or from animals tied to the wall and the vibrations they create due to their movements. An interesting method for determining if the noise transmitted is acceptable or not is determined by *alarife*, by order of the *alcalde*, by placing a bowel next to the edge of the wall in question filled with dry sand. If some of the sand spills from the bowl, during the vibrations, then the noise is determined as damage and its origin has to be stopped. This type of case has precedents during the Islamic period and even much later, such as the case recorded in the treatise of Ibn al-Rami in fourteenth century Tunis (Hakim 1986, p. 32, 33).

The rights granted by servitude is the second important principle that affected decisions. *Article 16* is about access to and from a property that is surrounded by other properties: the legal principle that is followed in a case as this is that no property shall be without an entry/exit. The *alcalde* must send in "good men", presumably the *alarife*, to the location to determine if there is another passage that does not cross other properties, and if there is no such possibility, then the shortest distance for access is determined between the property and nearest street. *Article 17* is about water that traverses a property, or originates there, and reaches somebody else's property. A number of situations and related conditions are indicated in this Article. Servitude rights, where they are needed, is an important principle that underlie the rules of the *OT*. This was the case in Roman law and the rules that were developed during the Islamic period as the evidence is available in the tenth century treatise of Ibn al-Imam, followed by the laws in the *Sieta Partidas* that were discussed earlier. The compact nature of historic and traditional towns, that are located on both the northern and southern coasts of the Mediterranean, would not have been possible to evolve without the application of the principle of servitude.

The rights of earlier usage is the third principle that had to be respected in decisions. Numerous rules in the *OT* embody the application of this right. For example *Articles 18, 19, and 20*, briefly discussed above, apply this principle. *Article 28* has this principle embedded in the rule that is indicated, namely that if walls are demolished and they are to be re-built they should follow the foundation alignment of the original wall(s). If there is an infringement, the *alarife* shall prohibit it by order of the *alcalde*.

Privacy of neighbors must be respected. The *OT* addresses infringements due to overlooking. The second issue of *Article 31*, discussed above, embodies this principle: namely locations or spaces and windows that allows visual access to a neighbor's private realm is not allowed and must be mitigated. The Article briefly provides detail for a specific case. *Article 34* specifically prohibits opening a door opposite a neighbor's door without the agreement of the latter. This rule applies to doors of shops and public baths that must not be opposite each other to avoid overlooking their interiors. Jean-Pierre Molenat (2000) cites case number 12 from Ibn al-Imam's tenth century treatise as an example of the longevity of these rules from the earlier Islamic period.

Rules for maintenance of streets and keeping them clean was found by Benito (1986) in folios as indicated. No one should discharge trash in front of their homes or on streets. They should burry it or take it outside the city (presumably outside the city walls) [folios 145–146]. If manure or trash is found on the street, the five closest neighbors will be accused unless they reveal who is responsible, if not they shall all be responsible to take the trash outside the city [folios 57–58]. Every Saturday inhabitants of a neighborhood had to sweep and clean the streets of their neighborhood. The owner or tenant of each house had to clean the area of the street adjunct to their house, and the trash accumulated had to be taken outside the city. The *almotacenes* (from the Arabic origin *al-muhtasib*) would inspect the results of the cleaning [folios 146–147]. The gravel that is left on the street from nearby construction or repair of a building, had to be placed against the wall of the building, and within eight days of the completion of the work it had to be taken outside the city [folio 58]. An animal that dies in a home has to be taken out the same day it died [folio 58]. The neighbors on a street have to take out any accumulated animal manure outside the city within three days, as required by the inspectors [folio 58]. Wagons used to collect manure must always be stored outside the city [folio 59]. It was prohibited for pigs to roam freely on streets or plazas, day or night [folios 94 and 113].

Having established the principles that underlie the rules of the *OT*, the following is a brief presentation of ***rules that are related to streets and buildings (mainly houses)***. *Article 3* is about the process of building houses and other edifices that result in establishing access ways in the form of streets, plazas and spaces formed by the junction of two houses or two streets named in the *OT* as *rinconadas*. These resulting spaces, i.e. streets, plazas and the *rinconandas* all belong to the King, i.e. to the municipality. Nobody can claim any of such spaces without the King donating it to that individual. *Article 25* addresses roof projections towards the street. It specifies that no building can extend its roof projection beyond a distance of one-third of the street width. This rule applies to projections from buildings across the street, which then allows the middle one-third of the street open to the sky for air circulation and to allow rain-water. The *alarife* has the power, by order of the *alcalde*, to demolish any roof projection that exceeds this allowance. *Article 26* is about *sobrados* (very likely from the Arabic *sabat*) which is a room bridging the street. Any owner building such a construction must allow a height clearance under the *sobrados* that would allow a knight in full armor to pass through, and if it is lower than this, the *alarife*, by order of the *alcalde*, shall have it demolished (no clearance dimension is specified as a part of this rule). Jean-Pierre Molenat (2000) cites case number 5 from Ibn al-Imam's tenth century treatise as an example of the longevity of these rules from the earlier Islamic period. In the latter treatise the clearance should allow a fully loaded beast of burden to pass through (approximately 3.50 m – see Hakim 1986, p. 21). *Article 35* prohibits the construction of a *poyos* (built-in bench) to be built against any wall that abuts a narrow street that would impede the traffic. The *alarife* can demolish such a bench by order of the *alcalde*. Addressing narrow streets imply the inclusion of cul-de-sacs. In the earlier Islamic period those were considered as jointly owned property by those who have access from it. In Spanish the term used for these types of streets/ access paths is *adarves* (from the Arabic *al-dareb*). Jean Passini's (2000) excellent study in which he traced the existence of *adarves* in twelfth century Toledo to their disappearance in the fifteenth century. He indicated this change on a map from an area of the city (see Figs. 3.1, 3.2 and 3.3). In essence, argues Passini, the conception of space as it related to streets, particularly *adarves*, changed during the Christian period that followed. All streets, regardless of their size or location, belonged to the King, i.e. the municipality. No direct mention in the *OT* of the conception of the *Fina*, that was an important concept related to streets and their use. Its usage is discussed in Ibn al-Imam's tenth century treatise. A brief definition is: the space immediately adjacent to the exterior wall of a building. Its width can vary between 1.00 and 1.50 m depending on the width of the street. It may be used for short temporary periods by the owner or tenant of the adjunct building (Hakim 1986). *Article 5* discusses the responsibility of those who come together to build a quarter, i.e. a group of houses and its streets, are responsible to build the cano (conduits or pipes that carry sewage) towards the main drainage of the village or town. Who is responsible for repairs is also indicated.

Rules that relate to buildings (mainly houses) are addressed through these elements: boundaries, shared or party walls, upper and lower levels of a building. With the exception of Articles 18 on baths and 19 on ovens, that are discussed above under the principle of avoiding and negating damage, all others relate to houses. On shared walls *Article 30* determines ownership agreement of shared walls recognized as such through a document, a witness, or by any other pact, or if it has beams (presumably on both sides for both houses sharing the wall). All these conditions are an indication that the wall is jointly owned, and the *alarife* will recognize it as such. The Article includes specific instructions in a situation when there is a jointly owned space between two properties and both owners want to build a new wall. *Article 23* deals with the lapse of time and its effect on determining ownership. Any man that benefits from a neighbor's wall and a year has passed and there is no evidence of a contract between the two parties, and the person who owns the wall swears that he did not know that his neighbor is using the wall and that he does not agree, the *alcalde* shall order the person using the wall to detach his use of the wall. However, if two or more years have passed, without complaint by the owner of the wall, the neighbor making use of the wall shall not lose its use, unless the owner of the wall can prove that he was away from the town during all of that period. *Article 4* addresses the issue of rainwater passage between the walls of two houses. If the rainwater is collected from both roofs then both parties benefit from it. However, if only one roof is the source, then the rainwater belongs to the owner of that roof. *Article 27* is about the collapse of a wall or of an old wall that is leaning and is in danger of collapse. If a complaint is received by *alcalde* that a wall has collapsed or there is a danger of collapse of an old wall that may cause damage, the *alarife* by order of the *alcalde* shall examine the situation and if necessary shall have it demolished before it kills somebody or create damage. If the owner of the wall is absent from the town, the *alarife* shall inform the *alcalde* and shall order it to be demolished. The *alarife* shall also estimate the cost and the wall's owner must eventually pay these costs. *Article 28* is about rebuilding a wall(s) that have collapsed. It should be built on the same foundation alignment of the original wall within the owner's plot boundary and no infringement towards the street is allowed. The *alarife*, by order of the *alcalde*, shall prohibit any infringement of this rule.

On the relationship of upper and lower construction. *Article 22's* title "Of houses that exceed in height other houses" and its content could imply the relationship between adjoining house on a slope or on top of each other. The house above must ensure that the rainwater evacuation shall not cause damage to the foundations of the house below. If the owner of the house above would like to build a *sobrado* or tower or a dovecote he shall be responsible for the cost of walls and foundations that are necessary. If, however, they agree to share the cost and the owner of the upper house overloads the walls and it collapses on the lower house, then the owner of the above house shall pay the damages to the owner of the lower house. The Article also specifies on who pays the cost, when the wall is shared, and one party refuses to pay for its rebuilding. *Article 29*'s language is not clear about the *sobrados* that are built, or rest on, other walls. These are structures that usually bridge over the street and require support on the other side of the owner's house. It mentions the obvious that the roof of the *sobrado* is its owner's responsibility. The owner of the lower house is supposed to strengthen the walls that are supporting it, and does not mention that this is the case when the *sobrado* is shared. However, *Article 26* is specifically about the *sobrado* that projects over and covers the street. The clearance under it shall be adequate to allow the passage of a knight in full armor, and if it is lower than that the *alarife*, by order of the *alcalde*, shall have it demolished. *Article 32* is on basements and wells: any owner of a house can dig a well, or a channel, or a basement, provided he does not create damage to a neighbor's adjacent wall. Before the commencement of the project, the neighbor shall be informed and shown a letter of an attorney stating so. This right to build is part of the right accorded to an owner of a property the freedom to build under or above his house provided no damage or danger will affect the neighbors.

On the purchase/sale, pawning, tenants, and heirs. *Article 36* on the division of constructed property among its heirs when one or more of the heirs contends over the division of a house, a *tienda* (tent), or *sobrado* (upper room), or bath, or *alfondiga* (hotel or similar use), or of a construction built of brick (*frogada*). The *alarife* shall judge the situation, by order of *alcalde*, with two men that are knowledgeable of construction, and if it is something that can be divided, then the *alarife* shall divide it and have the heirs cast lots for the various parts that result from the division of the property. If it cannot be divided then the *alarife* shall arrange that it shall be sold in auction for the best price and the proceeds are divided among the heirs.

The Article also addresses on how to deal with an heir who wants to obstruct division of the property for his own selfish reasons. *Article 37* on the purchase or sale of a construction that has flaws in it. This is based on the principle that a flaw in a property for sale must be declared by its owner to the buyer so that the price is adjusted accordingly. If the flaw is declared then the sale must be firm. If not, the *alarife*, with two associates, shall judge accordingly and determine a fare sale price that the buyer and seller have to accept. *Article 38* on pawning of a house or other construction (from the verb pawn, i.e. an object left as security for money lent). If a man accepts an item to be pawned which could be a house, an upper room, a hotel, bath, or a tent for storage, or any other construction, then such an item, while in the possession of the man that accepts it as a pawn, is damaged then he must repair it and keep it in good condition until the pawn is terminated. However, if the damage is caused by old age or rot then it is no fault of his. *Article 39* on the obligations of a tenant in a rented house: he is responsible for any damage to the walls, roof, beams, doors, or even tables and must pay for such damage and restore it to its original state by order of the *alcalde*. However, he shall not have to pay for damage to walls that lost their color, or are stained with soot, or part of the floor collapses as this type of damage is a part of the rent. Upon leaving the building he must ensure that it is clean and the privy is clear of dung.

   This covers all of the articles and their associated rules for the area of the city within the walls. The *OT* also contains *Articles 6 through 14 that are about elements located outside of the walls of the city*, such as those related to water and its distribution – mills, *anorias* (a wheel with buckets to draw up water), and small dams for diverting the water. Who is responsible for repair when mills are jointly owned? What are the punishments for those who damage any elements of the water distribution system? Those articles are not going to be elaborated here. See Figs. 3.4 and 3.5 for images of Toledo in 1930.

Alarife Rules for Building Activities in Cordoba from the Late Fifteenth Century/Early Sixteenth Century

Jesus Padilla Gonzalez's three studies (1983, 1984, 1996), included in the references, contain the following information about the institution of the *Alarife* from the late fifteenth century onwards to the eighteenth century, specifically to the date of publication in the year 1786 of the *Alarife* rules that this part of the chapter will draw on. The term *alarife* as an institution in Córdoba had a double meaning: (1) at the end of the fifteenth century it could be a synonym of *veedor* (overseer or inspector), or *alcalde* (mayor or judge) of any of the several construction occupations or trades in the city; (2) in the fifteenth century and specially in the sixteenth, the term *alarife* was used exclusively to designate two master masons *albañiles* or stone cutters *canteros*, or one master mason *albañil* and one master stone cutter *cantero*. These two masters were appointed by the city in perpetuity, or for a limited time, or annually depending on the historical time period in which the appointment occurred. Their job was to inspect *vistas de ojos* or bring into being *hacer condiciones* construction projects and public buildings in the city. They could also have the responsibility to perform the orders given to them by the judge or be consulted by a judge of the city about disputes related to constructions or buildings in the city. Furthermore, they also could function as surveyors or supervisors of surveyors, inspectors of bridges, drainages, walls, towers, streets, etc.

The term *Alarifazgo* could also have multiple meanings. First, it could designate a group of masters of different trades throughout the city. This is the most generic use of the word. Second, and this being the more specific use of the term, it signifies a group of inspectors or judges. Third, it could mean the institution made of the *alcaldes* (mayors or judges) and the *alarifes* of the city. Padilla Gonzalez, however, opts to use the term *alarifazgo* to signify the trade of *alarifes* from the point of view of an institution with legal powers in maters related to constructions in the city (1983, 58–60). The reminder of the article describes the historical evolution of the term *alarifazgo*. Padilla Gonzalez's (1984) article describes the election procedures of the *alarifes*, their activities in relationship to the city council, their judicial responsibilities, and their responsibilities within the guild of *alarifes*, and the fees they charged. He also points out that the institution of *alarifes*, in Cordoba, continued to the nineteenth century.

Jesús Padilla González indicates that *Libro 1° de las Ordenanzas de Córdoba* is the 'usual' or 'common' shortened name of manuscript number 39, section 13, of series 10 in the Archivo Municipal de

Córdoba (abbreviated in his 1983 and 1984 articles as A.M.C., in note 2, page 55 of the 1983 article, and in note 2, page 186 of the 1984 article). The complete title of the work according to the authors is: *Lybro Primero de las Ordenanzas que esta Muy Noble y muy Leal ziudad de Córdoua tiene para su gobierno, recopiladas con el nuevo yndize en el año 1716 siendo Escribanos Mayores de Cordoua D. Manuel Fernández de Cañete y D. Pedro Muñoz Touoso.* Furthermore, according to note 6, page 56 of his 1983 article the "Ordenanzas de alarifes de Pero López (*Hordenança de los alarifes*)" contains the 154 chapters or articles related to the *alarifes* and is dated from 1 February 1503. These 154 chapters are in the *Libro 1° de las Ordenanzas de Córdoba*, pages (abbreviated "ff") 131r. to 168 v. This same manuscript is also available in "Caja de Hierro" manuscript number 1778 and it is also in the Biblioteca Municipal de Córdoba with the title *Ordenanças de Alarife de esta M. N. y M. L. Ciudad de Córdoba, sacada a la letra de los originales que en su Archivo tiene dicha Ciudad para el uso de los Maestros de Alvañilería, y Carpintería de ella,* (Córdoba, Imprenta de Juan Rodríguez de la Torre, 1786). This last manuscript is located in the Biblioteca Municipal de Córdoba, shelf stack ("estantería") number 42, shelf ("tabla") 3, numbers 34 – folios 3–79. The cover is reproduced in Fig. 3.6, and the list of its contents and translations of selected articles are included in Appendix 10.

The framework of the topics that were used in the previous section for presenting the material of the *alarife* rules from early fifteenth century Toledo will be used to indicate where the articles, in the above-cited manuscript (i.e. *Ordenanças de Alarife de esta M. N. y M. L. Ciudad de Córdoba, 1786*) fit in. This is done to demonstrate the continuity of the rules from one city to another over a period of about one century, and are presented in Appendix 10. The number of each article, in Appendix 10, and its subject, as published in the *Ordenanças of 1786,* is listed sequentially followed by the number(s) of the Toledo framework to which it corresponds like this [# in Toledo framework]. The Toledo framework is presented here in more detail:

1 – Who are the *alarifes*?; 2 – Assignment and work of the *alarifes*; 3 – Avoiding and negating damage: Public and private baths; Ovens; Dovecotes; House that exceeds height of adjacent one; Old wall that

is feared to collapse; Smoke; Privacy – intrusion from a neighbor's window; Misuse of adjacent empty plot; Noise transmitted through wall; 4 – Servitude; Access to and from a property that is surrounded by other property; Water transverses other's property; 5 – Rights of earlier usage; Follow foundation of original wall. 6 – Privacy of neighbor must be respected; Door opposite door; 7 – Maintenance of streets and keeping them clean; Who is responsible for what; 8 – Streets and houses; Space on streets formed by junction of houses; Roof projection onto street; *Sobrados* (room bridging public street); Built-in bench on street; Who is responsible for building the sewage line; 9 – Rules related to houses; Shared walls; Lapse of time and effect on ownership; Rainwater passage between two houses; Collapse of wall and rebuilding it; 10 – Relationship between upper and lower construction; House that exceed height of adjacent house; *Sobrados* should allow a Knight with full armour to pass under; Basement and wells; 11 – Purchase / sale, pawing, tenants, and heirs; Division of property among heirs; Purchase of property that has flows in it; Pawning; Tenant's obligations.

The following is a statistical distribution of the rules, in the *Ordenanças of 1786*, according to the issues that they address as indicated by its number in the above framework: [3] Avoiding and negating damage – 23 %; [4] Servitude – 3 %; [5] Rights of earlier usage – 2.2 %; [6] Privacy – 3.6 %; [7] Maintenance of streets – 3 %; [8] Streets and houses – 15 %; [9] Related to houses only – 21 %; [10] Relation between upper and lower levels – 3 %; [11] Purchase, sale, etc. – 2 %. The first two topics, in the framework above, of the *OT (Ordenanzas de Toledo)* on [1] Who are the *alarifes*, and [2] Assignment and work of the *alarifes*, are also covered in similar stipulations in the Cordoba *Ordenanças of 1786* as 1 – Who are the *alarifes* and what are their qualities, and 2 – First thing the *alarife* has to do after being sworn in.

Twenty-three percent of the rules address the issue of avoiding and negating damage. Thirty-six percent are rules that address houses and as they relate to streets. This is a total of 59 % of the code. The rest of the rules ranging from 2 to 3.6 % each address other issues and topics of the framework above. The total is 76 % of the code. The balance of 14 % of the rules address issues that are absent in the earlier *OT (Ordenanzas de Toledo)*. They are: *Land use* – articles 101 on the prohibition of the location of an inn or tavern within a neighborhood, article 130 on where not to locate a laundry establishment, and article 105 on the conditions that permit selling merchandise on the street. *Solar access* – is covered by articles 50, 84, 87, and 128 on the respect for solar access to a neighbor, for example, the need to lower a party wall to allow solar access; trees that are within 3 f. from a neighbor's wall will likely block solar access; and rebuilding a damaged or collapsed roof must be done by ensuring that solar access reaches the neighbor. *Visual corridors* – techniques that would determine if visual access to a neighbor is damaging or not are covered by article 125. *Mater masons* – private individuals who hire master masons whose work infringes on the established rules of the *alarife* are addressed by articles 80, 81, 82, and 133. For a map of Cordoba in 1811, see Fig. 3.7. For recent air photos see Figs. 3.8 and 3.9.

References

Anderson, G. D., & Rosser-Owen, M. (Eds.). (2007). *Revisiting Al-Andalus: Perspectives on the material culture of Islamic Iberia and beyond.* Leiden/Boston: Brill.

Atkinson, W. C. (1960). *A history of Spain and Portugal.* Middlesex: Penguin.

Barbier. (1900, 1901). Translator from Arabic to French of al-Tutaili, Isa bin Musa (died 996 C.E.). Des droits et obligations entre proprietaires d'heritages voisins. *Revue Algerienne et Tunisienne de Legislation et de Jurisprudence* (Part 1 – Vol. 16, 1900 and Part 2 – Vol. 17, 1901).

Berger, A. (1953). Encyclopedic dictionary of Roman law. *Transactions of the American Philosophical Society, 43*(part 2). Philadelphia: American Philosophical Society.

Boisard, M. A. (1980). On the probable influence of Islam on Western Public and International Law. *International Journal of Middle East Studies, 11*(4), 429–450.

Burns, R. I. (Ed.). (2001). *Las Siete Partidas* (5 Vols., S.P. Scott, Trans.). Philadelphia: University of Pennsylvania Press.

Chalmeta, P., & Corriente, F. (Eds.). (1983). *Formulario Notarial Hispano-Arabe por el alfaqui y notario Cordobes Ibn al-Attar (s. X).* Madrid (Arabic and Spanish).

Comez Ramos, R. (1975). El Libro del Peso de Los Alarifes. *Las Actas del I Simposio Internacional de Mudejarismo* (pp. 255–267).

Goolam, N. M. I. (1999). Islamic influence on European legal philosophy and law. *Fundamina, 5,* 44–85.

el-Hajji, A. A. (1987). *Al-Tarikh al-Andalusi, 711–1492 C.E.* [The Andalusian History]. Damascus (Arabic).

Hakim, B. S. (1986). *Arabic-Islamic cities: Building and planning principles.* London: KPI.

Hakim, B. S. (1994). The 'Urf' and its role in diversifying the architecture of traditional Islamic cities. *Journal of Architectural & Planning Research, 11*(2), 108–127.

Hakim, B. S. (2001). Julian of Ascalon's treatise of construction and design rules from 6th-c. Palestine. *Journal of the Society of Architectural Historians, 60*(1), 4–25.

Hakim, B. S. (2008). Mediterranean urban and building codes: Origins, content, impact, and lessons. *Urban Design International, 13*(1), 21–40.

Hakim, B. S., & Ahmed, Z. (2006). Rules for the built environment in 19th century Northern Nigeria. *Journal of Architectural and Planning Research, 23*(1), 1–26.

Izquierdo Benito, R. (1986). Normas sobre edificaciones en Toledo en el siglo XV. *Anuario de Estudios Medievales, 16*, 519–532.

Molenat, J.-P. (2000). Les *Ordenanzas de los alarifes* de Toledo, comme temoignage sur la permanence de traditions d'epoque islamique. *Urbanisme musulman*(pp. 191–199). Madrid.

Padilla Gonzalez, J. (1983). "El Alarifazgo de Cordoba (1478–1516)" – Primera Parte. *Axerquia: Revista de Estudios Cordobeses, 8*, 53–82.

Padilla Gonzalez, J. (1984). "El Alarifazgo de Cordoba (Siglos XV y XVI)" – Segunda Parte. *Axerquia: Revista de Estudios Cordobeses, 10*, 183–206.

Padilla Gonzalez, J. (1987). Las ordenanzas de los carpinteros de Cordoba (siglos XV-XVI). *La Ciudad hispánica durante los siglos XIII al XVI: actas del coloquio celebrado en La Rábida y Sevilla del 14 al 19 de septiembre de 1981* (pp. 175–202). Edit Universidad Complutense, 1985.

Padilla Gonzalez, J. (1996). *Pedro Lopez II, Maestro Mayor y Alarife de Cordoba (1478–1507).* Cordoba.

Passini, J. (2000). L'urbanisme medieval toledan: decisions des juristes malikites et ordonnances municipales chretiennes de la construction. *Urbanisme musulman* (pp. 201–213). Madrid.

Ruiz, T. F. (1986). Law, Spanish. In *Dictionary of the middle ages* (Vol. 7, pp. 518–524). New York.

Scott, S. P. (Trans.). (1910). *The Visigothic Code (Forum Judicum).* Boston.

Shatzmiller, M. (1986). Review of P. Chalmeta & F. Corriente (Eds.). (1983). Formulario Notarial Hispano-Arabe por el alfaqui y notario Cordobes Ibn al-Attar (s. X), Madrid. *International Journal of Middle East Studies, 18*(4), 539–541.

Spain. (2007). Encyclopædia Britannica. *Encyclopædia Britannica 2007 ultimate reference suite.* Chicago.

Toledo. (2007). Encyclopædia Britannica. *Encyclopædia Britannica 2007 ultimate reference suite.* Chicago.

Torres Balbas, L. (1971). *Ciudades Hispano-Musulmanas.* Madrid.

Torres Marquez, M., & Naranjo Ramirez, J. (2012). El casco histórico de Córdoba y el primer plano de la ciudad: el «Plano de los Franceses» de 1811. *Eria: Revista Cuatrimestral de Geografía, 88*(2012), 129–151.

al-Tutaili, Isa bin Musa (died 996 C.E. – a). *Kitab al-Jidar*, verified by Ibrahim bin Muhammad al-Fayez, Riyadh, 1996.

al-Tutaili, Isa bin Musa (died 996 C.E. – b). *Al-Qada bil Marfaq fi al-Mabani wa Nefi al-Darar*, verified by Muhammad al-Numainij, Rabat, 1999.

al-Tutaili, Isa bin Musa (died 996 C.E. – c). *Kitab Nefi al-Darar*, verified by Ferid bin Sulaiman and al-Mukhtar al-Telili, Tunis, 2003.

al-Tuwaijri, Sulaiman. (1982). *Haq al-Irtifaq: Dirasa Muqarana* (Rights of servitude: A comparative study). PhD dissertation undertaken at Um al-Qura University, Makkah, and published online (Arabic).

Uthman, M. A. (1987). Fi shawari' al-medina al-Islamiyah wa turuqatiha [In the streets of the Islamic city]. *Al-Usur, 2*(part 2), 189–242 (Arabic).

Violich, F. (1962). Evolution of the Spanish City: Issues basic to planning today. *Journal of the American Institute of Planners, 28*(3), 170–179.

Fig. 3.1 Air photo of Toledo historic town in twentieth century (*Source*: Google Earth)

Fig. 3.2 The quarters of San Antolin and San Marcos: (**a**) circulation that shows the through streets and the cul-de-sacs during the Middle Ages. The Spanish term used for the cul-de-sacs is *adarves*; (**b**) the urban tissue of the same area in the twentieth century that shows *adarves* no longer exist due to their absorption by owners of the houses that they originally served (After Jean Passini (2000, p. 212))

Fig. 3.3 Air photo of the quarters of Toledo presented in Fig. 3.2 (*Source*: Google Earth)

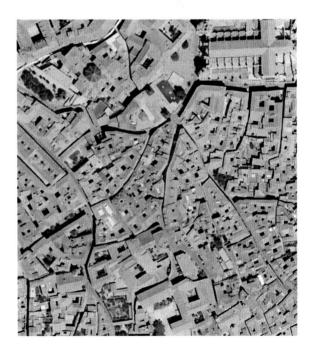

PLAZUELA DE SAN NICOLÁS

Foto Aldus

Fig. 3.4 Toledo, 1930. Plazuela de San Nicolas. This photo shows three types of upper level projections. Mules were used to carry heavy loads and small carts for moving heavy pots. The paving of the main street is different from the paving of the triangular surface of the plazuela. Photo (073) from the public website of Excmo. Ayuntamiento de Toledo: http://www.ayto-toledo.org/archivo/imagenes/fotos/1930/1930.asp

COBERTIZO DE SANTA CLARA

Fig. 3.5 Toledo, 1930. Cobertizo de Santa Clara. Rooms bridging the street at three levels. The upper room is of significance to the occupants as demonstrated by the decorative grill on the window. Photo (079) from the public website of Excmo. Ayuntamiento de Toledo: http://www.ayto-toledo.org/archivo/imagenes/fotos/1930/1930.asp

ORDENANZAS

DE ALARIFES

DE ESTA M. N. Y M. L.

CIUDAD DE CORDOBA,

SACADAS A LA LETRA DE LOS ORI-
ginales que en su Archivo tiene dicha Ciudad para el uso de los Maestros de Alvañilería, y Carpintería de ella.

CORDOBA.   MDCCLXXXVI.
En la Oficina de Don *Juan Rodriguez de la Torre.*
Con las licencias necesarias.

Fig. 3.6 Cover of the 1786 edition of the ordinances of *Alarifes* compiled by Pedro Lopez II, Grand Expert and *Alarife* of Cordoba from 1478 to 1507, confirming its long duration. Translation of this cover is in Part 2 of Appendix 10

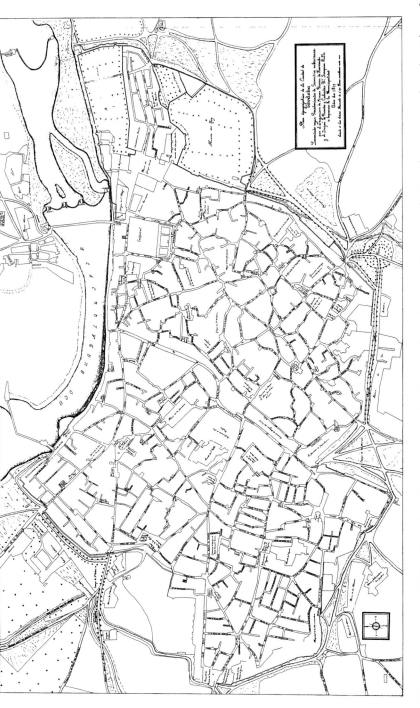

Fig. 3.7 Cordoba map of 1811. Note the existence and predominance of cul-de-sacs in the early nineteenth century, only a short time of 25 years after the publication of the Ordinances of *Alarife* in 1786. The caption in the box is: "Topographical plan of the city of Cordoba, drawn according to the principles of subterranean geometry by the mining engineer Baron of Karvinski and the engineer of bridges and roads Joaquin Rillo, in the year 1811. Funded by the Municipality". Note that the north direction is pointing down. Contemporary maps are usually drawn with the north direction pointing up

Fig. 3.8 Cordoba air photo of the historic area of the city during the twentieth century. Photo provided by Conjuncto Historico de Cordoba of the Gerencia Municipal de Urbanismo Ayuntamiento de Cordoba. North direction pointing down to match the direction in Fig. 3.7

Fig. 3.9 Cordoba, 2010. Oblique air photo of the historic sector of the city showing the famous mosque of Cordoba on the left foreground. The predominant typology of the clustered courtyard buildings is clearly evident (Photo by Rafael Tena Risquez, taken on December 28, 2010, and posted on http://cordobadesdeelcielo. blogspot.com.es/p/barrio-barrio.html)

Chapter 4
Conclusions

An underlying *goal* of all the codes that are discussed in Chaps. 1, 2, and 3 is *to deal with change in the built environment by ensuring that minimum damage occurs to preexisting structures and their owners, through stipulating fairness in the distribution of rights and responsibilities among various parties, particularly those who are proximate to each other. This ultimately will ensure the equitable equilibrium of the built environment during the process of change and growth.* Equitable equilibrium is a term this author uses to imply that fairness and justice must always be maintained between the rights of proximate neighbors to achieve harmony and goodwill.

The underlying *intentions* that are evident by a careful study of these codes are:

1. Change in the built environment should be accepted as a natural and healthy phenomenon. In the face of ongoing change, it is necessary to maintain an equitable equilibrium in the built environment.
2. Change, particularly that occurring among proximate neighbors, creates potential for damages to existing dwellings and other uses. Therefore, certain measures are necessary to prevent changes or uses that would (1) result in debasing the social and economic integrity of adjacent or nearby properties, (2) create conditions adversely affecting the moral integrity of the neighbors, and (3) destabilize peace and tranquility between neighbors.

A part of this chapter are Figs. 4.1–4.3 and Appendix 11.

B.S. Hakim, *Mediterranean Urbanism: Historic Urban / Building Rules and Processes*, DOI 10.1007/978-94-017-9140-3_4,
© Springer Science+Business Media Dordrecht 2014

3. In principle, property owners have the freedom to do what they please on their own property. Most uses are allowed, particularly those necessary for a livelihood. Nevertheless, the freedom to act within one's property is constrained by preexisting conditions of neighboring properties, neighbors' rights of servitude, and other rights associated with ownership for certain periods of time.
4. The compact built environment of ancient towns necessitates the implementation of interdependence rights among citizens, principally among proximate neighbors. As a consequence of interdependence rights, it becomes necessary to allocate responsibilities among such neighbors, particularly with respect to legal and economic issues.
5. The principle of interdependence allocates the right to a neighbor to abut a neighboring existing structure, but he must respect its boundaries and its owner's property rights.
6. The public realm must not be subjected to damages that result from activities or waste originating in the private realm.

The following are highlights of the issues and related cases in the built environment that are addressed by the codes:

Land use: location of churches or mosques, public baths, artisanal workshops, bakeries, and socially offensive uses
Views: for enjoyment such as the sea, mountains, and public gardens
Overlooking: visual corridors that compromise privacy generated by the location of doors, windows, openings, and heights
Houses and condominiums: involving acts that debase the value of adjacent properties, walls and floors between neighbors, and condominiums in multistory buildings
Walls: abutting and sharing rights; ownership rights and responsibilities
Drainage and hygiene: rain and wastewater drainage; responsibilities for cleaning septic tanks and removal of garbage
Planting: of trees, shrubs, and other vegetation
Streets: open-ended streets, cul-de-sacs, projections on streets, servitude, and access
Animals: cattle, sheep, chicken, birds, and bees

The nature of these codes are not to be viewed as being similar to contemporary planning regulations that are written to enforce an adopted master plan. Traditional towns, which are the subject of this book, were conceived and implemented according to known concepts and customary practices of a particular region. However, the incremental process of growth and change required that they follow accepted customary practices and rules known within the locality. These rules were formalized within the legal literature to provide local courts a framework for making sound and equitable decisions when two or more parties face conflicts resulting from changes and adjustments to their immediate surroundings. It is from this legal literature, examples of which are in Chaps. 1, 2, and 3, that we can identify specific rules and codes that were applied in the built environment of traditional towns.

Figure 4.1 portrays the conceptual representations of impacts on the local level (3 geometric shapes denoting 3 settlements) by *proscriptive* meta-principles and by *prescriptive* imposed laws. The diagram on the left represents a settlement's ability to respond freely to local conditions and requirements but is restrained by an over-arching set of meta-principles. This would result in settlements that are diverse in their physical form and exhibit distinct identity. The diagram on the right represents how prescriptions from a central authority, which are usually far removed from a locality, can inhibit creative solutions to local problems. Over time, the resulting settlements would tend to become similar to each other. The codes that are presented in this book contain both the proscriptive and prescriptive types, and we find that sometimes the same code contains both. Here is a definition/explanation of both types:

Proscription is an imposed restraint synonymous with prohibition as in "thou shalt not," e.g., you are free to design and manipulate your property provided you do not create damage on adjacent properties. *Prescription* is laying down of authoritative directions as in "thou shalt," e.g., you shall set back from your front boundary by (x) meters and from your side boundaries by (y) meters regardless of site conditions. Roman/Byzantine codes in many instances included specific numeric prescriptions, unlike their Islamic counterparts that tended not to include them.

Each traditional town had distinct features and a sense of place unique to its built form, whereas one can see the almost identical land-use patterns and built form features in the thousands of communities that were built in many countries, especially since the 1950s of the twentieth century.

Lessons for Contemporary and Future Practice

It is essential and instructive to understand the system and processes underlying the development of traditional towns and cities. Recent science can provide us with good analogies that clarify the phenomenon. John Holland's book contains useful insight (Holland 1995). In Chap. 1, he explains what a complex adaptive system is and how it works by identifying adaptive and aggregate agents. Individual agent's behavior is determined by a collection of rules that are a convenient way to describe agent strategies. These agents interact with each other according to rules that produce aggregation of agents at the next level, and those may again be aggregated to add new hierarchal levels. Rules can change as experience is accumulated. This is precisely what occurred in traditional built environments. What is also important to understand is that a complex adaptive system is nonlinear and dynamic that creates unpredictable and diverse results within the framework of rules. Although multitudes of changes do occur, particularly at the micro level, overall coherence of the character and identity of the town or city are not compromised (see Appendix 11 for definitions of these terms).

The study by Hakim and Ahmed (2006) demonstrates how the traditional city in the nineteenth-century Northern Nigeria embodies the characteristics of a self-regulating and adaptive system. The self-regulating aspect is a result of the decisions and actions of specific individuals in starting new compounds or small farms. In doing so, they respond to existing conditions on adjacent properties by adjusting their planning and design decisions. Over time, changes and adaptations occur in compounds as their owners adjust and adapt to changes in neighboring and contiguous compounds. The alignment of pathways and streets will be delineated and extended in response to the creation and/or changes of farm boundaries and compound walls.

Another important phenomenon that occurred in traditional towns is feedback. There are two types of feedback: negative and positive. It is the former that can handle random changes and a way of reaching equilibrium and equitability. Positive feedback repeats the same action again and again and is associated with top-down prescriptive codes as evident in current zoning laws. The relationship between proximate neighbors depends on decisions affected by negative feedback, such as when a window from one house overlooks the private domain of another as demonstrated by the codes in this book. The owner of the latter reacts by demanding that the window be sealed or removed. However, if the window was there before the new neighbor built his house, he must respond by laying out the house so that overlooking would not occur.

Emergent systems, such as what we find in traditional Mediterranean urbanism, depend on operating within boundaries defined by rules. The system's capacity for learning, growth, and experimentation derives from its adherence to these rules. Another important property in a living dynamic system is its network pattern. Networks of communications generate feedback loops, and such systems learn from mistakes. Thus, a community can correct its mistakes and regulate and organize itself by negative feedback.

It is extremely instructive for further understanding the underlying generative system and its codes that shaped traditional Mediterranean towns to use the analogy of the human or animal embryo. The following insight is from Lewis Wolpert's book (Wolpert 1991). He uses the term "generative program" as a framework for explaining how a generative system works:

> The embryo does not contain a description of the animal to which it will give rise, rather it contains a generative program for making it. It is like a recipe and different from a descriptive program, and a complex form can come from a simple program that is essentially contained within the genes that control cell behavior.
>
> There is no 'master builder' in the embryo. Each cell in the developing embryo has access to the same genetic information. A general principle of the embryonic organization is that 'small is beautiful'. There is no central government but rather, a number of small self-governing regions.

This is what occurs in a typical traditional built environment, i.e., the cell referred to above is the agent or individual household, and the embryo is the town under formation and once formed will continue to experience change and growth. The genetic information is the rules and codes that individuals follow without being dictated by a top-down authority. The small governing regions, the term used by Wolpert, correspond to neighborhoods in a town.

In a book by Virginia Postrel (1998), she asks in her introductory chapter: "How we feel about the evolving future tells us who we are as individuals and as a civilization: Do we search for *stasis* – a regulated, engineered world? Or do we embrace *dynamism* – a world of constant creation, discovery, and competition?"

Mediterranean traditional urbanism and its associated generative processes, rules, and codes generally represent dynamic systems that allow creation and discovery and celebrate bottom-up decision-making processes. Current zoning codes, and recent attempts to replace them with form-based codes, are stasis in nature and are regulated, engineered, and mostly based on top-down decision-making structures. Yet it should be noted that form-based codes, such as the SmartCode, do provide advantages that are absent in current zoning codes.

Postrel's general principles for dynamist rules are remarkably similar to the principles of rules and associated decision-making processes found in most traditional built environments around the Mediterranean. Postrel's five principles are as follows: "(1) Allow individuals (including groups of individuals) to act on their own knowledge; (2) Apply to simple, generic units and allow them to combine in many different ways; (3) Permit credible, understandable, enduring, and enforceable commitments; (4) Protect criticism, competition, and feedback; (5) Establish a framework within which people can create nested, competing frameworks of more specific rules." In general, therefore current types of coding, whether they are conventional zoning that dictate land use and enforce nominal prescriptive regulations for each use or form-based codes that require adherence to very specific stipulations related to the form of the building or clusters of buildings, are all top-down codes that are stasis in nature and cannot produce the dynamism discussed above.

On the question of how the law can be made to act dynamically, J.B. Ruhl's proposals are worthy of consideration (Ruhl 1996). He proposes to make rights-based common law, a system that is adaptive, a corner stone of the legal system in the USA. The three positive features of common law that he cites are as follows: (1) Common law changes slowly and incrementally because it is limited by the dimension of rights as exercised and enforced that allows it to evolve with society's needs; (2) the common law tackles issues as they come, keeps their components together because it is adaptive, and decides issues in their context, thus avoiding incomprehensible outcomes; and (3) the common law operates at the component interaction level versus current legal practice that, more often than not, tackles problems abstractly. The result is that the common law, because of its evolutionary qualities, is focused more on system structure and process, thus avoiding it to fall into stasis.

All of the above qualities of the common law are very similar to the legal structure and its associated processes found in traditional Mediterranean societies. It thus enforces the qualities of complex adaptive systems and its dynamic nonlinear nature. It helps to self-regulate legal decisions and promotes the emergent qualities in the built environment discussed earlier because it is essentially a bottom-up system that responds to local micro-conditions.

To further address the question on what are the lessons for contemporary and future practice, it should be remembered that modern towns and cities have employed many technologies that were absent in the past, specifically the car and its requirements for street design and parking including multistory parking structures and infrastructure technologies that include sewers, water, electricity, and communication lines. In addition, the contemporary city, at least since about the mid-twentieth century, has added various building types that did not exist in the past, such as airports, large hospitals, factories for numerous manufacturing processes, and so on. Therefore, it is necessary to demarcate the city into sectors that would require control and management of infrastructure and buildings that are for public use and that require precision and technological know-how for their construction and maintenance and the rest of most of the city that is dedicated to housing.

The lessons from the traditional Mediterranean experience, particularly its aspects of control, management, and coding, are primarily applicable to the housing sectors of contemporary and future towns and cities. The following essential principles, applicable to the habitat sectors of cities, can be adopted and applied:

- Habitat, or housing, formation and its subsequent growth and change over time should be formed and designed to behave as a *complex adaptive system.*
- The system must also be *self-regulating.*
- The system must rely on feedback. *Negative feedback* is what should occur during the process of self-regulation, as described earlier.

- The system must operate by a *generative program* and not a *descriptive program.*
- The generative program must be *nonlinear* in nature, i.e., it should rely on decisions that are informed by feedback.
- At the micro level, *agents* behave in *adaptive* ways, and they form the next level of *aggregate agents* who in turn form another layer and so on. An agent could be an individual or a household.
- The *responsibility* distribution between agents at various levels will require making changes to the current system of production and delivery, such as the role of the developer in assembling and subdividing land.
- The rule*s* and codes should primarily be based on intentions for performance and therefore should be *proscriptive* in nature. However, a minority of the codes might have to be *prescriptive*, particularly those related to technological elements such as the car and various infrastructure elements.
- The resulting system for habitat will be *dynamic* in nature, which means that *emergent* forms and configurations, particularly at the micro level, will be unpredictable. The resulting qualities of form will be unique to each location, thus enhancing the sense of place and identity at each micro level of the built environment. These unpredictable and sometimes surprising results will be evident from the level of the house design to the manner clusters of houses relate to each other, to the character of the public realm in streets, and to the level of a whole neighborhood.

To summarize, the above principles are therefore anchored in the following keywords: *complex adaptive system, self-regulation, negative feedback, generative program versus descriptive program, nonlinearity, adaptive agents, aggregate agents, responsibility distribution, simple rules, proscriptive versus prescriptive, dynamic versus stasis, and emergent form.* See definitions in Appendix 11.

Finally, in this chapter, I would like to briefly point out recent examples of attempts to work out alternatives to current practice in habitat production. The work of Christopher Alexander comes to mind for theoretical constructs, including his built and unbuilt projects. This is documented in his 4-volume book *The Nature of Order* (2002–2005). Volume 2 addresses process, and Volume 3 comprises many examples of built and unbuilt projects including a number of housing projects that attempt to recreate the underlying processes of traditional urbanism including the properties that are embodied in the list of keywords I have indicated above.

Leon Krier's Poundbury development, an extension of the city of Dorchester in Dorset, UK, is another example for attempting to recreate the character and sense of place of traditional towns and villages of that region. It is an example of a top-down structure of decision-making: from creating a general master plan to the manner in which the streets are laid out to the laying out the blocks for houses. The delegation for design of each building to a different architect, following a reasonably coherent code, is a process that is only partly similar to what occurred in traditional towns and has resulted in an environment with character and a sense of place. Needless to say, without Leon Krier overseeing the process at all its stages, the results might not have been as successful. This is very different from development of traditional towns that did not have a master planner overseeing its development. However, Poundbury may be viewed as a first step experiment toward future attempts that will embody more of the principles that are outlined above.

In his booklet, published by the Prince's Foundation in London, titled *The Architectural Tuning of Settlements*, 2008, Krier has a series of sketches showing the possibilities of the interaction of architecture and urbanism. One of his favorites is # IX, on page 27, that he designates as ideal. I have used this sketch to show the interface and location of buildings facing the public realm, denoted as "classical," i.e., designed according to top-down codes, and the location of buildings that follow a generative program denoted as "vernacular," which usually do not face significant public realm areas (see Figs. 4.2 and 4.3).

The SmartCode by Andres Duany et al., which is now in its version 9.2, is rapidly being disseminated in the USA via workshops, the Internet, and by other means. It is a model code that is designed to be adopted by local governments after changes are made to it by using a process of calibration. The code is based on seven zones along a transect covering areas from the natural to the urban core and special districts. The implementation of the code requires a top-down structure and technical expertise due to its many provisions that are mostly prescriptive. Calibrating the code to a specific locality requires thorough technical understanding of how the code works and very sensitive reading of a locality's characteristics to make it locally friendly. As it relates to the lessons and attributes of traditional urbanism discussed above, the basis for the code is a descriptive program that relies on prescriptive stipulations. It is stasis in nature and does not foster unpredictable emergent form.

A publication by this author (Hakim 2007) describes in detail the proposals and implementation measures for revitalizing a historic sector of the city of Muharraq, Bahrain, that include a control, management, and coding system inspired by the insight and lessons of the traditional experience.

We have seen from the material in this book how traditional towns located around the Mediterranean and beyond display individual uniqueness in their built form qualities and overall physical attributes including a strong sense of place. We also know from observation and research that residents develop a strong sense of attachment to their town and always remember with fondness the sense of place in and around their neighborhoods later on in life when they are living elsewhere in "modern" contemporary built environment settings.

The book also demonstrates and explains the typical coding system and its attributes that were used. What is remarkable, however, about this coding system and its related decision-making mechanism— particularly as it relates to building in sequence and the steps that are appropriate for each family and for each neighborhood—is that it clearly replicates natural phenomenon and related processes of inception, growth, change, rejuvenation, decay, and rebirth. The phenomenon of *Emergence* that was discovered and elaborated on within the last two decades by scientists from different disciplines confirms that these traditional towns follow models of sustainable natural processes.

In the current awareness among concerned individuals and societies about global warming, sustainability, democracy, and the strive to achieve justice and equity, we find inspiration and clear lessons to follow and implement now and in the future from the experience of traditional towns located around the Mediterranean and in countries that have traditionally followed a similar pattern of development.

References

Hakim, B. S. (2007). Generative processes for revitalizing historic towns or heritage districts. *Urban Design International, 12*(2/3), 87–99.

Hakim, B. S., & Ahmed, Z. (2006). Rules for the built environment in 19th century Northern Nigeria. *Journal of Architectural and Planning Research, 23*(1), 1–26.

Holland, J. (1995). *Hidden order: How adaptation builds complexity.* Cambridge, MA: Perseus Books Group.

Postrel, V. (1998). *The future and its enemies: The growing conflict over creativity, enterprise, and progress.* New York: Free Press.

Ruhl, J. B. (1996). Complexity theory as a paradigm for the dynamical law-and-society system: A wake-up call for legal reductionism and the modern administrative state. *Duke Law Journal, 45*(5), 849–928.

Wolpert, L. (1991). *The triumph of the embryo.* Oxford: Oxford University Press.

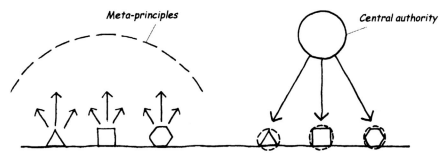

Fig. 4.1 Conceptual representation of the impacts on the local level (three geometric shapes denoting three settlements) by *proscriptive* meta-principles and by *prescriptive* imposed laws. The diagram on the left represents a settlement's ability to respond freely to local conditions and requirements but restrained by an overarching set of meta-principles. This would result in settlements that are diverse in their physical form and exhibit distinct local identity. The diagram on the right represents how prescriptions from a top-down central authority, far removed from a locality, inhibit creative solutions to local problems. Over time the settlements would tend to become similar to each other (Drawing by the author)

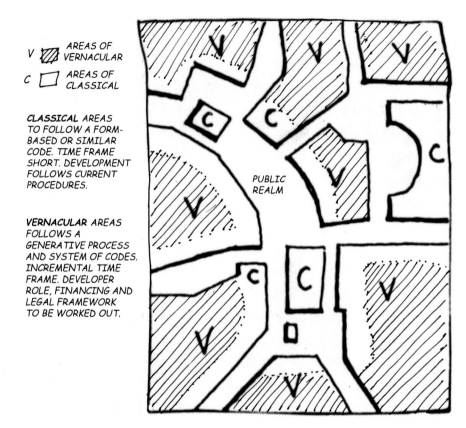

V ▨ AREAS OF
      VERNACULAR

C ▢ AREAS OF
      CLASSICAL

CLASSICAL AREAS
TO FOLLOW A FORM-
BASED OR SIMILAR
CODE. TIME FRAME
SHORT. DEVELOPMENT
FOLLOWS CURRENT
PROCEDURES.

VERNACULAR AREAS
FOLLOWS A
GENERATIVE PROCESS
AND SYSTEM OF CODES.
INCREMENTAL TIME
FRAME. DEVELOPER
ROLE, FINANCING AND
LEGAL FRAMEWORK
TO BE WORKED OUT.

PUBLIC
REALM

Fig. 4.2 The outline sketch is by Leon Krier from his booklet, published by the Prince's Foundation in London, titled *The Architectural Tuning of Settlements*, 2008. Krier has a series of sketches showing the possibilities of the interaction of architecture and urbanism. One of his favorites is # IX, on page 27, which he designates as ideal. I have used this sketch to show the interface and location of buildings facing the public realm, denoted as "classical," i.e., designed according to top-down codes, and the location of buildings that follow a generative program denoted as "vernacular," which usually do not face significant public realm areas

Fig. 4.3 The north side facade, facing south, of the Piazza del Campo in Siena. This image shows the facade architecture facing the Piazza is a result of the code that regulates the shape and size of the windows to achieve harmony and beauty, whereas the buildings in the back are a result of incremental change according to principles of a generative code. This is an example of what this author has suggested in Fig. 4.2 (Photo taken by Raoul Kieffer in October 2005. Permission granted by Raoul)

Appendix 1
Pergamon Law of the *Astynomoi* – Translated from the Original Greek by Sara Saba

Prescript:
[. . .] being *astynomos* he dedicated the royal law at his own expense.

Col. I
Let them inspect and take the appropriate decisions following the principles that seem just to them. In case these do not obey (this provision), after fining them with the penalty established by the law the *strategoi* shall leave the collection (of the money) to the *praktor*. (7) After assigning the work to bidders to restore the area to its original condition within ten days, the *astynomoi* who are in charge of collecting the due amount of money increased by half from those who did not comply, shall give their due to the contractors, and the rest to the treasurers. (14) If the *astynomoi* do not do as the law orders, the *strategoi* shall send out the contract, the *astynomoi* shall be charged with the surplus of the restoration cost and pay a fine of 100 drachmas in addition. (20) The *nomophylakes* shall collect from them immediately. Likewise, the same rule shall apply to others who do not comply. (23) Among the roads that run through the country-side, the main suburban roads (*leophoroi*) shall not be less than 20 cubits in width, the other streets not less than eight cubits, unless some use pathways as access to one another through the neighbor-hoods. (29) Those who have properties along the streets in each neighborhood at a distance of up to [?] stadia shall keep the streets

B.S. Hakim, *Mediterranean Urbanism: Historic Urban / Building Rules and Processes*, DOI 10.1007/978-94-017-9140-3,
© Springer Science+Business Media Dordrecht 2014

clean and passable[...] by contributing and repairing them together. If they do not comply the [?] shall confiscate [...]

Col. II
(48) [...] Those who have thrown out [...] the *amphodarchai* shall force (them?) to clean the area, as the law prescribes. Otherwise, they shall report them to the *astynomoi*. (52) The *astynomoi* shall leave the contract with the *amphodarches* and immediately collect the resulting sum from those who do not comply and fine them [...] drachmas. (56) If any one of the *amphodarchai* does not carry out any of the prescribed actions, he is to be fined twenty drachmas for each infraction by the *astynomoi*. (59) The revenues from the penalties shall be given monthly to the treasurers and be available, in case of necessity, for the cleaning of the (civic) areas, and shall not be diverted to another purpose. (65) The *astynomoi* shall take care of the collection and of everything else. If they do not attend to any of their duties, they shall be fined by the *strategoi* and the official in charge of the city 50 drachmas for each misdeed. The fine shall be redirected towards the activities that have been mentioned above. (72) Rubble: if people dig rubble or stones in the streets or make mud or make bricks or uncover conduits, the *amphodarchai* shall stop them. (76) If they do not comply, they shall report them to the *astynomoi*. These shall fine the transgressor five drachmas for each infraction and force him to restore everything to its previous condition and to cover the conduits. (82) If the residents do not comply, they shall assign the work within ten days and collect the resulting sum plus half from those who disobey. (86) Similarly, they shall force them to cover the already existing conduits. If the *astynomoi* do not do any of these things, they are liable to the same fines. (90) Collection: if any do not give their acquired share of the contract (for the collection) of dung or of the fines for the blocks that are cleaned at common expense, the *amphodarchai* shall give a pledge and give the document of the pledge to the *astynomoi* on the same day or on the next. (97) If no-one swears that the confiscated goods are his within five days, they shall sell them in the *phratry* or in the full market in the presence of the *astynomoi* and must convey the resulting [...] (102)

Col. III
They shall inspect them (?) and if they find they (?) are in need of repair, the owners shall repair them (?). (105) If any of them refuses,

the *astynomoi* shall assign the contract with a chosen person of those who have suffered damage. They (the *astynomoi*) shall collect as soon as possible three-fifths of the ensuing expenses from the disobedient person, two-fifths from the other one and hand it over to the contractors. (112) When common walls are in need of repair or have fallen down, if the neighbors use the walls in the same way, they shall contribute equally to the construction. (116) But if one house abuts the wall, while the other is freestanding, the one whose property leans (against the wall) shall pay two-thirds for the reconstruction, the one whose property is freestanding one-third. (121) Likewise they shall also pay if one has a two-floor structure, and the other a one-floor structure. (123) There shall be right of indictment before the *astynomoi* on the issue of common walls against the one who damages them and, if the defendants are found liable, having been defeated in a trial, they shall pay the damage caused to those (structures). (127) No one shall have the power to build on or cut through or in any other way damage common walls, unless they persuade the owners (to grant permission). (132) As to the neighboring walls that damage those who reside there, if the owners who have courtyards on the side of their neighbors want to build *peristaseis,* (136) they shall not be forbidden to build them [the *peristaseis*] (but they shall be) no wider than one cubit after covering them with stone copings, having built the outer wall of the *peristaseis* securely, if there is no bedrock, where the copings will be laid. (142) While paving, they shall not make the foundation higher than the rest of the open space, lest they block the water. (144) The owners of the *peristaseis* are the builders, while the neighbors (own) the places where they stand, when they have been paved, granted that they do not use them in any way that damages the other's walls. (149) They shall build the entrances of the *peristaseis* from their own houses. If according to the city architect and the *astynomoi* this is not possible, the neighbors shall provide entrance to those who come in for cleaning, likewise if the walls need repair if they collapsed. (156) Concerning those who enter for the purpose of malice, if they catch them, after the *astynomoi* make a judgment, they shall fine them five drachmas. (159) Nobody shall make trenches, plant pithoi, neither plan nor do anything else to someone else's walls or common walls, from which it would damage the wall. (163) Otherwise, if the owner files charges, the *astynomoi* shall investigate and make a determination, according to what seems fair to them. (166) As for the walls of other persons' houses that are about to fall, when the neighbors sue [. . .] the damage [. . .].

Col. IV
(171) they should compel (them) to clean underground conduits. (172) Fountains: the *astynomoi* shall be responsible for the fountains in the city and the suburban area, both that they are clean and that the underground conduits, which bring the water in and out, remain flowing. (176) If any need maintenance, they shall report it to the *strategoi* and to the official in charge of the sacred revenues, so that through them contracts may be made. (180) It shall not be possible for anyone to water animals, wash clothes, vessels, or any other thing at all at public fountains. (184) Anyone who does any of these things, if he is free, shall be dispossessed of the animals, clothes, and vessels, and be fined fifty drachmas (187); if he is a slave and does any of these things with his owner's approval, he shall likewise be dispossessed and flogged with fifty lashes in the pillory. (191) But if he acts without the owner's approval, he shall be deprived of what he has, and after being whipped with a hundred lashes, he should be detained in shackles for ten days and, when released, he shall be let loose with no fewer than fifty lashes. (196) To him who wants shall belong the right of seizure against all those who commit an illegal act against fountains; he who takes the seized property or reports to the *astynomoi* shall be apportioned half of the revenue realized from the seizure, and the rest shall be assigned to the maintenance of the Nymph's sanctuary. (203) Cisterns: after recording the cisterns existing in the houses the *astynomoi* in office shall deposit the records before the *strategoi* in the month Pantheios and see to it that the owners make them waterproof and that none of the extant cisterns are filled (with earth). (209) Otherwise after fining those who do any of those things 100 drachmas per cistern, they shall collect (the money) and compel them to clean them out. (212) If any had been filled in beforehand, they [the *astynomoi*] shall report to the owners, so that they are to clean them within eight months. (215) If they do not do so, after collecting the same fine from them, they shall compel these to clean them out. (217) The resulting revenue of the fines shall be handed in each month to the treasurers and shall be used for the

cleaning and maintenance of the cisterns and for nothing else. (221) The *astynomoi* shall compel whoever owns cisterns and by not plastering them damages the neighbors, them (to plaster the cisterns) after fining them and, if mandatory fines arise because of these, after collecting the money, the *astynomoi* shall render it to those who were damaged. (227) As for the *astynomoi* who do not deposit the record of the cisterns in the archive or do not act as the law orders, the *nomophylakes* shall collect 100 drachmas from them and assign it to the same funds. (233) Latrines: the *astynomoi* shall take care of both public latrines and the conduits from them and, for those that are not covered (236) [...].

* * *

This is the corrected and improved version of the translation of the Astynomoi Law that was first published in (Saba, 2012). It is reproduced in this appendix with permission of Dr. Sara Saba. The symbol [...] indicates that the original text is lost.

Reference

Saba, S. (2012). *The Astynomoi law from Pergamon: A new commentary*. Mainz: Verlag Antike, e.K.

Appendix 2
Justinian Code – Book 8, Title 10: Concerning Private Buildings (*De aedificiis privatis*)

8.10.11. Emperors Honorius and Theodosius to Severinus, Praetorian Prefect.

Projecting balconies, called *existai* in Greek, whether heretofore, or hereafter to be, constructed in the provinces, must be all means be lopped off unless there is a space of ten feet for free air between them. 1. Where private buildings are built up against public graneries, an interval of fifteen feet shall be maintained free from obstruction from projecting balconies. 2. We prescribed this interval also for all who wish to build, so that if anyone attempts to build within ten feet, or to have a balcony within fifteen feet (respectively as mentioned) he may know that his structure will not alone be demolished, but the house itself will be confiscated to the fisc. Given September 29 (423). Bas. 58.11.9.

8.10.12. Emperor Caesar Zeno, pious, victor, triumpher, the always specially to be revered Augustus to Adamantius, City Prefect. Given between (476 and 479).

Desiring our subjects to enjoy freedom from litigation, as well as to be freed from external wars, we always give them warning beforehand. We accordingly enact the present law, which sufficiently shows the good suggestions of Your Magnificence to us, and how prudently we define what may solve difficulties.

1. We shall to some extent avoid words ordinarily used in governmental affairs and shall employ those which are more commonly known so that no one who comes in touch with this law will need an interpreter.

B.S. Hakim, *Mediterranean Urbanism: Historic Urban / Building Rules and Processes*, DOI 10.1007/978-94-017-9140-3,

1a. We have learned from the report made to us by Your Magnificence, that the law of our father Leo, of immortal memory, which he made for people in this city who wanted to build, has become ambiguous in several particulars through doubts raised by men who interpret badly the direction therein, that those who restore their buildings shall not increase the former size thereof, lest they cut off the light and view of the neighbors, contrary to the former situation, without adding what shall be done, if the builder (owner) has received permission by pact or stipulation to change the structure if he wishes.

1b. We, therefore, ordain that if a builder (owner) has such pact or stipulation, he may build according to the terms thereof, although he thereby injures the neighbors who are bound thereby.

2. And since the same constitution provides that a man who builds must leave a space of twelve feet between his house and that of his neighbor, and adds "more or less," which leads to the greatest obscurity – and an ambiguity is hardly suited to clear up a doubt – we, more clearly, order that there shall be twelve feet of space left between the houses, from top to bottom. A man who complies with this requirement may erect his house to any height desired, and may have windows for his view as they say, or for light according to the imperial legislation, whether he wants to build a new house or repair an old one or reconstruct one consumed by fire.

2a. But no one shall, in this space, be permitted to shut off from a neighbor's house the direct and unobstructed view which he has, standing or sitting in his house, of the sea, (and shall not force him) to turn or look sideways or put his body in a forced position, in order to see the sea.

2b. Nothing was said in former legislation about gardens or trees, nor is anything added herein about them; for there should be no servitude as to them.

3. If a man builds a house and an alley or street more than twelve feet wide intervenes (between his house and that of a neighbor), he shall not on that account be permitted to occupy any part of the alley or street, adding it to his property; for the provision for twelve feet of space between houses is not made in order that public property may be encroached upon, and used for buildings, but in order that the

spaces between houses shall not be less than that, and any space in excess of that shall remain as it is, and will not be permitted to be diminished, and the rights of cities will be protected.

3a. If the shape of an old building is such that the space between it and the neighboring building is less than twelve feet, its height shall not be increased, nor shall windows be cut, unless ten feet of distance intervenes; and even then no window[s] for view can be constructed, as stated, which were not there before; but windows for light may be constructed six feet from the ground, and no one must, with the light-giving windows being opened at the stated altitude of ten feet, make what is called a false floor, and thereby circumvent the law.

3b. For if that were permitted, windows for light would, by reason of the false (high) floor, serve for purposes of view and would be too near to the neighbor. We forbid that to be done; provided, however, that we do not take away any right, which may exist by reason of any pact or stipulation.

4. Besides, since a former law ordained that houses previously consumed by fire might be reconstructed to a height of a hundred feet, although a neighbor's view of the sea might be obstructed, and desirous to rid that law of its ambiguity, we order that such right shall exist as to houses burned down as well as to those which are repaired, and as to houses not heretofore existing, but now erected, and as to those which are not damaged by any fire but are in ruin through age or other cause. The construction of such house may proceed without hindrance, though the view of the sea from another house may be obstructed, provided that there is a distance of a hundred feet between it and its surrounding houses.

4a. Any view of the sea, however, from a kitchen, toilet room, nook, stairs, passage-way or from what are commonly called gang-ways (*basternia*) may be obstructed, by a man wanting to build within one hundred feet, provided the intervening distance is twelve feet.

4b. These provisions apply where no agreement exists to build otherwise; for if there is such agreement, the building may be constructed according to its terms though no such interval is left, and although the parties who made the agreement or their successors in interest have their view of the sea obstructed, since rights acquired by pacts ought not to be nullified by general laws.

5. We likewise ordain that sun-rooms (*salaria*) shall not be constructed of beams and poles merely, but in the Roman shape, and an interval of ten feet shall be left between two sun-rooms opposite each other.

   5a. But if this cannot be done on account of the narrowness of the space, the sun-rooms shall be constructed diagonally from each other.

   5b. If the alley itself is not wider than ten feet, neither party shall undertake to construct sun-rooms or projecting balconies.

   5c. And these structures built according to these directions shall be fifteen feet high from the ground, and shall not be supported (on the outside) by any perpendicular columns of wood or stone or by walls set in the ground, lest the air under the sun-rooms, built at the height aforesaid, be shut off, or the alley and public way be narrowed thereby.

   5d. We also forbid the construction of stairs leading from the alley to the sun-rooms, so that by more careful construction, and by the fact that sun-rooms are not too close to each other, danger from fire threatening the city and the owners of houses – would that it did not exist – may be diminished and become scarcer and maybe more easily warded off.

   5e. If a sun-room or stairway is constructed contrary to our law, it shall not only be torn down, but the owner of the house shall also be fined ten pounds of gold and the masterbuilder or contractor who constructed it shall pay another ten pounds of gold, and if the man who erected it cannot pay the fine on account of poverty, he shall be scourged by lashes and expelled from the city.

6. In addition we order that no one shall hereafter be permitted to close up several columns on the public porticos, from the so-called mile-column to the capitol, with booths constructed of boards only, or put up in some other manner, between the columns.

   6a. But structures of that kind shall not exceed six feet in width, with the walls toward the street, and seven feet in height, and a free passage from the porticos to the street shall in any event be left in the space between four columns.

6b. Besides, booths or shops of that sort shall be decorated on the outside with marble so as to be an ornament to a city and a pleasing sight to the passers-by.

6c. Shops erected between columns in other parts of the city may be constructed of the size and in the manner as Your Magnificence deems for the city's interest, preserving equality for all, so that a right granted to one may not be denied to another.

7. We also embrace in the law that honest men shall not be wronged by the fraud of malicious disputants. For many men, induce by envy, and without having sustained any harm, raise a dispute against those who want to build, and delay the work, so that the man who had commenced to build, and who is then forbidden to do so, is compelled not only to leave his work incomplete, but, in addition thereto, the money with which he had hoped to erect the building is eaten by the law-suit; and what is more absurd than anything else is that when the decision is in his favor, he is still enmeshed in indissoluble chains while the man who hindered the construction appeals and takes the time granted therefore, delighted to have obstructed the work to the great injury of his neighbor.

7a. We accordingly order that if an appeal is taken from the decision of the trial judge in suits of this kind, the winner or loser, alone or with the opponent, may, as soon as the report or written draft (of the proceedings) is made by the judge, go before the tribunal of Your Magnificence without awaiting for the regular time, and having called the opponent in the usual manner, if absent, lay the decision of the judge before you, so that the cause may be lawfully ended without delay, and so that, if winter is at hand or approaches, the man who wants to build and is unjustly forbidden to do so, may not suffer intolerable injury while waiting for the long time given for appeals.

7b. In like manner, if anyone wants to appeal, objecting to the decree of Your Magnificence, the consultation, as it is called, shall be made immediately, and the loser as well as the winner may, in the usual manner, open the examination of the decision in our imperial palace without any delay.

7c. And everyone, moreover, must bear in mind that if he tries to stop anyone from building, he must, if defeated, make good all the damage caused by him, including the value of the material spoiled or deteriorated during the time of the litigation; further, if a man undertakes to build contrary to law, he must, if defeated, make good the damage of the man who forbade him to do so, and who was compelled to commence a suit in connection therewith.

8. We further direct that every suit of this kind (in this city) shall be disposed of by the decision of the judicial tribunal of Your Magnitude alone, and not other of the illustrious magistrates shall hear it, and none who are engaged in such litigation shall have the right to make any objection to the jurisdiction of the court by reason of their imperial service, in order to evade the judgment or the payment of the damage awarded by the decision of the glorious prefect of the city by the decision of the referee appointed by him; but the defeated party shall be forced to pay by the staff of Your Magnificence, without the right to object to the jurisdiction of the court.

9. Your Magnificence, moreover, shall see that no contractor or artificer leaves any work uncompleted, but must compel the man who commenced the work, upon receiving his pay, to complete the work or to pay the damage sustained by the owner thereby, and all loss of profit by reason of the non-completion of the work, and if a defaulting contractor is, per chance, a pauper, he shall be whipped and expelled from the city.

9a. Another man of the same trade shall not be prevented from completing a work commenced by someone else, which, we have learned, that contractors or artificers have attempted against builders, they themselves not finishing the work which they commenced, and not allowing others to do so, but seeking to inflict intolerable damage on owners who prepared to build.

9b. And if, moreover, a man refuses to finish a building commenced by another, merely for the reason that someone else commenced it, he shall suffer the same penalty as the man who abandoned the work.

Note by Fred H. Blume.

Holmes, William Gordon (1905) *The Age of Justinian and Theodora*, pp. 42–43, gives a good picture of some parts of Constantinople in the 6th century, which illustrates some of the legislation mentioned here. He says:

"A main street consists of an open paved road, not more than 15 feet wide, bounded on each side by a colonnade or portico. More than fifty of such porticoes are in existence at this date, so that the pedestrian can traverse almost the whole city under shelter from sun or rain. Many of them have an upper floor, approached by wooden or stone steps which is used as an *ambulacrum* or promenade. They are plentifully adorned with statuary of all kinds.

*** On the inside the porticoes are lined for the most part by shops and workshops. Opening to them in certain positions are public halls or auditoriums, architecturally decorative and furnished with seats, where meetings can be held and professors can lecture to classes on various topics. Between the pillars of the colonnades next to the thoroughfare we find stalls and tables (limited to six feet of length and seven of height) for the sale of all kinds of wares. In the finer parts of the city such stalls or booths must by law be ornamentally constructed and encrusted outside with marbles so as not to mar the beauty of the piazza. At the tables especially are seated the money-changers or bankers, who lend money at usury, receive it at interest, and act generally as the pawnbrokers of the capital. Such pleasant arcades have naturally become the habitual resort of courtesans, and they are recognized as the legitimate place of shelter for the houseless poor. The open spaces to which the Latin name of forum is applied are expansions of the main streets, and like them, are surrounded on all sides by porticoes.

*** Few of them (the private streets) are more than ten feet wide, and this scanty space is still more contracted above by projecting floors or balconies. In many places also the public way is encroached upon by Solaria or sun-stages, that is to say, by balconies supported on pillars of wood or marble, and often furnished with a flight of stairs leading to the pavement below. In such alleys low windows, affording a view of the street, or facile to lean out, are considered unseemly by the inmates of the opposite houses. Hence mere light-giving apertures, placed six feet above the flooring are the regular means of illumination. Transparent glass is sometimes used for the closure of windows, but more often we find thin plates of marble or alabaster with ornamental designs, figured on the translucent substance. Simple wooden shutters, however, are seen commonly enough in houses of the poorer class.

*** Between 476 and 479 Zeno, taking advantage of an extensive fire, promulgated a very stringent building act (C. 8.10.12) contravention of which renders the offending structure liable to demolition, and inflicts a fine of ten pounds of gold on the owner. The architect also becomes liable in a similar amount, and is even subjected to banishment, if he is unable to pay. By this act, which remains permanently in force throughout the empire, the not very ample width of twelve feet is fixed for private streets; solaria and balconies must be at least ten feet distant from similar projections on the opposite side, and not less than fifteen feet above the pavement; while stairs connecting them directly with the thoroughfare are entirely abolished. Prospective windows are forbidden in streets narrower than the statutory allowance of twelve feet."

8.10.13. Emperor Justinian to John, Praetorian Prefect.

Doubt has arisen as to whether the constitution of Zeno of blessed memory directed to Adamantius, City Prefect, treating of servitudes, is purely local and its rules applicable to and required to be observed only in this city (of Constantinople), leaving the ancient rules, contrary thereto, in force in the provinces. Deeming it unworthy of our times that one law should apply in this imperial city, and another in the provinces, we ordain that the above constitution shall apply in all cities in the Roman empire alike, and everything shall be done according to the rule therein stated, and if any rule contained of the ancient law is changed thereby, the changed rule shall also be enforced in the provinces by the presidents thereof. Rules of the ancient law not changed by the law of Zeno shall remain in full force and effect everywhere. Given at Constantinople September 1 (531).

From:
http://www.uwyo.edu/lawlib/blume-justinian/ajc-edition-2/
University of Wyoming, College of Law
George William Hopper Law Library
Annotated Justinian Code
Translated by Fred H. Blume, Edited by Timothy Kearley (Second
Edition, 2008).

Appendix 3
The Roman-Byzantine Building Regulations by Vasso Tourptsoglou-Stephanidou

Foreword

The organizing of the housing areas of Byzantine towns and cities is to remain presumptive as long as it relies exclusively on the sparse excavations accomplished and on the few surviving edifices of that era. The medieval central area of Corinth does reveal a street pattern and an arrangement of houses and workshops, but only on their foundation level and as an upper layer of classical, hellenistic and roman constructions.[1] On the other hand, Mystras is a relatively well preserved unit but its low density, the sharp inclination of the ground on which it was built, and the historical occasions responsible for its founding would not characterize it as a typical Byzantine town. Besides, the remains of its residential areas are relatively late, dating from 1300–1700.[2]

Other important sources which are often used for the reconstruction of the image of typical housing areas in Byzantine Cities are the contemporary literature (historical, ecclesiastic etc.), the Byzantine painting (miniatures, icons, frescos etc.) and the urban legislations of the time. For the purpose of our research the third source of

---

A part of this Appendix are Figs. A.1 to A.9 located at the end of this appendix.

[1] R. Scranton, *Mediaeval architecture in the central area of Corinth*, Corinth, v. XVI, American School of Classical Studies, Princeton (N. Jersey 1958) pl. VI.

[2] Α. Ορλάνδος, Τα παλάτια και τα σπίτια του Μυστρά, Αρχείον Βυζαντινών μνημείων της Ελλάδος, τ. Γ (1937), pp. 6–114.

B.S. Hakim, *Mediterranean Urbanism: Historic Urban / Building Rules and Processes*, DOI 10.1007/978-94-017-9140-3, © Springer Science+Business Media Dordrecht 2014

information was employed since we consider it as the most objective
one, at least as far as the intentions of the legislator are concerned.
We really do not believe that this legislation was systematically
applied throughout the empire; nevertheless it still remains a more
trustworthy and positive source of knowledge in comparison to the
subjective and often motivated literary information and to the depictions of edifices in the peculiar perspective used by the Byzantine
painters.

Since this legislation really constituted a comprehensible corpus, it
is interesting to know the kind of urban problems these laws were
aiming to control. Even more, if building restrictions or regulations
were provided only by official laws or by customary ones as well, the
influence they imposed on each other and, if possible, their duration
through time.[3]

I. Introductory Notes on Basic Concepts of the Byzantine
   Legislation on Neighboring Properties and Reference
   to Its Sources

In the Roman and Byzantine Civil Law a distinction is made between
two kinds of property rights. This distinction differentiates between
private "things" ('res') and non-private ones. In the former case such
privately owned "things" are subject to exchange while in the latter,
they are not. Among the non-private things the law includes (a) the
things common to all people ("res omnium communes") such as
air, running water, the sea and the sea shore, (b) the public things
("res publicae") such as roads, rivers, seaports, things one may freely
use but not own, (c) the things which belong to the community ("res
universitatis" or "res communes") such as theaters, arcades, baths and

---

[3] At this point I wish to thank my dear friend Niki Proussanidou- Vaitsou for
correcting my English in the present text. This article is an extended summary of
a chapter of my treatise, Περίγραμμα βυζαντινών οικοδομικών περιορισμών (από
τον Ιουστινιανό στον Αρμενόπουλο και η προβολή τους στη νομοθεσία του
νεοελληνικού κράτους), Εταιρεία Μακεδονικών Σπουδών, Θεσσαλονίκη 1998
(*An outline of Byzantine building regulations: from Justinian to Harmenopoulos
and their influence on the legislation of the New Hellenic State*, Society of Macedonian Studies, Thessaloniki 1998).

(d) the things belonging to the divine law ("res juris divinis") that is churches and holy relics ("res sacrae"), cemeteries, and tombs ("res religiosae") and city walls, portals etc. ("res sanctae"). We must note that here the term "things" does not denote only tangible things (moveable or immovable) but also certain rights on these things, for instance the rights to inheritance or usufruct or use or servitude or habitation etc. The present article concentrates only on private immovable things and on rights of servitude, to the extent that they both refer to the building procedures and restrictions as well as to the problems that such activities cause to the adjoining properties.

The research covers two categories of Law: the official and the customary law. Concerning the official law we have used as sources the Theodosian Code, the three parts of Justinian's Corpus Juris Civilis and his Novels, the Basilika and other earlier or more recent law compilations, official or private, which communicate the Byzantine civil law up to 1345.[4] As for the customary law, we refer mainly to the "laws" of Julian of Ascalon, well known by their insertion in Leon's VI Book of the Prefect ("ἐπαρχικὸν βίβλιον") and in Harmenopoulos' Hexabiblos.[5] We also refer to the Syro-roman Lawbook, an assortment of laws introduced and applied in the Middle East around the 5th century.[6]

We believe that up to the reign of Leon I, the early Byzantine legislation on building procedures and restrictions follows at a very close pace the Roman one. We conclude this from the edicts found in the 15th Book of the Theodosian Code ("on public works") as well as from the edicts which were later inserted in Justinian's Code and Digest and whose original provenance might be attributed to the lost chapter 24 of the 4th Book of the Theodosian compilation ("on private and public buildings"). Even more, since the Roman

---

[4] C. Pharr, *The Theodosian Code and Novels and the Sirmodian Constitutions*, Greenwood Press, New York 1969 (1952) = C. Theod. / T. Mommsen-P. Kruger-P. Scholl (Kroll), *Corpus Juris Civilis*, v. I-III, Weidmann 1970–73 (1906–1912) = C, D, N / H. J. Scheltema–N. van der Wal–D. Holwerda, *Basilicorum libri LX*, Groningen 1955–1988 = *Jus Grecoromanum*, 1931 = J.G.R.

[5] Πιτσάκης, Κωνσταντίνου Ἀρμενοπούλου, Πρόχειρον νόμων ἡ Εξάβιβλος, Αθήνα 1974 = Harm.

[6] K. G. Bruns - E. Sachau, *Syrisch-romisches Rechtsbuch aus dem funften Jahrhundert*, Aalen 1961 (1880) = Lawbook.

legislation had incorporated certain ancient Greek laws, such as Solon's law on distances from adjoining properties, those laws, after their insertion in the Law of the Twelve Tablets (Dodecadeltos, table VII) were later included in the Digest and from then on were often repeated in the Byzantine legislation.

A great innovation of the urban legislation is owed to an edict issued by the emperor Zenon (474–491), issued between 476–479. It is a corpus of building restrictions concerning Constantinople addressed to the city's Prefect Adamantius and it is included in Justinian's Code (C 8,10,12) in the Greek language. With a new edict at 531, Justinian extended its initially local application throughout the Byzantine empire, only the cases where existing ancient customary laws of a province were not opposed by the new law. In these instances, the old law was to be applied (C 8, 10, 13). Besides his valuable contribution to the expansion of the application of Zenon's edict, Justinian issued three novel constitutions concerning affiliated subjects. Two of them elucidated Zenon's law about the rights of view towards the sea (N. 63 of 538 and N. 165), while with the third (N.122 of 543) he instructed the laborers and the masons to be reasonable with their demands for fees etc. But even these new constitutions of Justinian may be considered as extensions of Zenon's law.

Modifications or further elaborations on the official law concerning buildings are not apparent up to the end of the Byzantine era, with the sole exception of Leon's VI two novel constitutions. These constitutions refer to the construction of balconies (N.113) and to the distances that should be kept between an edifice and the boundaries of originally rural estates (N.71). All the law compilations or private law manuals posterior to C.I.C. repeat Zenon's law, often paraphrasing its contents or changing the order of its passages. Yet, we must also refer to a number of edicts of the 10th century, issued probably as a monography with the title "The Prefect's Book" ("ἐπαρχικὸν βίβλιον"), which comprise a series of ordinances of the occasional Prefects of Constantinople addressed to the trade unions ("συντεχνίες") of the capital. The major aim of this compilation of ordinances is to set rules on the practice of each special trade and to confirm the State's surveillance on the commerce. In doing this it often limits the practice of some trades into certain areas of the capital and appoints distances to be kept between trade establishments of the same kind. The title 22 of this monography covers the leading instructions on the practice of masons and of other special technicians of the same trade. The text is very interesting since it insinuates ways for solving discordances between clients and laborers and appoints time guarantee for the secure construction of buildings. Up to this time, this guarantee was only available for public buildings.

Yet, the main reason we refer to the Prefect's Book[7] at this point is not merely the content of its title 22. At the end of a manuscript copy of this book, dated from the 14th century (manuscript of Geneva, No. 23), there were found as a supplement 48 "laws" under the odd superscription "Prefects" ordinances compiled by the architect Julian of Ascalon out of the laws, that is the customs of Palestine ("ἐπαρχικὰ ἀπὸ τῶν τοῦ Ἀσκαλωνίτου Ἰουλιανοῦ τοῦ ἀρχιτέκτονος ἐκ τῶν νόμων ἤτοι ἐθῶν τῶν ἐν Παλαιστίνῃ"). These 48 "laws" describe several building restrictions and other affiliated subjects which, according to the title, were valid in Palestine and possibly within the larger area of the Middle East, about the beginning of 6th century. This very ancient series of "laws" was included in the Prefect's Book of the 10th century in the form of an either symptomatic or organic supplement of this compilation, since it also treated problems of the professional practice of tradesmen. This is accurate for a large part of these "laws". But there exists some others which form by themselves an almost complete corpus of building regulations, different from the ones found in Zenon's edict, the official legislation always valid in the Byzantine era. The problem must have become more acute after 1345, when Harmenopoulos included Julian's "laws" in his compilation Hexabiblos, side by side with the Zenonian laws. The great importance which was attributed to Hexabiblos during the centuries of Turkish occupation and later on, up to the mid of the 19th century, carried over in time the problem of the coexistence of two differing types of building restrictions.

---

[7] J. Nicole, *Le livre du Prefet,* Variorum Reprints 1970 (1893), p. 371–392 / J. Coder, *Das Eparcherbuch Leons des Weisen*, Osterreichische Academie der Wissenschaften, Wien 1991. Julian's laws are partly included in a manuscript of the 14th cent. (Codex Panagiou Taphou 25) and to their complete extent, in a more recent one, dating from the 16th cent. (Codex Serdicensis, gr. 144), probably a copy of the Geneva manuscript.

Before we proceed to the analysis of building restrictions, both official and customary, which were supposed to be applied during the Byzantine era, it is important to explain two basic institutions of the Roman and Byzantine law: The first one concerns the proprietary rights of the owner of the land over the things built or grown on it. The second deals with the power attributed to rights of praedial servitude to interfere with building legislation and often to prevail over it.

Referring to the first, it is well known that in Greece, up to 1929, the official law accepted that in urban and suburban areas the Roman institution of vertical co-ownership was the only valid one. That is, the owner(s) of a plot or a field or a vineyard was also the owner of what was constructed or planted on it ("εἴκει τὰ ὑπερκείμενα τοῖς ὑποκειμένοις"). This general rule, which also allowed co-ownership in ideal fractions and co-ownership "pro diviso" (that is, in the vertical sense), did not recognize or accept the horizontal co-ownership. Of course there existed some exemptions, mainly in the islands of the Cyclades, where the horizontal co-ownership was practiced in a peculiar way, in accordance to the local customs. Yet, these exemptions were considered by the Greek law as the result of the application of rights of servitude rather than as the enforcement of a different institution, even a customary one. Nevertheless, the horizontal co-ownership in these insular areas must have followed in a subtle way the ancient Greek law, where the ownership of the subsoil, the soil and the crops grown on it sometimes belonged to different persons.[8] In urban or suburban areas of ancient Greece this institution was not prevailing, either because the urban low density did not evoke the practice of horizontal co-ownership, or because the intrinsic meaning of the Greek "οἶκος" did not encourage it. The Byzantine official law preserved the Roman institution of vertical co-ownership, at least as far as urban and suburban areas were concerned, while very early some exceptions were allowed in the agricultural areas with the practice of "ἐμφύτευσις".

The customary law in the Middle East and specifically that of Palestine, as it is rendered to us by Julian's "laws", is differentiated on this point. It appears clearly in certain "laws" that the practice of horizontal co-ownership was the common rule. This fact is further

---

[8] Π. Ζέπος, ιδιοκτησία κατ' ορόφους. (Ν 3741/1929) Αθήναι 1931, σ. 10–11.

clarified by the manner in which the costs for the impairment of buildings were divided among co-owners and by the prohibitions set for the establishment of workshops offending the environment on the lower level of multistoried edifices.[9] We note the same practice described in the Syro-roman Lawbook in reference to a two storied dwelling with different owners on each floor.[10]

The second important institution to be analyzed here is that of the rights enjoyed by contracting a praedial servitude. Servitude is called the "real" right of acquiring partial authority over an alien property for the benefit of a person of another property. In cases where persons are benefited by this right, the servitude is called personal; in cases where a property is benefited, praedial. Usufruct, or use of an alien property, for instance, are personal servitudes, since people are benefited. But the right of way through an alien field or terrain, or the right to support one's edifice on a neighbor's exterior wall are praedial servitudes because the immovable "things" (a field or a house) are being benefited. Depending on the location of a property (in cities and towns, or in the fields), the praedial servitudes are distinguished as "civil" and "rustic" (rural).

The acquisition of rights of praedial servitude is accomplished in several ways: The common methods are by: (a) a written official agreement between the two parties (dominant, servient), (b) an oral agreement accompanied by a written declaration of the servient party, (c) long use, that is by the informal but not furtive use of these rights over the servient property for 10 or 20 years – depending on the presence or the absence of its proprietor on site – without any formal complaint.

The rights of servitude thus acquired, carry also a date of expiration. This is either stated in the initial agreement or follows naturally the demolition of the dominant or servient property or the annulment of the purpose of its acquisition. But most often the rights of servitude expire by non usage; that is by not making use of these rights for 10 or 20 years in "rustic" servitudes. In the case of "civil" servitudes it is also required that by this time, the owner of the servient property has constructed something or has taken some measures which disable the

---

[9] Harm. 2,4 § 18, 20, 29, 40, 42.

[10] Lawbook §98 (London manuscript), p. 273–74.

application of the servitude's rights, with no formal complaint being deposed by the owner of the dominant property.

Rights of servitude, as long as they were properly acquired and maintained, were highly respected, that even the official law could not abrogate them. This is apparent in Zenon's edict where almost all of his restrictions include the condition that if there exists a right of servitude which allows something different, the servitude must be maintained. Even more, the first part of his edict, which concerns the already existing edifices, deals with them as if there exist mutual rights of servitude between them (of light and aspect). Justinian's more recent edict (C 8.10.13 of 531), which expands the applications of Zenon's laws throughout the empire, refers to them as laws "quae de servitutibus loquitur". As we shall see further on for some cases, properly acquired rights of servitude can be put to an end or expire when the proper distances defined by Zenon are applied.

In the customary law of Palestine, according to Julian, the effect of newly contracted rights of servitude on the building restrictions is almost non-existent. It is remarkable that among Julian's 48 "laws" the term "servitude" appears only twice, quite by chance in the §82 and in its full meaning in §26 (about taverns). Nevertheless, in §35 (about light apertures) and in §75 (about rainwater spouts) old rights of servitude are described by the use of the term "νόμη".

II. Building Restrictions Prior To Zenon's Edict

We do not claim that a thorough research was made of the Roman building restrictions. Here we only refer to the relative laws or even to the relative hints we found in the incomplete Theodosian Code and in Justinian's C. I. C. which we suppose were, or should have been, applied in construction during the early Byzantine era.

(a) Proper distances between buildings

- According to Gaius, the Law of the Twelve Tablets included Solon's law on distances.[11] Gaiusas passage was inserted in the

---

[11] Tablet VII, of the Law of the Twelve Tablets (K. G. Bruns, *Fontes Juris Romani Antiqui*, Gradenwitz, Aalen 1969 (1909), p. 27.

Digest (D 10.1.13) in an incomplete form while later in Prochiron and in the Synopsis Basilicorum,[12] we come across it in a somewhat differing form. Nevertheless, in the above compilations only part of Solon's law is included, that which defines distances between boundaries and constructions of several kinds (buildings, retaining walls, pits and cesspools, trees etc.) in rural areas, while his restrictions for constructing buildings in cities are omitted.[13]

– Festus writes that the Law of the Twelve Tablets also included a condition demanding the existence of a specific distance between adjoining buildings ("Ambitus-dicitur circuitus aedificiorum, patens-pedes duos et semissem"), that is an open space of 2,5 roman feet away from the boundaries.[14] This is the "legitimum spatium" which Papirius Justus refers to in his treatise on the Law of the Twelve Tablets, part of which was later included in the Digest (D 8.2.14). He writes that the emperors Antonius and Severns declared by a rescript that in the case of vacant ground which is not burdened with a servitude, its owner may build on it providing he leaves the

---

[12] Gaius, book IV, *ad legem XII tab.* (D 10.1.13): "ἐάν τις αἱμασιὰν παρ' ἀλλοτρίῳ χωρίῳ ὀρύγῃ, τὸν ὅρον μὴ παραβαίνειν· ἐὰν τειχίον, πόδα ἀπολείπειν· ἐὰν δὲ οἴκημα, δύο πόδας. ἐὰν δὲ τάφ(ρ)ον ἢ βόθρον ὀρύττῃ, ὅσον τὸ βάθος ἦ, τοσοῦτον ἀπολείπειν, ἐὰν δὲ φρέαρ, ὀργυιάν. ἐλαίαν δὲ καὶ συκῆν ἐννέα πόδας ἀπὸ τοῦ ἀλλοτρίου φυτεύειν, τὰ δὲ ἄλλα δένδρα πέντε πόδας". In the Synopsis of Basilicorum (K, IX, sch. 33) it is quoted: "εἰ δέ τις ἐν ἀγρῷ βούλοιτο κτίσαι, τόξου, βολὴν ἀπὸ τοῦ ἀγρογείτονος ἀπεχέτω ἢ ὀργυιάν" (ζέποι J.G.R. τ. Ε, σ. 342). The fathom usually equals 6 Byzantine feet, that is equal to 1.87 m. Prochiron 38, 50–51: "ἐάν τις δημοσία ὁδὸν ἤτοι παρ' ἀλλοτρίου χωρίου ὀρύττῃ, τὸν ὅρον μὴ παραβαίνῃ· ἐὰν τειχίον, πόδα ἐνὰν ἀπολείπῃ· ἐὰν δὲ οἴκημα, πόδας 6. ἐὰν δὲ τάφ(ρ)ον ἢ βόθρον ὀρύττῃ, ὅσον τὸ βάθος εἴη, τοσοῦτον ἀπολείπῃ, ἐὰν δὲ φρέαρ, ὀργυιάν. εἰ μήπω φρέαρ προυπάρχῃ τοῦ γείτονος καὶ διὰ τοῦ καίνου ἔργου βλάπτεται. ἐλαίαν δὲ καὶ συκῆν πόδας ἐννέα ἀπὸ τοῦ ἀλλοτρίου φυτεύειν, τὰ δὲ ἄλλα δένδρα πόδας πέντε".

[13] According to U. E. Paoli ("La loi du Solon sur les distances", *Altri studi di Diritto Greco e Romano*, Milano, 1976, p. 571–583). Solon's law is completed as follows: ". . . ἐὰν δὲ οἴκημα δύο πόδας. ἐὰν δὲ ἐν ἄστει οἰκοδομῇ, ἢ χρήσθω τοῖς οὖσιν ἀποδοὺς τὸ ἥμισυ τῶν ἀναλισκομένων, ἢ ἀπολειπέτω τὸ ἥμισυ ὧν γέγραπται. ἐὰν δὲ τάφ(ρ)ον . . ."

[14] Bruns, *Fontes*, p. 26.

"legitumum spatium" between his building and a neighboring tenement building ("insula"). According to Tacitus (Ann. 15, XLIII), following the great arson of Rome at 64, Nero restored the application of the "ambitus", possibly neglected by this time, by not allowing construction of party-walls between dwellings but each having its own surrounding wall.

– According to an edict by the emperors Arcadius, Honorius and Theodosius at 406 (C.Theod. 15.1.46 / C 8.10. 9) aiming to limit the danger of fire expansions, private and public buildings should keep between them a distance of 15 feet, while in a more recent edict, at 423, Honorius and Theodosius (C 8.10.11) defined the proper distance between private edifices to at least 10 feet. As for the public buildings it is clear that the open space of 15 feet refers to all sides of the structure, while this is not so clear in the case of private buildings where the distance of 10 feet rather appears to refer only to their fronts.

(b) Construction of balconies (Fig. A.7a)

The early Roman laws did not allow the construction of balconies in projection. According to a comment by the jurist J. Paulus (3rd cent. A.D.), which was later inserted in the Digest (D 8.2.1 pr.) and in Basilika (B 58.2.1), in situations where public ground or a public roadway lies between two estates, the existence of a servitude giving right to insert a beam or to have a roof or other structure projecting from a building, or to discharge rainwater from eavesdrips, is prevented. The reason is that the air space above such ground must be kept clear.

Nevertheless, in 348 B.C., the censor C. Maenius constructed balconies facing the forum, for viewing the games performed. Thus, this kind of constructions took his name, called thereafter "maeniana". During the reign of Valentianus I and Valens, the prefect of the city of Rome Vettius Agorius Praetextatus (367–368 A.D.), restoring the old roman laws, issued the order that all the city's "maenianae" as well as the walls of private houses leaning to sacred buildings should be removed.[15] Some years after Praetextatus' order,

---

[15] Ammianus Marcellinus, *Histoire,* XXVII, 9 §10. According to H. E. Dirksen ("Das Polizei-Gesetz des Kaisers Zeno iiber die bauliche Anlage der Privathauser in Konstantinopel", *Philologische und historische Abbandlungen der Koniglichen*

in 389, an edict issued by the emperors Valentianus II, Theodosius I and Arcadius ordered the prefect of Constantinople to demolish the private buildings attached to public ones (C. Theod. 15.1.24). Ten years later, in 398, Arcadius and Honorius issued another, more specific, on the same subject. According to it, all the lean-by buildings ("parapetasia") and all the structures joined or attached to private and public edifices should be demolished, as measures taken against fire expansions and in order to secure the width of the roads and the pedestrians' circulation under the porticos (C.Theod. 15.1.39 / C 8.11.14). Dirksen is of the opinion that balconies were also included in the term "parapetasia" but this might not be exact.[16]

It appears that the above prohibitions were gradually withdrawn some years later. In 423 Theodosius and Honorius issued an edict defining the conditions under which the projection of balconies were allowed in the provinces of the empire. Namely: a distance of 10 feet should be kept between projections of private buildings and of 15 feet between private and public ones. As we will see in Zenon's edict, by the end of the 5th century the practice of constructing balconies projecting over roadways was already extended to the capital.

(c) The height of buildings

According to Strabo, emperor Augustus defined by law the maximum height of the buildings of Rome to 70 feet (about 20,77 m), while later Trajan (98–117), reduced it to 60 (17,76 m).[17] This height allowed the construction of 5–6 different floors and it was often used to its full extent in the erection of "insulas", that is multistoried tenement houses, a very useful arrangement for housing the thriving population of Rome. Similar housing needs must also have existed in Constantinople of the 5th century, since contemporary literary sources protest about the closeness of the housing quarters.[18] Anyway, it is rather

---

Akademie der Wissenschaften zu Berlin (1844), Berlin, 1846, p. 101) the order of 367–368 concerned Constantinople. We think that Ammianus' text clearly refers to Rome, since at this time Praetextatus was the prefect of this city.

[16] Ibid, p. 101.

[17] L. de Beylie, *L' habitation byzantine,* Grenoble-Paris, 1902, p. 3–4.

[18] Greek term, *Histoire nouvelle,* II, 35.2.

certain that only during the reign of Leon I (457–474) there were taken some measures for the increase of the permitted height of a certain category of edifices.

III. Zenon's Edict (474–491)

Zenon succeeded his father-in-law Leon I in 474, co-reigning with his son Leon II, who passed away some months later. After some civic riots in 476 he was established as the sole Emperor. His reign was seriously troubled by the invasions of Ostrogoths in Byzantine territories as well as by religious discordances.[19]

The edict we intend to analyze is addressed to the city's prefect Adamantius (474–479), probably an old associate in the expedition against the Ostrogoths.[20] In these circumstances we believe that the edict was published between 476 and 479. It is included in Justinian's Code (C 8.10.12) and, besides being one of the longest edicts, it is curiously enough rendered in the Greek language.

As it appears from the preface of the edict, the prefect Adamantius confronted some problems in his effort and duty to apply the existing building laws in the capital. That is, the ante-Zenonian legislation we have already mentioned and some more recent laws issued by Leon I and Zenon himself. The new edict aimed to clarify the law to the citizens so that they would have no need to ask for help in order to comprehend it.

(a) Regulations concerning the old (pre-existent) edifices (§1a–1b)

The "conditions" of the existing building of Constantinople should not be disarranged by innovations. Speaking of "conditions", the edict names only the amount of natural light coming in from the apertures ("φῶτα") and the view enjoyed through the windows of an edifice ("ἄποψις"). But since the incoming amount of natural light is relative

---

[19] By 488 the Ostrogoths began evacuating the Balkan peninsula intending to direct their army against Italy. Their withdrawal coincided with the end of the great invasions which took place during the 5th century. (*Ιστορία του Ελληνικού έθνους*, τ. Ζ., Εκδοτική Αθηνών, Αθήνα 1978, p. 132).

[20] Ibid, p. 129.

to the distance of the neighboring building, to its height as well as to the number and kind of the existing apertures, all these factors must also be taken to account. Considering the existing conditions firmly established and respected, every innovation made should follow the old forms ("τὸ παλαίον σχῆμα"), that is, no new apertures must be opened and the heights and the distances of the neighboring buildings must remain unchanged. Yet, in cases where either existent or later acquired oral or formal rights of servitude benefit one of the two adjoining estates, the dominant one is allowed to alter its old form at the expense of the servient one, according to the rights acquired (rights of light, or of aspect, etc.). It is then allowed to augment its volume in the horizontal or the vertical sense, lessening thus the incoming amount of light or obstructing the view of the servient property. It has been already mentioned that in Zenon's edict the existing edifices are treated as if they were under some mutual obligation of servitude. We now see that it is possible that one party can be unbound of this obligation by acquiring from the adjoining property new rights of servitude which allow him to do certain things, otherwise prohibited. Later on we shall see that both parties may be unbound by keeping between their buildings the proper distances defined by Zenon's edict.

(b) Regulations concerning new edifices (§ 2–3b, Fig. A.1a, b)

It is probable that during his early reign Zenon issued a law which defined that all newly erected edifices in Constantinople should keep a distance of about 12 feet from each other. The obscurity of this law must have created some problems in the cases where distances less than 12 feet were applied. With the new law it is firmly stated that this distance should be applied throughout the entire height of all kinds of buildings; that is, the newly erected, the renovated and the ones reconstructed after the great fires of 465 and 469. The law does not mention anything about the roof's projection, an issue which was later included in a Leon's VI novel constitution (N. 113). The law also states that this distance of 12 feet between buildings allows the construction of all kinds of desirable apertures, namely normal and high-level windows. The only exception to this rule concerns the cases where a newly erected edifice (or renovated or reconstructed) hinders with its volume the view of the sea which up to that time was enjoyed by the neighboring building. Meaning that, once acquired, this privilege cannot be deprived, because it is considered as a servitude of aspect gained by long use. Yet, the notion of view in the above case was strictly limited in situations where the view of the sea was concerned and did not include other worthy views of nature, such as gardens or woods, since the latter views "were neither foreseen by the prior laws nor will be added by the present; because it is not convenient to maintain such a servitude" (§2–2b).

Although the distance of 12 feet is the rule, in cases where the distance between two edifices is found larger, that is the roadway is wider, the excess in the width must be preserved and not be appropriated by the neighboring estates ". . . so that the rights of the city are maintained" (§3).

Since the capital's dwellings were already old and its urban growth limitless, it was thought necessary to allow some minor renovations in existing old buildings which did not conform with the distance of 12 feet between each other. So the law offered some variations in its application in cases the existent distance ranged between 10 and 12 feet. While this category of old buildings was neither allowed to change its volume in the horizontal or vertical sense, nor to open new regular windows, it was permissible to construct new high-level windows ("φωτιστίκαι θύριδες") on the condition that they were set 6 feet off the floor and no mezzanine platform was erected in between, converting the high-level windows into proper ("παρακυπτικά"). Yet, even in this case, if a different arrangement was agreed upon between neighbors, these prohibitions could be removed (§3a–3b).

(c) Regulations concerning the maximum allowed height of edifices and the obstruction of the sea view (§4–4b, Figs. A.2 and A.3)

During Leon's I reign two great fires are mentioned in Constantinople (465 and 469). Up to the last century, this city was very vulnerable to fires, set either by hazard or by arson, since its housing density was high and the building material used is mostly timber. Wood was abundant, very cheap to get and very safe during earthquakes, the second serious pest of the region. Therefore it is natural that the

Byzantine legislation on accidental or intentional fires was both particular and severe.[21]

Intending to encourage the reconstructions of some housing quarters, probably just after the fire of 469, Leon I issued an edict allowing the owners of burnt up edifices to reconstruct them to the height of 100 feet (31,23 m), regardless of the probable obstruction of the sea view enjoyed by neighboring buildings. Leon's laws, which are only mentioned in Zenon's edict (§4), insinuate both his agony for the rebuilding of his capital and the fact that keeping the view of the sea unobstructed was an old and respected practice. This extremely gratuitous allowance to this specific category of properties is modified by Zenon's edict to the extent that this height, from now on, is allowed for all buildings of the capital (new, renovated, reconstructed), as long as they keep a distance of 100 feet from the existing buildings enjoying the view. Constantinople, with its hills and descending terraces, is a city inclining towards its surrounding seas. Yet the inclination is not in most cases so steep and the distance of 100 feet not large enough as to allow the erection of edifices 100 feet high without obstructing the view of the sea. It is rather an act of compensation towards the edifices which can no longer enjoy the sea, providing them with a larger frontal space, that is, better natural light and good aeriation.

The space of 100 feet was necessary only in cases in which the view was enjoyed from the main living quarters of the edifice and not from the auxiliary ones, such as staircases, corridors or privies, where the distance of 12 feet was considered enough. Yet, even here, private or formal agreements between the interested parties might abrogate the law and the previously dominant edifice (the one with the view), following such an agreement, might be rendered to a servient one, having no more right to protest formally against the erection of a new edifice obstructing its view, since

---

[21] In the Digest: D 8.12.13 / D 9.2.27 §7-12 / D 9.2.30 §3/ D 19.2.9 and II /D 43.16.1 §8 / D 43.24.7 §4 / D 47.9.1 §2-3/ D 47.9.3 §7/ D 47.9.9 / D 47.9.11 / D 47.9.12 §1/ D 48.8.10 / D 48.19.28 §12. Also in *Ecloga Legum Isaurorum* 17, 40–41 and in most of the posterior official and private law compilations *(Leges rusticae, Epanagoge, Prochiron, Basilica, Epitome, Synopsis Basilicorum, Epanagoge aucta, Synopsis minor, Prochiron aucrum,* etc.).

"...it is not proper that existing agreements are overruled by general laws" (§4–4b).

The law concerning the view of the sea is the only one in Zenon's edict which retained its local character, being exclusively applied in Constantinople, although this is not mentioned in Justinian's edict of 531 (C 8. 10. 13).[22] It must also be noted that the maximum allowed height of buildings (100 feet) is neither repeated in more recent law compilations nor substituted by another.[23] On the contrary, keeping the view of the sea unobstructed appears to have been quite an important matter, since we find it included in almost all the later formal law compilations, as well as in the customary law up to 1826.[24] Justinian himself issued two novel constitutions on this subject (N 63 in 538 and N 165) of which the first one is worth noting.

As it always happens, at that time there were some swindlers who tried to erect edifices high enough as to hinder the neighbor's view of the sea without leaving open the required distance of 100 feet. In order to achieve this without openly breaking the law, they began by erecting a non-purpose construction, perhaps only a high wall (".... καθάπερ τι παραπέτασμα") setting it at a distance of 100 feet away from the building with the view, obstructing the latter and at the same time canceling every right of its owner to protest. Later on, they built a proper house in the intermediate space, only 12 feet away from the existing building. When things calmed down and the scheme followed was less obvious, they demolished the non-purpose construction, to the effect that it was they now who enjoyed the view, without having yielded part of their terrain as a compensation to the offended neighbor. This fraud was considered by Justinian as good as robbery ("vi bonorum raptorum") and all those involved were heavily fined in gold (the owners as well as the magistrates who allowed it to happen).

(d) Regulations concerning the construction of balconies (§5–5e, Fig. A.7b)

---

[22] The exception is first noticed in "Prochiron" (πρόχειρος νόμος) 38,5, repeated in B 58.11.12 and explained thoroughly in the "Practica ex actis Eustathii romani" (Greek name) 18,5 in the case of a dispute at Chrysoupolis.

[23] It only appears in a vague manner in B 58.11.11.

[24] See footnote 40.

During the time following the edict of 423, which allowed the construction of balconies in the provinces, this practice must have somehow been extended as well in the capital. In his edict Zenon sets some additional, quite important at the time, requirements allowing the realization of this sort of constructions, without in fact trespassing the guidelines of the former edict, that is the necessary distance of 10 feet between the balconies. The new conditions set aim at facilitating the circulation on the roads and at restraining fire expansions. As for the circulation, the edict sets for the balcony a minimum height of 15 feet (4,70 m) off the road level, which is considered quite adequate, since a loaded camel with its rider on is not higher than 3,20 m.[25] Even more, the balconies should be constructed without any supports underneath (walls or columns), that is they must be propped cantilevered structures, thus facilitating full access along the roadway and preserving its width. As for measures against fire, it is proposed that the balconies should not be constructed exclusively with wooden beams and planks but also in the "roman way" ("...τῷ τῶν λεγομένων ῥωμανισίων οἰκοδομεῖσθαι σχήματι"), meaning probably the supporting of the floor's timber construction on stone or marble projections off the main wall. The edict also prohibits rising open staircases leading from the road to the balcony, obviously as a measure for fire protection and in order to preserve the road's full width. As for the distances between balconies, they should be 10 feet apart and if the roadway is not wide enough to allow two balconies facing each other, they should be constructed one by one, i.e. probably offsetting each other. As for roads less than 10 feet wide, no balconies are permitted.

The law about balconies cannot be overruled by private agreements since those projections partly overlay public spaces on which such rights of servitude are not allowed. Yet they are permitted over private properties, terrains or buildings.[26] The violators of this law are heavily punished with fines in gold (the owner, the architect or the constructor) while the workmen who have executed them are beaten and sent to exile.

---

[25] B. S. Hakim, *Arabic-Islamic Cities: Building and Planning Principles*, London, New York, 1986, p. 21.

[26] D 9.2.29 §I / B 58.10.76.

In his edict Zenon uses for the balconies the term "solaria" ("ἡλιακός"). Yet, "solarium" is a term with an ampler meaning since it signifies all building spaces wholly or partly open to the sun; for instance, a terrace over a building ("δωμάτηρος ἡλιακός"), open or partly covered with a roof, with or without a colonnade in front, is also a solarium. On the ground level arcades or "portici" ("στοαί, ἔμβολοι") are also called solaria. Balconies in the above case, either as projections of the terrace or as independent projections from the main volume of the building are also solaria. This last form of solaria, the projecting balconies, are found all over the world in a variety of forms: As plain projections of the floor, or covered as well with a roof, or partly covered around with some lightweight material, or all covered around, leaving only light apertures etc. The last mentioned form of balcony is widely known as *sahnisi* or *erker*.[27]

(e) Trade establishments in public spaces(§6–6c)

Arcades, that is solaria on the ground level, were a very common architectural form in the Byzantine cities, either due to the climate or owing to the historical continuity of the place and the people. Constantinople's main avenue, the Mesi Odos, originally planned by Constantine the Great, began its course from the square of August-eum, traversed the city in the E-W direction and joined the Via Egnatia through the Golden Gate. It was the most important and commercial road of the city, traversed the fora of Constantine, of Theodosius, of the Taurus and of Arcadius and was lined on both sides with arcades. At its easterly starting point, there stood a pillar called Milian on whose vertical surface there were engraved the distances between the capital and the major cities of the empire. Under the arcades lining the Mesi Odos were concentrated most of the "cleaner" commercial activities of the city, in small shops divided from each other by walls or planks. These shops were municipal property ("res universitatis"), rented to the tradesmen. Since the city's commercial activities were so thriving, it is probable that those arcades were so crowded that there was no free space left either for the customers or the passersby. With his edict Zenon tries to

---

[27] Ν. Μουτσόπουλος, Η αρχιτεκτονική προεξοχή – το σαχνίσι, Εταιρεία Μακεδονικών Σπουδών, Θεσσαλονίκη 1988, σ. 319–372.

control this overcrowding under the arcades of Constantinople, by setting rules on the density and the size of the shops along the Mesi Odos, from Milion up to Capitolium (approximately by the forum of Theodosius), and by authorizing the city's prefect to act likewise for the space under the capital's other arcades. The shops along the Mesi Odos should be no more than 6 feet wide and their maximum height up to 7 feet. He also orders that the series of shops should be interrupted at intervals, leaving free passage across the arcades of a width equal to the distance of 4 columns, a practice which is found in similar constructions in the agora of Corinth (200 A.D.).[28] These regulations, like the ones about balconies, cannot be overruled by private agreements since the arcades are part of the city's property.

(f) Directions concerning building procedures and practice (§7–9b)

Zenon's edict closes with two more items which, although they do not describe building restrictions, they do aim at solving problems arising between neighbors in the event of new constructions, innovations and reconstructions or in disputes between landlords and contractors (masons or architects) who undertake the projects.

The first item deals mainly with the proper legal procedures to be followed in cases of denunciations made by interested parties against the erection of new edifices (§7–8). With the second item Zenon attempts to settle the usual disputes between owners and masons about salaries due or demanded, or about malpractice or refusal in completing constructions which other masons started and never completed. (§9–9b). Both subjects are too important to be briefly discussed here since they are amply covered by the Byzantine legislation. We shall only note that in the title 22 of the Book of the Prefect (10th century) there is a minute analysis of the mutual obligations of employers and employees, the proper legal actions for settling their disputes, the penalties for violating their contract and, last but not least, the setting of time guarantee as to the artistic and safe construction of the edifice, valid of course only when no calamities have intervened. The time guarantee for buildings in which quick-lime was used in the mortar between stones and bricks is fixed to 10 years, while for those where only plain mud was used, to 6 years.

---

[28] Scranton, *Corinth*, pl. III.

According to a law of 385 (C.Theod. 15.1.24 / C 8.11.8 etc.), time guarantee for public buildings was already fixed to 15 years.

Zenon's edict is not only the first complete law of the western world on building restrictions and urban regulations but also the last one to be conceived in the Byzantine era. Its restrictions were repeatedly included unchanged in almost all the posterior law compilations, private or official, even in the last important one, the Basilika. By the mid of the 14 century, they were also included side by side with the customary "laws" of easterly origin, in Harmenopoulos' Hexabiblos. Due to this last manual they remained alive, either included in the local customary laws or just in the conscience of the people as the legal inheritance of the Byzantine emperors. Their application was valid up to the mid of the 19th century, that is the early years of the establishment of the new Hellenic State.

Of course this corpus of laws is not to be considered complete in several points. An example of this deficiency is manifested in the law on distances which refers only to edifices facing each other across a roadway. Since the danger of fires is omnipresent in the edict, one naturally expects that some relative measures are also taken for the side and back boundaries of the buildings. Furthermore, there is no elucidation as to the building system of housing which is to prevail in the capital: whether the system is to be an attached one or a detached (surrounded by open space), as was used for public buildings (C. Theod. 15.1.46 of 406 / C 8.10.9). In the latter case there is no clarification as the relation of open spaces on the side and back boundaries of the edifice with the "legitimum spatium" of the law of the Twelve Tablets. Zenon's edict gives no apparent answer to this problem allowing us thus to search for it.

There is no doubt that by the 5th century Constantinople was already a well populated city. According to Zosimos, the dwellings in the housing quarters adjoined each other, the density was high and the streets narrow.[29] More recent depictions of the city show crowded and dense housing areas and sparsity of open spaces. Yet, even if this

---

[29] Ζώσιμος *Histoire* II 35.2: ". . .καὶ τὰς οἰκήσεις οὕτως εἶναι συνεχώρησαν συνεχεῖς ὥστε καὶ οἰκουροῦντας καὶ ἐν ταῖς ἀγυιαῖς ὄντας στενοχωρεῖσθαι τοὺς ταύτης οἰκήτορας καὶ μετὰ κινδύνου βαδίζειν διὰ τὴν τῶν ἀνθρώπων καὶ ζῴων πολυπλήθειαν. . . ."

was the common practice, we must not exclude the possibility that there should have existed cases where dwellings of status were erected at some distance from their side and back boundaries. The question is how wide this space might have been and what allowances it carried along as to the construction of light receptors, such as normal or high-level windows, since we have already mentioned the care with which the discrimination between these two kinds of apertures was made. Searching out this point, the Syro-roman Lawbook, a law compilation of the 5th century applied in the Middle East, is of some help. In this compilation it is maintained that the legislation included derives from Constantine, Theodosius and Leon, that is, Constantine the Great, Theodosius II and Leon I, Zenon's father in law and predecessor. In a passage of the Lawbook's Syrian translation (§120, London manuscript), there appear some restrictions as to distances between buildings and boundaries, ranging from 0–4 yards, according to the functional elements foreseen on their respective facades (apertures, rainwater spouts). The important point in these restrictions is that they refer to distances between buildings and their side boundaries, while Zenon's edict appears to refer to distances between buildings across a roadway. According to the Lawbook, if one wishes to discharge rainwater from a spout, or to open a narrow window no more than one yard wide, he must keep a distance of two yards away from his boundaries. If the window is to be wider, the open space must be four yards, while in the case of mere opening a high-level window, it is not necessary to keep any distance at all. This described arrangement means that buildings can be adjoined or not depending on the structural elements of their side-facades (Fig. A.4). As for the metrical relation of the yard mentioned in the Lawbook's to the Roman or Byzantine one, this is really a problem. A passage of this compilation (§119 London manuscript/ §83a Paris manuscript) defines the metrical system valid in the region of the Middle East by the end of the 5th cent. (1 mile = 1000 "passi" = 500 "ακαῖνες", each subdivided to 8 yards). Yet, experts on metrology[30] decided that the author of this passage must have

---

[30] Th. Mommsen, *Syrisches Provinzialmass und romischer Reichskataster*, Hermes III (Berlin, 1869) p. 429–438 / Fr. Hultsch, *Metrologie*, Graz, 1971 (1882), p. 582–584 / K. G. Bruns–E. Sachau, *Rechtsbuch*, p. 285–286.

mixed up in his estimations of Roman feet (0,295 m.) with philetaerian ones (0,350 m.), rendering thus the metrical definition useless. So we must simply regard the yards mentioned in the text as being either Roman (0,443 m.) or philetaerian ones (0,525 m.). In this case 8 (4 + 4) yards equals to 3,54 or to 4,20 m., while 4 (2 + 2) yards, to 1 ,72 or to 2, 1 0 m. respectively. These dimensions do not coincide either with the 2,5 + 2,5 feet of the Law of the Twelve Tablets (1,47 m = "legitimum spatium") or with the 10 feet of Honorius' and Theodosius' edict (2,95 m.).

These clues found in the Syro-roman Lawbook lead to the conclusion that at least as a principle, the "legitinum spatium" was still applied up to the 5th century in cases where openings or rainwater discharges were foreseen, but certainly in no other situations. Revaluing accordingly the text of the edict of 423 (C 8.10.11) stating generally that private buildings should keep a distance of 10 feet between them, we may conclude that this earlier law did not refer only to the front elevations but also to the rest of them, depending on the structures foreseen or realized there. Zenon must have followed the same train of thought. Being forced by circumstances to enlarge the space between the buildings' front elevations from 10 to 12 feet, he kept silent about what should happen on the other elevations, obviously considering that the same practice should be applied in cases of windows etc (Fig. A.5). This conclusion is further confirmed by a statement of obscure origin found in a law manual compiled by Michael Attaliatis, a jurist of the 11th century (Νομικον Ποιημα, 34,9). In this law it is stated clearly that, since the formal law failed to decide about the proper distance of edifices which are to be built near a boundary wall or near the property of a neighbor, what prevailed according to the Quaestorium was the custom to keep the distance of 6 feet off the boundaries. The same distance of 6 feet is quoted in Prochiron (beginning of 10th century) and in Synopsis Basilicorum (middle of 10th century). In Prochiron the extract repeats the phraseology of Solon's Law on distances (D 1 0. 1.13) and differs only on the distances between buildings (6 feet instead of 2).[31]

---

[31] See footnotes 12–13 and I. Ζέπου, Νομοθεσία του Σόλωνος, ΕΚΕΙΕΔ, τ. 18 (1971) σ. 53.

IV. "ἐπαρχικὰ", ἀπὸ τῶν τοῦ Ἀσκαλωνίτου Ἰουλιανοῦ τοῦ
ἀρχιτέκτονος ἐκ τῶν νόμων ἤτοι ἐθῶν τῶν ἐν Παλαιστίνῃ
("**Prefects' Ordinances Compiled by the Architect Julian
of Ascalon Based on the Laws, that Is the Customs,
of Palestine**")

We have already mentioned the historical background of this manual.
The "laws" included were compiled at an obscure date, certainly after
476–479 (Zenon's edict) and possibly even after 531 (Justinian's
edict expanding Zenon's law throughout the empire). Yet, the origin
of some of them in the form of unwritten customary laws may be
considered even earlier.[32] They were initially applied in the Middle
East but already by the 10th century they were transplanted to Constantinople and, either by chance or intentionally, were introduced as
a supplement to Leon's VI "Book of the Prefect". Since their later
inclusion in Harmenopoulos' Hexabiblos, their influence, if not
exactly their application, was expanded through the Balkan region
and the Greek peninsula and was maintained up to the mid of the 19th
century. We have also mentioned that since these "laws" describe the
building practices in the region of the Middle East, it is probable that
they may be related to the regulations described in the Syro-roman
Lawbook. It was further explained that through these "laws" it
becomes apparent that the practice in the region was that of the
horizontal co-ownership and not the Roman institution of the vertical
ownership. Last but not least, it is important to notice that Julian's
"laws" do not appear to lose their validity by opposing rights of new
servitudes agreed upon, as in the case of Zenon's edict.

Julian's "laws" constitute by themselves a more or less complete
corpus of building regulations, just like Zenon's. But since they enter

---

[32] Julian is not a fictitious person since his name and profession are mentioned in a
letter written by the neoplatonic philosopher Aeneas Gazaeus. The date of the letter
is uncertain but it is asserted that the philosopher lived about the turn of the 5th
century, certainly before 534. In his letter Aeneas asks Julian to repair some minor
defects in the construction of a fountain in his gardens, appraising at the same time
its splendor. It is well known that Aeneas kept a successful school of rhetorics in
Gaza and this makes him almost Julian's compatriot since the two cities (Gaza and
Ascalon) lie close together (Enea di Gaza, *Epistole*, a cura di L. Massa Positano
(Collana di studi greci, XIX), Naples 1950, p. 17, 53).

into minute details, specifying situations and conditions instead of generalizing them, they fall short of juridical expression. Yet, they certainly surpass Zenon's edict in the platitude of the thematic areas included. The "laws" cover directions for establishing particular workshops in housing areas, give practical answers to structural problems, propose structural building details, instruct the cultivators as to the manner plantations should be organized, set rules about the proper distribution of the expenses concerning building repairs among the co-owners etc. Nevertheless, it is not only the rich thematic areas which are approached that render these "laws" so important but also the manner in which the building problems are analyzed and solved. These "laws" reveal a solid knowledge of building practice, allowing no doubts that Julian was an architect-constructor of a remarkable sensitivity in anticipating the effects of nature's basic elements (fire, earth, air and water) on building materials, during the process of constructing shelter and other kinds of human accommodations.

In this article we will only analyze the building restrictions comparing them to the corresponding ones of Zenon's edict. Yet, we'll yield to the temptation to present a specimen of the essence of this compilation by referring also to some directions on the installation of workshops in housing quarters and to some examples of practical solutions given to structural problems.

(a) Regulations concerning distances between buildings (§23, 28, 33, 35, 36, 75, in the numerical order of Hexabiblos. Figure A.6a, b, c, d, e)

If somebody wishes to erect a one-story building, with all kinds of apertures on its elevation, he can do so by keeping a distance of 10 feet away from the neighboring building (§23). By keeping this distance one may also add another floor on a ground level building but in this case apertures are not allowed. In the event that the opposite edifice is of some importance, either in volume or in quality, the newly added floor must be kept at a distance of 20 feet (and not 10) in order not to obstruct it visually. At this distance all kinds of apertures are allowed (§28). The same distance should also be maintained when some new opening have to be pierced on a blind wall of an edifice which faces a neighboring building with apertures on its front wall. In cases where only new high-level windows are to be opened on an existing blind wall, no specific distance is required but that they must be set 3,5 yards higher from the floor level, so as not to be used as proper windows (§33). We believe that this circumventive approach made in articles 28 and 33 really means that one-story buildings with all sorts of apertures may be erected at a distance of only 10 feet away from existing ones, while for multistoried ones the proper distance is 20 feet in case proper windows are to be opened. This is also the explanation Harmenopoulos gives in his comment in article 33 and in this sense the "law" was understood and probably applied during the following centuries.

Julian refers also to another kind of apertures, besides proper and high level windows, the "τοξίκαι θύριδες", that is loopholes which were opened on the lower part of the walls of multistoried dwellings in the Middle Ages, usually for defensive reasons. It is very probable that these loopholes are related to the narrow windows, less than a yard wide, which were mentioned in the Syro-roman Lawbook. If a dwelling possesses such apertures looking toward a vacant piece of land whose owner later on wishes to build something on it, there exist two possible solutions: in case the loopholes are more than 10 years old and constitute the sole source of light in the chamber, the owner of the vacant lot must build at a distance of 3 1/3 yards away from the wall with the loopholes. In case the loopholes are either new or there is light coming into the chamber from another side, the new building may be erected in contact with the existing wall, blocking its loopholes (§35). Of course, this case defines clearly an old right of servitude concerning light.

The owner of a vacant lot, who wishes to construct an edifice on it, must also keep the distance of 3 1/3 yards in case the neighboring building possesses old rainwater spouts discharging water into his land (§75). Yet, in another passage, Julian notes that when there are no openings on the existing building but only spouts discharging rainwater into the vacant lot, the latter owner is allowed to erect his new edifice attached to the existing one, lengthening the spouts and making sure that the rain water discharges onto his new roof without damaging the neighboring wall (§36).

It is clear that Julian's "laws" constitute a corpus of building restrictions according to which (a) new one-story buildings with windows are allowed to be erected at the distance of 10 feet away from existing ones ("law" closely related to the edict of 423 and somehow to the instructions about opening wide windows of the Syro-roman Lawbook), (b) new multistoried buildings with windows are allowed at a distance of 20 feet from each other ("law" with no apparent relation to prior legislation), (c) The existence of necessary old loopholes or of old rainwater spouts compel the owner of a former vacant lot to keep his new edifice 3 1/3 yards away from the neighboring one ("law" reminding us of the "legitimum spatium" of the Law of the Twelve Tablets but also of the instructions of the Lawbook about narrow windows), (d) opening new high-level windows is always allowed as long as they are constructed 3,5 yards above the ground floor, ("law" partly similar to Zenon's and to the Lawbook's instructions). Evenmore, considering the exact wording of Julian's "laws" we note that they appear to be applied all around the building and not only on the road side.

(b) Regulations concerning the construction of balconies (§32, Fig. A.7c)

Julian's "law" about balconies generally coincides with the edict of Honorius and Theodosius of 423 and with that of Zenon, because it also defines the distance between balconies to 10 feet at least. Yet, in the case described (§32) there is also the condition that balconies may only be constructed on walls where the opening of a normal window is permitted. Since balconies are necessarily constructed on the upper stories of buildings, where opening a window presupposes the distance of 20 feet, it is clear that for Julian there are two necessary conditions for the realization of this kind of projections: a distance of 20 feet between opposite buildings and distance of 10 feet between the projections' outer limits.

There is no doubt that Julian's "law" about balconies is less elaborated than Zenon's, since there is neither mention of the manner of their construction nor of their height above the road level.[33]

---

[33] In Cyprus, after the island was sold to Guy de Lusignan (1192), the Assises of the Kingdom of Jerusalem and Cyprus were applied initially as customary and, later on, as official law. In a passage of the compilation which deals with civil rights of the burgesses *(Assises de la Basse Cour or de la cour de Bourgeois)* the conditions for the construction of balconies are defined in a quite different manner (fig. A.7. d). That

(c) Practical solutions to structural problems (§30,29)

In the event that someone wishes to replace a pier standing on the ground level of his building with a column, he must make sure that the diameter of the new column is no less than half of the width of the pier. If the replacement is to take place in an upper floor, then he should not allow the base of the new column to lean upon the lower pier directly, but he should place in between a "ἱμάντωμα" (a layer of materials, wood or mortar for the even distribution of the vertical forces), 8 fingers thick, which is about 15,6 cm (§30).

In case the owner of the ground floor story of a building has either narrow windows on his outer wall or no windows at all and wishes to enlarge them or to pierce the wall in order to open new ones, he is allowed to do so only if such apertures already exist on the wall of the upper story. But even in this case he must make sure that the vertical limits of the new openings are 6 fingers (about 12 cm) narrower on each side than that of the upper floor's windows (§29).

(d) Regulations concerning the maximum allowed height of edifices and the obstructed view (§47–51, Fig. A.8)

Julian's "laws" do not set a maximum height for buildings, obviously because this might be considered unnecessary for the regions where his law manual was applied. Amongst the examples he uses the highest building mentioned reaches 20 yards and consists of 3 proper stories and one on the semi-basement level (§40).

Regarding the view which is enjoyed from the apertures, Julian's "laws" investigates the problem quite thoroughly. It is not only the view of the sea, the shores, the villages by the seaside or that of the bays and the anchorages that is important, but also the view of the gardens and the woods. Looking at the mountains is also considered a view, writes Julian, repeating an otherwise lost extract of the jurist Papinianus. Yet, the most important point is that Julian does not consider only nature as worthwhile looking at, but men's artistic creations as well, the "δημοσία γραφή", a term which might include besides pictorial artistic creations and plastic ones.

---

is, each balcony's projection should not cover more than 1/3 of the public roadway's width. (Κ. Σαθας, Ασίζαι του Βασιλείου των Ιεροσολύμων και της Κύπρου, Μεσαιωνική βιβλιοθήκη, τ. 6, Αθήναι, 1972/1877, cod. A σ μ στ cod. B σ μ δ).

Eyesight, according to Julian, is the acutest human sense, enabling one to look at the sea as far as 40 miles, at the gardens and woods as far as 20 miles and at the artistic creations up to a distance of 200 yards. Yet, this does not mean that one should not be allowed to build in between, because thus neither cities nor villages would ever have existed. Therefore, he sets or repeats some rules as to the minimum distances necessary for keeping the view unharmed: in cases where the view of the sea or the mountains of an existing edifice is in danger of being obstructed by the erection of a new construction, the latter must be set at least 100 feet away. If it is the view of gardens or woods or artistic creations that is being obstructed, then the proper distance of the new building should be no less than 50 feet. We should note here that in Zenon's edict it is specifically emphasized that the aspect toward gardens and woods was not considered as a view to be respected, neither by the ancient law nor by the present one. We really do not know if Julian repeats here some ancient law which Zenon ignored or an ancient custom of Palestine which according to Justinian's edict of 531 (C 8.10.13) never lost its validity.[34] The hypothesis that this series of "laws" was compiled closely after September 531 is based on the possibility that, following the above edict, some order was issued demanding from the provinces' officials a written outline of the old customary laws still valid in their region.

(e) Regulations concerning establishments for workshops (§ 13–22, 25–27, Fig. A.9)

In the articles 13–22 and 25–26, following the numerical order of the Hexabiblos, Julian makes a list of several handicraft establishments whose everyday function, owing to the materials used and the means of elaboration (fire), usually harm the neighboring or overlaying dwellings. This list is useful both as a source describing the way these workshops functioned and as a supplement to the ordinances included in Leon's Book of the Prefect. Yet, the focus here is not on the relation between tradesmen and purchasers or tradesmen and the State, but exclusively on the harmful effects the function of these establishments

---

[34] C 8.10.13: " … ceteris videlicet omnibus, quae non per Zenonianam legem innovata sunt, sed veteribus legibus comprehensa, in sua firmitate in omniloco manentibus".

had on their immediate environment. Although Julian might have also been some kind of a city official, in his regulations concerning workshops he appears as a sincere architect aiming at keeping records of his professional experiences in a rather instructive manner.

A characteristic sample of his experiences as an architect is the arrangement he proposes for the construction of new private baths in a housing quarter (§13). The importance of public and private bathing establishments in the Byzantine and Muslim world is well known and it is noteworthy that in fact Julian's "laws" begin with this sort of edifices. At its most simple forms, a bathhouse is composed of an antechamber, the bathing rooms and the furnace where water is being heated. Naturally there is also a chimney pipe leading the smoke to the open air. According to Julian, unlike bakery ovens which burn only during the night, the bathhouses' furnaces burn continually during day and night. Since the smoke which comes out of the chimney pipe is naturally a great nuisance to the dwellings, one should try to minimize its harmful effects. Julian attends to the problem by concentrating on three facts: (a) the microclimate of the region, that is the direction of the prevailing winds during winter and summertime, (b) the customary human trend of keeping the windows closed during wintertime and open during the summer, and (c) the natural flow of the dispersing smoke which mostly affects the higher floors of the buildings closer to the chimney pipe.

Keeping these facts in mind and using also his experiences, he comes up with a diagram of the minimum allowed distances between the baths furnace (it would have been more exact to use the chimney as the focus-point) and the neighboring environment. Of these three facts, the last two are standard while the first one may be considered as variable. So it is not important if the microclimate defined in the example is that of Palestine or Constantinople or a fictitious one, since the system may work anywhere. Anyway, in the region described the prevailing summer winds blow from the N-E direction while in winter from the S-W. As for the existing buildings surrounding the bathhouses' site, they are distinguished in three hazard groups, depending on their height and on the apertures they have towards the furnace. The multistoried dwellings with apertures, the multistoried ones without apertures or the dwellings on the ground floor with apertures, and the buildings on the ground floor without apertures.

As we will shall see, the constructor of the bathhouse would likely have a rough time finding the right position for erecting it.

The most risky position of the furnace is when it lies at the N-E of existing multistoried buildings with openings; the reason being that during summertime, the winds, blowing from the N-E, carry the smoke towards a S-W direction creating nuisance to the dwellings through the open windows. Therefore, the proper distance to be kept is 30 yards. If the furnace of the bath is to be placed at the S-W of buildings of the same hazard group as above, the proper distance is 20 yards, because in this case the wind carries the smoke towards the dwellings only in winter, when the openings remain closed. Those distances are reduced to 1/3 of the initial ones for the second hazard group (10 and 6,66 yards respectively) and are almost diminished in the cases of dwellings on the ground floor without apertures (5 and 3,33 yards), depending on whether the furnace is located in a N-E or a S-W direction (Fig. A.9).

Julian's distances are usually measured in feet and in yards. Since the metrical system of the Byzantine empire should not be considered fixed through time and region, we have every cause to presume that the "foot" and the "yard" initially used by Julian were somewhat different in length from the ones valid during the 10th century in Constantinople or from the foot and yard in use during 1345 in Thessaloniki, where probably the Hexabiblos was compiled. It is certain that by the turn of the 5th century the metrical system used in the Middle East was either the Roman, or the philetaerian one (1 foot = 0,350 m, 1 yard = 1,5 feet = 0,525 m.). We are rather inclined to assume that Julian referred to the latter since its use was more common in everyday life. On the other hand, in the Geneva copy the group of Julian's "laws" is introduced by an almost complete extract of Heron's treatise "περὶ μέτρων". There it is plainly stated that there are two kinds of "yards", one equal to 2 feet and another to 1,5 feet, whose specific use, according to Schilbach[35] is not clearly discerned. An incomplete rendering of Heron's same extract is also included in many manuscripts of the Hexabiblos with only one kind of yard mentioned, that equaling to 1,5 feet. So, the yard used by Julian (0,35x 1,5 = 0,525 m.) during the 10th century might have

---

[35] Er. Schilbach, *Byzantinische Metrologie,* Munchen 1970, p. 20–21.

corresponded either to 0,624 m., that is to two Byzantine feet (0,3123x2) or to 0,468 m. (0,3123x1,5), while to the reader of the Hexabiblos only to 0,468 m.

Without commenting on the actually limited distances proposed, in this "law" exists an organized reasoning leading to a system of general application. Perhaps today we would have also taken into account the heating capacity of the furnace, since it affects the amount of smoke discharged, but certainly this is too great a demand to make upon an architect of the 6th century.

Julian uses a similar system for the placing of bakeries' ovens in the middle of housing quarters (§14), of tile-and pottery-kilns (§15), and of furnaces for preparing gypsum (§16). Further on the list deals with other kinds of workshops, whose common characteristic is the use of fire in their daily function, proposing either general or specific limitations on their setting. The workshops mentioned in the "laws" are lime-kilns, dye-houses, glassworks, blacksmith shops, brine and oil shops and rope-manufacturing shops (§17–22). There are also proposals for establishing stables and brothels (§25,27).

It is also interesting to look at his proposals for the arrangement of wine-shops (§26). It is necessary to explain beforehand that, at least in Constantinople, these establishments opened at 8:00 a.m. and closed at 8:00 p.m., that there was a State control of the capacity of the serving vessels[36] and that their proprietors, as well as their customers, were considered as persons of ill-fame. Evenmore, that the existence of a resting place for pack-animals in or nearby the wine-shops was rather convenient, since these places were usually frequented by travelers.

According to Julian, the main entrance to a wine-shop or public house had to be offset from the door of the dwelling across the roadway in order to eliminate the harm created by direct overlooking, noises and by unpleasant odors. The same restrictions are valid for the setting of entrance doors of stables (§25,27). This practice is well known in the Islamic cities of the Magreb, in cases the roadway is less than 7 cubits wide (3,25–3,50 m).[37] The wine-shop's activities should be limited only in its interior space and no spreading is allowed

---

[36] Leon's Book of the Prefect, 19, §1–4.

[37] Hakim, *Arabic-Islamic Cities*, p. 38.

outdoors, in terraces or under kiosks along the roadway or the market place. The provision of resting places for pack animals is undesirable, and if possible should be avoided, since it is harmful for the pedestrians.

The few passages about structures, workshops and wine-shops, which we have analyzed above, are only a sample of the rich experiences included in Julian's "laws". These instructions certainly deserve, transcending the limits of the field of Law, to enlighten other sciences too.

V. Epilogue

We now reach the most peculiar stage of the evolution through time of the Byzantine building regulations (restrictions or Limitations: "περιορισμοί"). It is well known that Harmenopoulos used in his compilatory manual "Hexabiblos" all sorts of old and current law sources[38] and that one of them was certainly Leon's "Book of the Prefect". Since the manuscript he used for his compilation included Julian's "laws" of Palestine, Harmenopoulos also inserted them in the most relative chapter of his manual, in Book 2 ("περὶ νόμης καὶ δεσποτείας"), title 4 ("περὶ καινοτομιῶν"). Under this title 4 of the Hexabiblos were also included laws about rights of servitude and several passages of Zenon's edict. As we have already mentioned, this juxtaposition of differing laws must have caused uncertainties and misunderstandings as to which law was to be applied. Otherwise the Hexabiblos (1345), the most serious law-manual of the Byzantine civil law present during the Turkish occupation, was regarded by the Greek people as the major law-source expressing the Emperors' legislation. But, while by this time the Hexabiblos was often used as the main source for more recent compilatory law-manuals, it was not amply used for bestowing justice. Only after Spanos's printed translation was published in (1744) did the Hexabiblos prevail over all other law-manuals in status and in use. Its inherent and sentimental values as well as its convenient division in chapters, rendered it so important a manual that a decree issued by the newly established

---

[38] Πιτσάκης, Αρμενοπουλος, εισαγωγή.

Greek government (23.2.1835) declared that "The civil laws of the Byzantine Emperors included in Harmenopoulos' Hexabiblos are to have the validity of State laws until the publication of the new civil code whose drawing up we have already ordered. But customs established, either by long and uninterrupted use or by court decisions, are to prevail over the law in the regions where they were established". This promised new Civil Code was published only in 1946. It is only natural that during the first post-revolutionary years it would have been extremely difficult for jurists and statesmen to realize that the title 4 in the 2nd Book of the Hexabiblos included not only imperial laws but also customary "laws" of Palestine. No discrimination was ever made at that time so that all the laws of the 4th title, even differing in their origins, were considered valid.

But even earlier, by the end of the 18th century, some passages of Hexabiblos were already included in the local customary laws which flourished in several Greek autonomous regions, mostly in the insular communities.[39] There is a legal document of the local administration of Naxos[40] dated on 15 October 1826, a few years after the declaration of the Greek independence, concerning a dispute between two civilians. The defendant was on his way to erect an edifice in the town of Naxos at a distance of 4 feet from an existing old building, offending its lighting and interrupting its view of the sea. The local court decided that this should not be allowed because, according to Harmenopoulos, the distance between the buildings should be at least 10 to 20 feet (depending on whether the new edifice was to be erected in villages or towns). Evenmore, because ". . .according to the ancient

---

[39] A vivid example of this case is apparent in the legislation of the island of Samos. There, since 1744, the predominant official law was that of Harmenopoulos' Hexabiblos. The use of this law manual prevailed during all the political changes which occured on the island, that is between 1821–1834, 1835–1849 and 1850–1900 (date of the introduction of the new civil code) but always in coexistence with the local customary law. This common law, as it was recorded by government officials in 1847 and 1860, appears to derive also from the Hexabiblos. So we have a case where both official and customary laws coincide as to their common source (Αλ. Α. Σεβαστάκης, Δίκαιο και δικαστική εξουσία στη Σάμο, 1550–1912, Αθήναι 1986).

[40] Ι. Βισβίζης, Η πολιτική δικαιοσύνη κατά την ελληνικήν επανάστασιν μέχρι του Καποδιστρίου, Αθήνα 1941, σ. 488–489.

customs of Naxos, which are in accordance with the code of Laws of the ever memorable Christian emperors of Constantinople, . . .nobody is allowed to deprive his neighbor of the view of the sea, the valley and the mountain, or obscure his lighting by erecting a building. . .". Yet, these laws to which the local administration refers to, do not exactly originate from the Byzantine Emperors but from the customary laws of Palestine, as they were recorded by an architect from Ascalon.

We are not sure if it was the discovery of this fact or the strong inclination towards a European urban planning system, which soon prevailed in the new Greek State, but from 1849 the situation changed. Arios Pagos, the Supreme Court of Greece, decided that since the building restrictions included in the Hexabiblos, were under the responsibility of the police authority, they should normally be part of the Public Law and not of the Civil one, meaning that they ceased to be included in the decree of 1835 as valid Laws and thus could not be effective anymore. This verdict[41] opened the way to westernized urban planning, with all its positive and negative features, for the newly organized Greek State.

Acknowledgement This article is published with the permission of the author and the publisher. It is reformatted to fit the formatting style of this book. It was first published in 2000, and the full reference is: Vasso Tourptsoglou-Stephanidou, "The Roman-Byzantine Building Regulations". *Saopstenja*, 30–31 (1998–1999), Belgrade 2000, pages 37–63.

References

Byzantine legal compilations and sources: *Theodosian Code; Corpus Juris Civilis; Leon's Novel Constitutions; Basilika; The Prefect's Book;* Harmenopoulos's *Hexabiblos; The Syro-roman Lawbook; Synopsis Basilicorum; Ecloga Legum Isaurorum; Prochiron Legum; Practica ex actis Eustathii Romani.*
Bruns, K. G. (1969). *Fontes Juris Romani Antiqui.* Aalen: Gradenwitz.
De Beylie, L. (1902). *L'habitation byzantine.* Paris: Grenoble.
Dirksen, H. E. (1944). Das Polizei-Gesetz des Kaisers Zeno uber die bauliche Anlage der Privathauser in Konstantinopel. *Philogische und historische Abhandlungen der Koniglichen Akademie der Wissenschaften zu Berlin.*

---

[41] A.Π/ 291/1849.

Hakim, B. S. (1986). *Arabic-Islamic cities: Building and planning principles.* London.

Hultsch, Fr. (1882). *Metrologie.* Graz.

Massa Positano, L. (Ed.). (1950). Enea di Gaza. *Epistole.* Naples.

Mommsen, Th. (1869). Syrisches Provinzialmass und romischer Reichskataster. *Hermes III*, Berlin.

Paoli, U. E. (1976). La loi du Solon sur les distances. *Altri Sudi di Diritto Greco e Romano.* Milano.

Schilbach, Er. (1970). *Byzantinische Metrologie.* Munich.

Scranton, R. (1958). *Mediaeval Architecture in the Central Area of Corinth* (vol. 16). Princeton.

References in Greek (listed sequentially as they occurred in the text)

Α. Ορλάνδος, Τα παλάτια και τα σπίτια του Μυστρά, Αρχείον Βυζαντινών μνημείων της Ελλάδος, τ. Γ (1937), pp. 5–114.

Π. Ζέπος, ιδιοκτησία κατ' ορόφους. (Ν. 3741/1929), Αθήναι 1931.

Ζέπου, *Jus Grecoromanum,* Αθήναι 1931.

Ιστορία του Ελληνικού έθνους, τ. Ζ., Εκδοτική Αθηνών, Αθήνα ,1978.

Ν. Μουτσόπουλος, Η αρχιτεκτονική προεξοχή, Θεσσαλονίκη, 1988.

Σαθας, Ασσίζαι του Βασιλείου των Ιεροσολύμων και της Κύπρου, Μεσαιωνική Βιβλιοθήκη, τ. 6, Αθήναι, 1972 (1877).

Πιτσάκης, Κωνσταντίνου 'Αρμενοπούλου, Πρόχειρον νόμων ή Εξάβιβλος, Αθήνα 1974;

Α. Σεβαστάκης, Δίκαιο και δικαστική εξουσία στη Σάμο, 1550–1912, Αθήνα 1986;

Ι Βισβίζης, Η πολιτική δικαιοσύνη κατά την ελληνικήν επανάστασιν μέχρι του Καποδιστρίου, Αθήνα 1941.

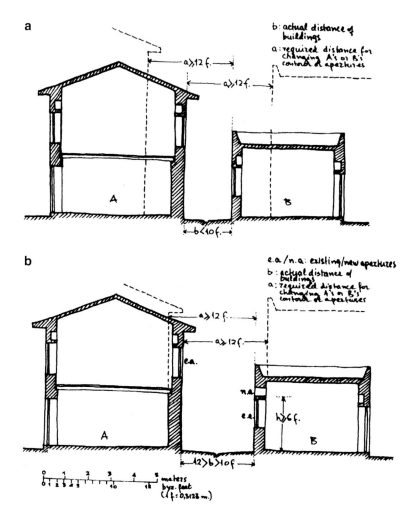

Fig. A.1 Limitations to change in private buildings as determined by road width, according to Zenon's edict (C 8.10.12–3a): (**a**) when road width is less than 10 feet, no change is allowed, and (**b**) when road width is between 10 and 12 feet, only new high level windows are allowed that are 6 feet from the internal floor level. Byzantine foot = 0.3123 m.

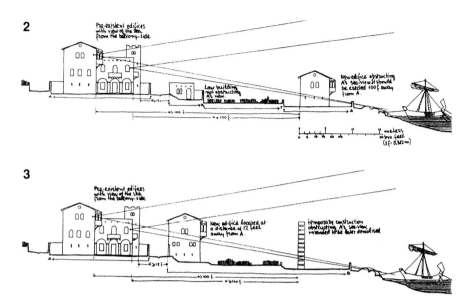

Figs. A.2 and A.3 top (2) Servitude to protect the view of the sea, according to Zeno's edict (C 8.10.12–4), and below (3) Circumventing methods for obstructing the view of the sea (Justinian's Novel Constitution, Number 63). Byzantine foot = 0.3123 m

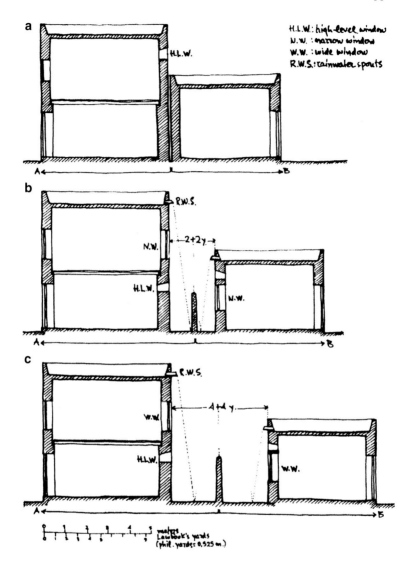

Fig. A.4 Distances between buildings at their side and back boundaries that allow change, according to (Syro-Roman Lawbook): (**a**) opening high-level windows is allowed when buildings are abutting each other as shown, (**b**) when there is a distance of 2 yards from the boundary, new narrow windows, and/or adding rain spouts are allowed as shown, and (**c**) when there is a distance of 4 yards from the boundary, opening new regular sized windows is allowed. The yard in the Syro-Roman Lawbook = 0.525 m

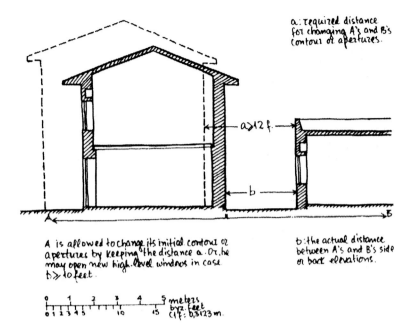

a: required distance for changing A's and B's contour of apertures.

a⟩12 f.

A is allowed to change its initial contour or apertures by keeping the distance a. Or, he may open new high-level windows in case b ⟩⟩ 10 feet.

b: the actual distance between A's and B's side or back elevations.

0 1 2 3 4 5 meters
                   byz. feet
0 1 2 3 4 5   10   15 Cl f: 0.3123 m.

Fig. A.5 Probable interpretation of Zenon's edict on what is allowed or disallowed on a building's side or back elevation. Byzantine foot = 0.3123 m

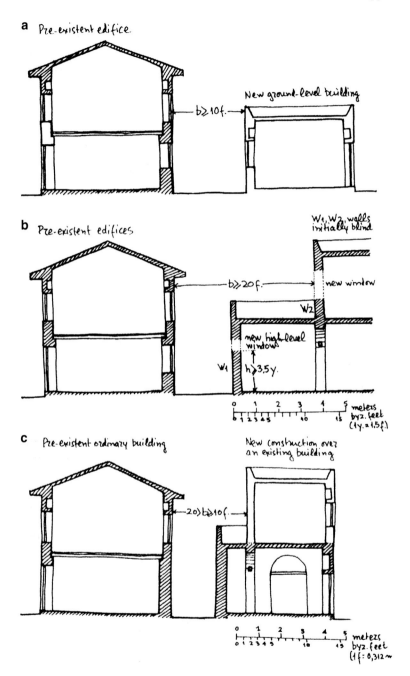

Fig. A.6 Required distance between buildings that allow proposed change or new construction (Julian's rules as numbered in Harmenopoulos's *Hexabiblos* (2, 4 [23], 33, 28, 35): (**a**) a one-story building is allowed, in towns and villages, at a distance of 10 feet from an existing building; (**b**) opening regular sized and high-level windows on a former blind wall that faces windows of an existing building is allowed. For the regular sized window when there is a distance

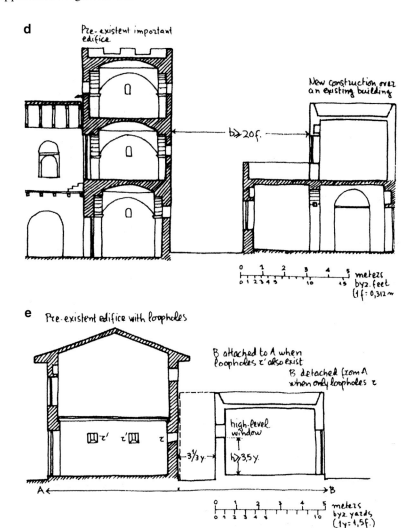

d Pre-existent important edifice

New construction over an existing building

b>20f.

0 1 2 3 4 5 meters
0 1 2 3 4 5   10   15 byz. feet
                         (1f: 0,312m

e Pre-existent edifice with loopholes

B attached to A when loopholes z' also exist

B detached from A when only loopholes z

high-level window

-3⅓y.→ b>3,5y.

A←   →B

0 1 2 3 4 5 meters
0 1 2 3 4 5   10   byz. yards
                     (1y: 1,5f.)

Fig. A.6 (continued)   of 20 feet, and for high-level windows they must be at a distance of 3.5 yards from the floor of the room as shown. The yard = 1.5 Byzantine foot. Therefore 3.5 yards = 5.25 Byzantine feet which is 1.64 m; (**c**) new construction over an existing building that faces another pre-existing building is allowed at a distance of less than 20 feet but no window openings can be opened; (**d**) when the pre-existing building in condition (c) is an "important" structure then the necessary distance must be at least 20 feet; (**e**) right of servitude to light: when a new building is to be built abutting an existing building that has loopholes (small openings for light), two possibilities: 1) if the loopholes are old and constitute the only source for light, then the new construction must be setback 3.33 yards from the existing building, 2) if the loopholes are less than 10 years old, or there are other sources for light, then the new construction can abut the existing building. Byzantine yard = 1.5 feet, therefore 3.33 yards x 1.5 = 5 feet which is = 1.56 m

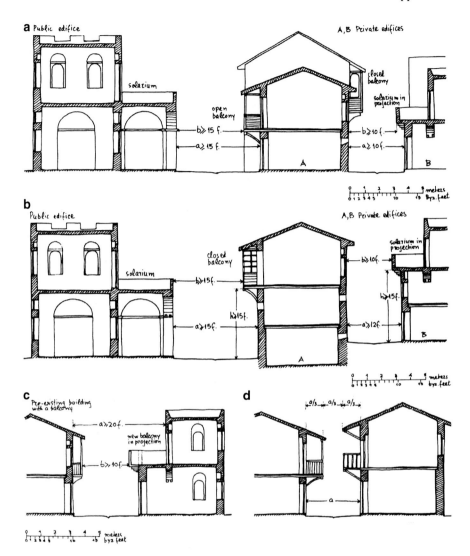

Fig. A.7 Construction of balconies: (**a**) Balcony construction according to (C 8.10.11) of the year 423 C.E.; (**b**) Balcony construction according to Zenon's (C 8.10.12); (**c**) Balcony construction according to Julian's rules as numbered in the *Hexabiblos* (2, 4 [32]); (**d**) Balcony construction according to the *Assises of Cyprus* (A [146]). Byzantine foot = 0.3123 m.

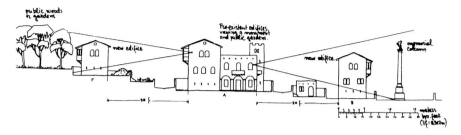

Fig. A.8 Servitude of views toward gardens and wooded areas and toward artistic objects or paintings should be at least a setback of 50 feet for a new building per Julian's rules as numbered in the *Hexabiblos* (2, 4 [48, 49]); the setback distance for a new building from one that enjoys the view of the sea or mountains is 100 feet, *Hexabiblos* (2, 4 [47, 51])

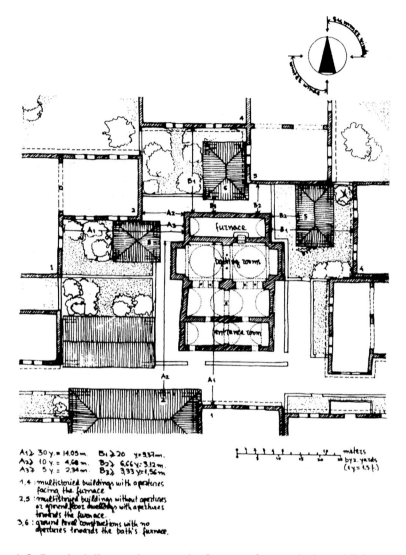

A₁≥ 30y.= 14.05m.   B₁≥ 20   y=9.37m.
A₂≥ 10 y.= 4.68 m.   B₂≥ 6.66y.=3.12m.
A₃≥ 5 y = 2.34 m.   B₃≥ 3.33 y=1.56m.

1,4 : multistoried buildings with apertures
       facing the furnace

2,5 : multistoried buildings without apertures
       at ground floor dwellings with apertures
       towards the furnace.

3,6 : ground level constructions with no
       apertures towards the bath's furnace.

Fig. A.9 Required distance between the furnace of a new bath establishment and the surrounding dwellings according to the rules set out by Julian and as recorded in the *Hexabiblos* (2, 4 [13]). The differentiation of the distances depends on the orientation of the furnace, the location of windows of the existing nearby dwellings, and the direction of the prevailing winds during the summer and winter. For a clearer interpretation of these conditions, see Fig. 6 in (Hakim 2001). To convert Byzantine yards to meters: yard x1.5 Byzantine feet x 0.3123 = meters

Appendix 4
Prochiron Legum: Background and Text

Background

The sources for the *Prochiron Legum* are the *Ecloga* dated to 741 CE
(Burgmann, "Ecloga", ODB 1991), and the later *Procheiros Nomos*
dated to 872 CE (Schminck, "Prochiron", ODB 1991). The *Ecloga* is
in the form of a synopsis of Justinian's *Corpus Juris Civilis* from the
first half of the 500's CE. The *Ecloga* was issued by Leo III and
Constantine V. It constituted a corpus of secular law unrivaled until
the end of the 9th century (Burgmann, "Ecloga", ODB 1991).
It continued to be the official exposition of the law until the publication of the *Procheiros Nomos* by Basil I, the emperor whose reign is
867–886 CE and the founder of the Macedonian dynasty that dates
from 867 to 1156 CE. The *Ecloga* was used as a precedent to the
Procheiros Nomos in form and substance (Freshfield 1930). It dates to
872 CE (Schminck, "Prochiron", ODB 1991). It does not seem that it
was superseded by any other official publication. And in the 14th
century Harmenopolis seems to treat it as still in use at his time and
uses it as the basis to his manual the *Hexabiblos*, as he explains in its
Introduction (Freshfield 1930).

In Calabria and Puglia people continued to be the subjects of the
Byzantine empire until the Norman conquest in 1060 CE. During the
reign of Basil II (976–1025) the Eastern Byzantine government
attempted to restore authority in Calabria and Puglia. It is either in
the reign of Basil II, or earlier, that the first edition of the *Prochiron
Legum* was composed in Calabria. According to Freshfield it was
copied at Soverato, a village near Cantanzano in Calabria. It has no

B.S. Hakim, *Mediterranean Urbanism: Historic Urban / Building Rules
and Processes*, DOI 10.1007/978-94-017-9140-3,
© Springer Science+Business Media Dordrecht 2014

preamble and is not dated. It was compiled for use in Calabria and shows that the *Ecloga* held its place and continued to be used concurrently with the *Procheiros Nomos* in Southern Italy. The first chapters and the one on crime of the *Prochiros Legum* were taken from the *Ecloga*, while all but the last two chapters are taken from the *Procheiros Nomos* (Freshfield, 1930).

According to Francesco Brandileone the *Prochiron Legum*, known as the "Vatican Greek Codex 845", was first revealed by B. Capasso in 1867 CE as a hand written manuscript in Greek on 142 octavo folios in two columns (Brandileone, 1895). Many of the articles within the chapters of the *Prochiron Legum* clearly show the adaptation of earlier Byzantine codes to be compatible with local customary practices in Southern Italy. The editor replace technical terms with common words and simplified the sentences so that the reader could understand the meaning and purpose of each article (Brandileone, 1895). Brandileone uses a deductive method to determine the time and place of compilation of the *Prochiron Legum* as follows:

- It was compiled in the Greek area of Southern Italy.
- The compiler was not a clergyman, as he disregarded important religious provisions.
- He lived a distant from the sea, as specified by certain punishments that were associated with the sea to be replaced by a river.
- Sicily should be excluded for the reasons given by Brandileone.
- He lived closer to Cosenza than to Reggio, because the Lombard principles he introduced were more common in the north than in the south of Calabria.
- Brandileone noted that the compilation has also made use of the *Epitome Legum*, which is dated to 914 CE (Schminck, "Epitome Legum", ODB 1991), and therefore it must be dated after 914 CE. The latest date for its compilation is no later that the second half of the 11th century.

Brandileone also discusses a later edition of the *Prochiron Legum*, and he says that it is not possible to determine from the text to whom to attribute the work of the earlier or later editors (Brandileone 1895). However, he seems to be certain that the first editor wrote it between 980 and 1050, i.e., within the span of those 70 years. This is compatible with Freshfield's estimation for the first edition of the *Prochiron*

Legum, i.e. most probably during the reign of Basil II (976–1025). Freshfield also mentions in his Preface (Freshfield, 1931) that it was revised in the reign of the Norman King Roger II (1105–1154). Brandileone interprets the date of the revised edition of the *Prochiron Legum* to the first decade of Roger II's kingdom. According to historical data Roger II began his personal rule in 1112 CE, and became King of Sicily in 1130. Therefore the date of the revised edition would be between 1130 and 1140 CE. This means that the second edition dates over a century later than the original first edition.

The following image is from folio 60 of the manuscript as it was reproduced by Brandiloene and Puntoni (1895). It is located in their book between pages 222 and 223. The page is folded down on itself and the text seen is not continuous.

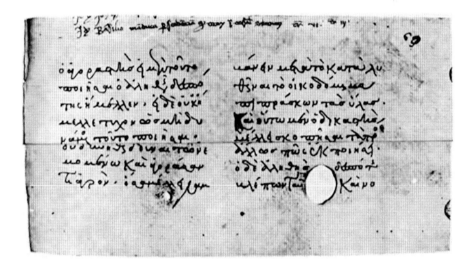

The following sentences from article 34 can be seen in the image of the manuscript's Greek text:

If the current owner has spent more than the land itself was worth it suffices that the applicant matches its actual value.

It can also be decided that, if the previous owner is ready to go to the current occupant and offer all the amount he could get, including what he has added to the field, then the previous owner shall be allowed to do so.

Text

(Chapter 33)

1. A person creates a new work, when he builds a wall anew or pulls it down and alters the original aspect of it.

2. If your servant is engaged in building I can legally give him a notice in regard to new building. But your servant cannot give a valid notice to another person engaged in building.

3. If the matter concerns several persons in regard to the building a notice to one of them suffices; and it will hold good and be reckoned as given to all the owners concerned in the undertaking. If after notice given one of the owners continues to build, the others will not be affected or liable; for the work done by one shall not prejudice those who took no part in it.

4. We decree that anyone who wishes to renovate an old building shall not change the old plan of the house, nor shall he be permitted to deprive his neighbors of light and view unless perchance he has either by contract or agreement a servitude which grants and permits him to change the form of the building as he may like and wish. For the person who has this right of 'servitude' may build without hindrance as he wishes even if perchance he prejudices his neighbors since the servitude was constituted by contract or agreement. When two houses stand 'over against' one another, that is to say are placed contiguously to one another, a space of 12 feet must intervene between them beginning from the foundations and be so separated from the adjoining house. And each party can raise his building as high as he wishes and open prospect windows whether he builds a new house or rebuilds an old one destroyed by fire.

5. In this blessed city the view of a neighbor who only claims (is entitled to) 12 feet cannot be taken away if he can see the sea directly standing or even sitting in his dwellings, and is not obliged to turn about and obtain a sideway view of the sea. If however there is a space of 100 feet between two dwellings one owner can build without hindrance and deprive his neighbors' view of the sea.

6. Where anyone has a view of the sea from a kitchen, bath, steps or terrace then another person can build within the 100 feet and

without any impediment deprive his neighbor of a view. If however there is an agreement which concedes and permits building the agreement shall hold good even if it damages the neighbor's view of the sea, or if he who is now the owner has so agreed or the former owner did so. For a general law cannot over-ride servitudes properly created (that is by agreement).

7. One joint owner of property cannot impose a servitude on the property jointly owned without the knowledge and consent of the other joint owner.

8. A right of 'view' does not apply to a tree or to a garden.

9. Anyone building premises where an alley or lane intervenes is not permitted to appropriate the excess by which the alley or lane exceeds the width of 12 feet. For the law as to 12 feet is not prescribed to the public detriment but only to prevent less than 12 f. between two houses. When therefore the alley or lane is more than 12 feet wide the excess cannot be appropriated but must be kept for the public. Should the space between two old houses be less than 12 feet no one can raise his house beyond the original height or open windows other than those which already existed. Wherefore if the space intervening be 10 feet then the person building is not allowed to make prospect windows unless he already had them. But he can make lights at a height of 6 feet from the ground. No one is allowed to make a false floor in his house and so convert a light into a prospect window.

10. No one who is a joint owner of a party wall can pull it down and build it up again without the knowledge and consent of the other common owners: for he is not the sole owner of the wall.

11. There is no restriction on building on vacant land, that is in a place where a building can cause no damage to neighbors.

12. Anyone desiring to build or heighten a tumbled down house must not obstruct his neighbor's light or otherwise damage him: and he can be compelled to retain the former style and the plan of the original scheme of the house.

13. Anyone who can legally raise his house can do so provided he does not impose a 'burden' on his neighbor's house. Similarly he must not impose a servitude more burdensome than is appropriate thereto.

14. No one can forbid his neighbor and prevent him from opening a doorway on to the public highway. Provided he does not injure the highway.
15. If a spring from which a person draws water runs dry, and subsequently it flows again in the former course and such person again draws water as before, the servitude for him to draw water from it is reinstated as he formerly had it.
16. No one is allowed to make an oven or kindle a fire on a party wall lest the wall be injured.
17. Where anyone builds a chimney and smoke issuing from it is a nuisance to dwellers in houses above, such dwellers can effectively and legally compel the builder to prevent the smoke unless perchance a servitude or other legal right for the smoke to issue exists. But on the other hand we decree that dwellers above, who throw water or ordure down and injuriously affect those dwelling below, are forbidden to do so. Inasmuch as a person can only act in his own house so as not to injure others. And we decree likewise regarding offensive smells.
18. If your wall inclines toward my house and leans forward I can compel you to straighten it and prevent it from falling and injuring my house.
19. If a tree stands in my neighbor's yard and throws out great roots which injure the foundations of my house, then with the antecedent order of the Archon I can compel him to cut them off.
20. If anyone forcibly opens windows in derogation to another person's premises he can be compelled to restore the building to the former state at his own cost.
21. No one can deposit manure near another person's wall unless a servitude or some agreement or other right to do so exists.
22. If rain gutter tiles need renovating we order that each proprietor shall repair the pipes of the gutter beginning in his own premises and continuing till he reaches the premises of his neighbor.
23. In the same way the beds of water-courses, that is to say water conduits serving gardens, plantations and vineyards, must be cleaned and repaired, each proprietor beginning on his own premises and continuing up to that of the adjoining owner. And where the bed of the water-course passes through his garden he

must dig it out, remove the mud and sodden soil and clean it and throw the refuse on his garden.

24. The following agreements are not effective. If I agree with you that I am not allowed to make a fire on my hearth in my house, or kindle a fire, or rest or wash in it. For if agreements of that sort are made they are void altogether and ineffective.

25. Agreements made contrary to law or to good custom shall, we decree, have no force. And that applies also to ambiguous law.

26. A vendor who sells a house and in general terms tells the purchaser, 'this house which I am selling to you is subject to a servitude,' is not obliged to sell the house freed from that encumbrance. Wherefore should there even be no servitude he can impose one upon it and make it subject to the vendor's or any other strange house. But if the vendor say specifically my house is for sale and is subject to a servitude in regard to the owner of such a house and conveys the servitude to him there can be no question.

27. A species of servitude exists when a person is prevented from emitting smoke from a chimney or the furnace of a bath house on to his neighbor's premises or to throw slops or water down on to them.

28. If I am bound to you by a servitude not to build, and I do build, and a long time elapses, that is 30 years, the servitude is extinguished through the effluxion of time.

29. I can build a stair against a party wall since no damage ensues.

30. If you owe me a servitude not to heighten your building in such a way as to impede the light of my house which pertains to me because I had lights which come through windows in my house, and I obstructed them 10 or 20 years ago, that is to say closed them up, and in that state they continued for the said periods, the consequence is that my right to the servitude expires, if you raise your house and it so remained raised for 10 or 20 years. For observe that in that case I did not exercise my right to servitude since I kept my windows obstructed and closed and you rightly obtained freedom (from the servitude) to raise your house higher, which freedom you could not a quire if I had not closed my windows; and so my right to exercise the servitude ceases. If however when my windows were closed you did nothing to your

house by raising it my right to exercise the servitude remains to me whole as it was at the outset. And if after 10 or 20 years I open my windows and then you wish to heighten your house I can legally prevent you from so doing.

31. If I have a servitude which entitles me to place my joists, that is my beams, and apply and support them in your wall and insert them in joist holes made in your wall, then if I remove my joists and for 10 years I do not replace them in the joist holes, leaving the holes open as they were when I took the joists away, then the prescription (against me) does not run in your favour. But if, when I removed my joists, you close up the joist holes and they remain so closed for 10 or 20 years you obtain freedom from the servitude due to me. For you have acquired the 'dominium' by usucaption by keeping the joist holes closed for that time. If however you leave them open and do nothing but leave them in that condition the servitude to me is preserved and I can replace the joists in the joist holes made aforetime.

32. Every servitude and usufruct arising there from is lost if it is not exercised for 10 years if the parties interested are present, or for 20 years if absent.

33. If a purchaser in good faith does not know that the property he acquired belonged to anyone but the vendor, he is a purchaser in good faith. If the purchaser subsequently learns that the property belonged to anyone other than the vendor, that is a stranger to the purchaser, and nevertheless proceeds to erect a building, then if later on, the true owner comes to claim the property the purchaser cannot claim expenses incurred but he can take away the building materials provided he does so without injuring the owner of the property, that is to say without injuring the property.

34. If an individual has built on or farmed the land of another that he bought in good faith and then the land is (re) claimed by the previous owner, a fair judge will evaluate the case according to the people and circumstances. Suppose, for example that the previous owner would have made the same improvements to the land as the current owner. If he wants to get his land back, he must at least match the increased value that occurred in the land. If the current owner has spent more than the land itself was worth it suffices that the applicant (previous owner) matches its

actual value. If, for example, the current owner was so poor that to make these expenditures he was deprived of his home and the tomb of his ancestors, then the judge would consider it sufficient if the previous owner (the applicant) be allowed to remove what he can, provided that the land does not suffer and not be of less value than it was before any new construction. It can also be decided that, if the previous owner is ready to go to the current occupant and offer all the amount he could get, including what he has added to the field, then the previous owner shall be allowed to do so. In such a case, we should not encourage abuse, such as an occupant who wants, for example, to remove paintings that adorned the walls out of spite or a sense of revenge. But if it is deemed that the first owner is willing to (re) sell his assets immediately upon recovery, he must meet all costs. If he refuses, the current occupant will be ordered to restore the assets only after such costs have been deducted.

35. If anyone obtains property in bad faith and alienates it, that is parts with, sells, donates, exchanges or in any other way disposes of it, and the true owner being cognizant and knowing that the matter concerns and pertains to himself does not intervene and make a legal claim against the person who has obtained it by purchase, gift, otherwise, he shall not have the legal right of recovering it, if he is on the spot, within 10 years, if he is absent, in 20 years. If however the true owner was not aware that the property belonging to him had been disposed of (in the several manners indicated) we declare that the true owner's remedy of recovery shall not be barred by 10 or 20 years prescription, but only by 30 years, since the person who acquired the property cannot declare 'I am the bona fide possessor ' because he acquired it from him who obtained it mala-fide. And in regard to the prescriptive periods of 10, 20 or 30 years we make this further provision that if the true owner during part of the currency of such prescriptive periods was absent and for another part was present then for calculating the prescriptive period against him, there shall be added to the years of his presence the years of his absence.

36. If anyone takes proceedings against another in regard to realty which the possessor did not hold by lawful means, and is not yet

excluded by the 30 years prescriptive period, and has not lost his cause of action, he can rightly claim and recover the property itself. Neither time nor custom will confirm transactions based upon false premises.

37. A proprietary title to a person is acquired in 3 years provided that possession is uninterrupted, that is undisputed by a sworn declaration.

38. Anyone who has servitude to pasture and water cattle on your farm can acquire the right of building a shed on it.

39. If anyone attempts to build near a threshing floor and by doing so injures the owner thereof the builder can be legally restrained from building.

40. If one person conducts water from another farmer's land and the farmer, knowing it, silently acquiesces for 3 years, he cannot prevent such person because the right becomes prescriptive in 3 years. If the farmer forbids the user such person cannot claim his expenses for making the water conduit and the farmer becomes the owner of the conduit.

41. If the person who owned a house (either the original owner or the builder) was unable to prohibit the passage of water his purchaser cannot prohibit it either since it is apparent that the purchaser bought the property subject to the encumbrance.

42. Inferior, that is to say lower lying, lands are subject to a silent servitude to upper lands, to receive water flowing down from them, obtaining, as compensation for the burden imposed, the 'fatness' of the upper lying lands.

43. If I have not availed myself of a servitude belonging to my farm for 5 years and I sell it, the 5 years are reckoned for a purchaser thus. If the purchaser does not exercise the right within the next 5 years the servitude ceases. If we require 10 years to expire before one party is freed from the servitude we also require the same period to expire before the other party loses the right by not using it. And we are not concerned to enquire whether only one or several persons did not avail themselves.

44. If anyone ploughs up a public road, that is to say land belonging to another estate not abutting on his own land, he shall forfeit the equivalent of 50 *nomismata*.

45. Anyone ploughing (or digging) near another person's farm must leave a space of 8 feet from the (common) boundary; if it is a wall boundary then up to 1 feet; if a dwelling house 6 feet; anyone digging a tomb or a pit shall leave between such excavations and the boundary a space equal to the depth of such excavations; if a well then a fathom unless the neighboring owner has a well which is injured by the new work. For planting olive or fig trees a space of 9 feet must be left from the (common) boundary; and in the case of other trees 5 feet.

46. If I have a water conduit near your farm then the following servitude tacitly inures to me; if I wish to repair the banks you must allow space enough for me and my workmen of ingress and egress so that I can have access to the right and left bank and a right to deposit soil, stones, and wood material and chalk and sand to repair it.

47. If I sell a part of my land to you and agree with you that you shall bring water through it and the legal time goes by and the water-course is not made, my legal right is preserved. If however I made it but did not use it until after the 10 years expired, that is the legal period, my right to the servitude expires.

48. If there is enjoyment of servitude rights one year out of two or one month out of two, then the time allotment must be doubled in order to compensate for non-use. The same applies for servitude rights of access. But if such rights were relinquished to just one day out of two or only during the day or only during the night, such rights would be lost through non-use. Indeed, if servitude rights were established to be used by the hour or one hour per day, then such rights would be lost through non-use since normally such rights are continuous.

49. Where limits and boundaries are in litigation the plea of 30 years prescriptive occupation and not 10 or 20 years applies.

50. When a question of ownership of boundaries arises the judge must either rely upon the boundary marks or the public records made before the suit arose. Unless it is proved that the boundaries were changed by the occupier from time to time, or for a time. For if that happened the boundaries must be deduced according to the arrangement made by those fixing them and not by the ancient boundaries.

51. If a public road is destroyed either by an earthquake or by the inundation of a river the owner of the adjacent land is obliged to permit a right of way across his land so that the public can pass over it.

52. If a river flows between my land and yours and then other soil accrues to mine gradually and imperceptibly, so that no one knows to what extent or when the accretion happened, the soil so accrued becomes my property and is mine. If by the violence and spate of the river a part of your land is taken away and added to my land it is manifest that the accrued land remains your property; for the accretion did not happen gradually and imperceptibly.

53. The period for taking every action which affects a venerable foundation whether personal or hypothecary must not exceed 40 years; so however that the 'exceptiones temporales competentes' in regard to each of the charitable houses are applied at the proper times. 'Personal' means when a person is in possession of a farm belonging to a venerable house, sells it and can defend his title by pleading the prescriptive possessory period of 40 years. 'Hypothecary' means when a mortgage was given and 40 years elapse, and no claim was made on the person who had it or on his son or his grandson.

54. If a free person is injured, compensation shall be made for the cost of medical treatment and the loss of work, that is for such time as elapsed while the person injured could not exercise his business or do his duties at home; the compensation is to be reckoned after that manner and not for the disfigurement inflicted. For the body of a free person cannot be valued.

55. It does not seem to us to be unfitting to decree that those who are excommunicated for crime shall not be prescribed by prescriptive period. That is to say those who are sentenced to punishment forbidding them to leave the city on account of crime be it adultery, theft, or slander shall not be prescribed in regard to their property. Banishment is sufficient for them.

56. Nor shall (prescriptive) time be reckoned against those who are absent on Imperial service, and as long as they are so absent, and until they return (Freshfield thinks that where soldiers are concerned this privilege was only accorded to them while they were on active service).

57. The deaf, dumb, mad, insane, and the prisoner of war shall not be prescribed by the period of 10 or 20 years. For the time begins to run for a captive when he returns from captivity and for sick persons when they are restored to health.

58. If a spring from which a person draws water runs dry for some time and then flows again in its own channels, the servitude is renewed and restored, as before.

59. Anyone who sells defective or rotten timber, and did so in ignorance of the defect, shall be liable to repay the price he received in excess of the true value of it. If however he knew the defect and did not reveal it to the purchaser but concealed it and so deceived the purchaser, he shall be liable to pay whatever damage the purchaser suffered by reason thereof. If therefore the house built with defective timber falls down he will be liable to the purchaser for the estimated value of the house.

References

Brandileone, F., & Puntoni, V. (1895). *Prochiron Legum: Pubblicato Secondo il Codice Vaticano Greco 845*. Roma: Istituto Storico Italiano, Fonti per la Storia d'Italia.

Brandileone, F. (1895). Studio sul Prochiron Legum. *Bullettino Dell'Istituto Storico Italiano, 16*, 93–126. Roma.

Burgmann. (1991). Ecloga. *The Oxford dictionary of Byzantium.*

Freshfield, E. H. (1930). The official manuals of Roman law of the eighth and ninth centuries. *The Cambridge Law Journal, 4*(1), 34–50.

Freshfield, E. H. (1931). *A provincial manual of later Roman Law: The Calabrian Procheiron – On servitudes and bye-laws incidental to the tenure of real property*. Cambridge: Cambridge University Press.

Schminck. (1991). Prochiron. *The Oxford dictionary of Byzantium.*

Appendix 5
Samples of 13th and 14th Century Italian Urban Statutes

Arezzo, 1327: *Statuto di Arczzo (1327)*, ed. G. Marri Camerani (Deputazione di Storia Patria per Ia Toscana, sezione di Arezzo, Fonti di Storia Aretina, i, Florence, 1946).

Ascoli, 1377: *Statuti di Ascoli Piceno dell' anno MCCCLXXXVII*, ed. L. Zdekauer and P Sella (Fonti dell'lstituto Storico Italiano peril il Medioevo, *47*, Rome, 1910).

Bergamo, 1331: *Lo statuto di Bergamo del 1331*. ed. C. Storti Storchi Milan: Giuffre, 1986.

Bologna, 1250: *Statuti di Bologna dall' anna 1245 all' anna 1267*, ed. L. Frati (Monumenti istorici pertinenti aile Provincie della Romagna, serie i (Statuti), 3 vols., Bologna, 1869–77).

Bologna, 1288: *Statuti di Bologna dell' anno 1288*, ed. G. Fasoli and P. Sella (Studi e Testi, 73, 85, Citta del Vaticano: Biblioteca Apostolica Vaticana, 1937, 1939).

Ferrara, 1287: *Statuta Ferrariae anno MCCLXXXVll*, ed. W. Montorsi (Ferrara: Cassa di Risparmio di Ferrara, 1955).

Florence, 1322–25: *Statuti della Repubblica Fiorentina*, ed. R. Caggese, i, *Statuto del Capitano del Popolo degli anni 1322–25* (Florence: Tip. Galileiana, 1910).

Florence, 1325: *Statuti della Repubblica Fiorentina*, ed. R. Caggese, ii, *Statuto del Podesta dell' anno 1325* (Florence: Tip. Galileiana, 1921).

Milan, 1216: *Liber consuetudinum Mediolani anni MCCXVI*, ed. F. Besta and G.I. Barni (Milan: Giuffre, 1949).

Modena, 1327: *Statuta civitatis Mutinae anno 1327 reformata* (Monumenti di Storia Patria per le Provincie Modenesi, serie Statuti, i, Parma, 1864).

Parma, 1255: *Statuta Communis Pannae digesta anno MCCLV* (Monumenta Historica ad Provincias Parmensem et Placentinam pertinentia, Parma, 1856).

Parma, 1266: *Statuta Communis Pannae ab anno MCCLVI ad annum circiter MCCCVl* (Monumenta Historica ad Provincias Parmensem et Placentinam pertinentia, Parma, 1857).

Perugia, 1342: *Statuti di Perugia dell' anno MCCCXLl1*, ed. G. degli Azzi (Corpus Statutorum ltalicorum, i, Rome, 1913).

B.S. Hakim, *Mediterranean Urbanism: Historic Urban / Building Rules and Processes*, DOI 10.1007/978-94-017-9140-3,
© Springer Science+Business Media Dordrecht 2014

Piacenza, 1327: *Statuta van a civitatis Placentiae* (Monumenta Historica ad Provincias Parmensem et Placentinam pertinentia, Parma, 1860).

Pistoia, twelfth century: L.A. Muratori, *Antiquitates Italicae Medii Aevi,* iv (Milan, 1741): 'Statutum civitatis Pistoriensis anno Christi MCXVII et circiter anno MCC condita una cum notis cl. v. Huberti Benvoglienti.'

Pistoia, 1296: *Statutum potestatis communis Pistorii anni MCCLXXXXVI,* ed. L. Zdekauer (Milan: apud Ulricum Hoepli, 1888).

Reggio, 1242: *Consuetudini e statuti reggiani del secolo XIII,* ed. A. Cerlini, i (Corpus Statutorum Italicorum, 16, Milan: Hoepli, 1933).

Rome, 1363–70: *Statuti della citta di Roma,* ed. C. Re (Rome: Tip. della Pace, 1880).

Sassari, 1316: 'Gli statuti della repubblica sassarese, testo logodurese del secolo XIV', ed. P.E. Guarnerio in *Archivio Glottologico Italiano,* xiii (1892–94), 4–103.

Siena, 1262: *Il Constituto del Comune di Siena dell' anno 1262,* ed. L. Zdekauer (Milan: Hoepli, 1897).

Siena, 1309: *Il Costituto del comune di Siena volgarizzato nel MCCCIX-MCCCX,* ed. Mahmoud S. Elsheikh (Citta di Castello, 2002).

Treviso, 1283–84: *Gli Statuti del Comune di Treviso (sec. XIII-XIV),* ed. B. Betto (Fonti dell' Istituto Storico Italiano per il Medioevo, 109, Rome, 1984).

Verona, 1276: *Gli statuti veronesi del 1276 colle correzioni e le aggiunte fino al 1323,* ed. G. Sandri (Venice: R. Deputazione, 1940).

Appendix 6
A Selection of Rules from Central and Northern Italy During the 12th to 14th Centuries

Siena: Rule for maintaining the harmony of windows that overlook the Piazza del Campo. This rule was first published as statute no. 5 in 1297, and as no. III.37 in the 1309 statutes. Both original versions are in Italian. Braunfels reproduced it as document # 1 in his appendix (Braunfels, 1953), and recently Fabrizio Nevola provided an English translation (Nevola, 2009). The following version is from Nevola:

> "We also rule and order that if any house or palace should be built on the Campo market square, that if these houses or palaces should face onto the Campo, then these facades should be built with windows divided by colonettes, and have no overhanging structures. And the city magistrate (*podesta*) must ensure that this ruling is enforced. And whosoever should ignore these rulings and build a house or palace without applying said demands will be condemned by the lord magistrate of Siena to a fine of 25 *lire*. And if the magistrate should omit to apply the fine, he shall likewise have 25 *lire* detracted from his salary."

Siena: Rule for prohibiting building overhanging jetties or balconies facing the Piazza del Campo. This rule was first published in the statutes of 1297 and later as no. III.261 in the statutes of 1309. Braunfels reproduced the original Italian as document # 2 in his appendix (Braunfels, 1953). Fabrizio Nevola provided an English translation (Nevola, 2009). The following version is from Nevola:

> "Also, with this ruling it is established that by a clause of the Statute of the Commune of Siena, that whosoever builds a house facing onto the Campo of the market, should construct windows with colonettes and not over-hanging balconies or jetties (*ballatoi*), and it is also ruled by this clause

B.S. Hakim, *Mediterranean Urbanism: Historic Urban / Building Rules and Processes*, DOI 10.1007/978-94-017-9140-3,
© Springer Science+Business Media Dordrecht 2014

that those houses that are already built around the Campo should not be modified by the addition of balconies. It is also ruled that no one, from this day forth, should build or renew or make any form of balcony or overhanging structure of any sort on buildings around the Campo, and also on any tower house or palace projecting from its walls. And whosoever should ignore these rulings will be condemned to a fine of 25 *lire*. And furthermore they will also be obliged to tear down and remove any such balcony or overhang. And this clause was ordered in the Year of Our Lord 1297 on 10 May."

Florence: Petition by members of the Merchant Guild of Florence in 1363 regarding the configuration of residential buildings surrounding the Piazza San Giovanni. Published by Braunfels as document # 7 in his appendix (Braunfels, 1953). Translated from the Latin by Giovanni de Venuto with the assistance of Tiziana Destino:

"By the Consuls the officials of the kallimal art of Florence of the *opere ecclesie* and the construction site of the Church of *San Giovanni Battista* in Florence, it is said that after the houses of the aforementioned construction were built, by the square of the said church, some small houses remained that are in such a state that they disfigure the appearance and beauty of the entire aforementioned square. It is encouraged to refurbish them in a way that all those who are inhabiting Florence in the area of *Santa Reparata* by the square on the one side and the road that is called *dei Spatari* on the other side, and the house of *Lapo Donato Viviani* and of his brothers on the other side, and any or other things that are relevant to the houses should be required to and must, within the next year, have removed entirely every door of those houses (such as those doors that open into the square or on the side of that square) and any other element pertaining to them, and build or have built a wall on the said side that is properly plastered and polished, of a height of at least 16 arm-lengths [about 9 meters], and ensure the beauty of the recently constructed wall of these houses on the side of the square, and with doors and windows appropriate to what is referred to before."

Bologna: On paving in front of houses and responsibility for maintenance. – The issue of responsibility is an important consideration of a sound generative process. – Translated by Trevor Dean from the *Statuti di Bologna dell' anno 1288*, from the section on refuse collection (Dean, 2000):

"We establish that whoever has paving in front of their houses is to maintain it, and if it is broken, to redo it at their expense.", and "if there remains any unpaved road in the city or suburbs, and a majority of the neighbours of that district wish to pave it, then it is to be paved and all the neighbours are to be compelled to contribute.", and "We order that everyone must remove, from the street in front of his house, mud, earth, grape skins, . . . and all other dirt. . ."

Bologna: An example of enforcement of the statute as recorded in the *Achivio di Stato*, Bologna Commune, Capitano del Popolo:

On 13 October 1376: "Domenico di Nanne da Viadagola and Filippo di Cavalino, inhabitants in the Capella SS Jacomo e Filippo, found by me to have a pipe over the public roadway from which water fell into public space, contrary to the statutes."

References

Braunfels, W. (1953). *Mittelalterliche Stadtbaukunst in der Toskana*. Berlin: Verlag Gebr. Mann.

Dean, T. (2000). *The towns of Italy in the later middle ages*. Manchester: Manchester University Press.

Nevola, F. (2009). Ordering the piazza del Campo of Siena (1309). Translated from Italian. In K. L. Jansen, J. Drell, & F. Andrews (Eds.), *Medieval Italy: Texts in translation*. Philadelphia: University of Pennsylvania Press, (pp. 261–264).

Appendix 7
Ibn al-Imam's 10th Century Treatise from Tudela: Goal, Intentions and Content

Underlying **goal** of the treatise:

The goal is to deal with change in the built environment by ensuring that minimum damage occurs to preexisting structures and their owners, through stipulating fairness in the distribution of rights and responsibilities among various parties, particularly those who are proximate to each other, to ensure the equitable equilibrium of the built environment during the process of change and growth. This is achieved by taking into consideration the overarching generic rule to avoid harming others and where necessary to provide legal solutions for servitudes affecting buildings and land.

Underlying **intentions** that are evident from the analysis of the rules in the treatise:

1. Change in the built environment should be accepted as a natural and healthy phenomenon. In the face of ongoing change, it is necessary to maintain an equitable equilibrium in the built environment.
2. Change, particularly that occurring among proximate neighbors, creates potential for damages to existing dwellings and other uses. Therefore, certain measures are necessary to prevent changes or uses that would (i) result in debasing the social and economic integrity of adjacent or nearby properties, (ii) create conditions adversely affecting the moral integrity of the neighbors, and (iii) destabilize peace and tranquility between neighbors.

B.S. Hakim, *Mediterranean Urbanism: Historic Urban / Building Rules and Processes*, DOI 10.1007/978-94-017-9140-3,
© Springer Science+Business Media Dordrecht 2014

3. In principle, property owners have the freedom to do what they please on their own property. Most uses are allowed, particularly those necessary for a livelihood. Nevertheless, the freedom to act within one's property is constrained by preexisting conditions of neighboring properties, neighbors' rights of servitude, and other rights associated with ownership for certain periods of time.
4. The compact built environment of ancient towns necessitates the implementation of interdependence rights among citizens, principally among proximate neighbors. As a consequence of interdependence rights, it becomes necessary to allocate responsibilities among such neighbors, particularly with respect to legal and economic issues.
5. The public realm must not be subjected to damages that result from activities or waste originating in the private realm.

The nature of the **rules** and their impact:

The rules imbedded in Ibn al-Imam's treatise can be described as being *proscriptive* followed by all parties involved in a specific location. This would make their implementation very sensitive to a locality's unique conditions, resulting in built form that is unique to its surrounding conditions and by extension contributing to an overall dynamic built form of the town or city.

This type of rules must be distinguished from those that are *prescriptive* in content that specifies conditions and measurements and their application everywhere regardless of the unique attributes of a specific location. In essence imposing a preconceived notion everywhere devised by a top-down authority. This would result, with the passage of time, in sameness and repetitive patterns that would inhibit creative solutions to local problems. This is the situation today with the housing sector in many countries, particularly since the mid-20th century.

The 49 cases in Ibn al-Imam's treatise (al-Tutaili, Isa bin Musa, died 996 C.E. - c) may be grouped under the following seven categories that I have determined. Each case is a discussion, by Ibn al-Imam, of the various opinions from different earlier and contemporary jurists for appropriate rules to solve a given problem. Sometimes opinions differ providing options for solving a specific case.

The case numbers are indicated between brackets before a title for its content:

1- **Land / Building Use**: (1, 2, 3, 6, 7) – servitudes between houses; (31, 32, 34) – servitude access; (24, 25) – usage in other's property; (15, 16) – ovens, shops and other uses.
2- **Streets**: (26, 27, 35) – right-of-ways for streets; (28, 29, 30) – damage to streets; (33) – on private streets.
3- **Walls**: (18, 19, 22, 23) – on party walls; (4, 5) – projections from walls; (20, 21) – the leaning wall.
4- **Overlooking / Privacy**: (12, 13, 17) – overlooking from windows and doors; (14) – overlooking from a minaret.
5- **Drainage and Hygiene**: (8) – rainwater drainage; (9) – removal of garbage; (10) – cleaning toilets; (11) – garbage on nearby plot.
6- **Plants / trees**: (39, 40, 41, 42, 43, 44) – issues related to trees; (36, 37, 38) – damage issues.
7- **Birds / Bees / Animals**: (45) – pigeon cotes; (46) – selling animals; (47) – damage from animals; (48) – damage to plants; (49) – on bees.

Reference

al-Tutaili, Isa bin Musa (died 996 C.E. – c). *Kitab Nefi al-Darar*, verified by Ferid bin Sulaiman and al-Mukhtar al-Telili, Tunis, 2003.

Appendix 8
Ibn al-Attar's 10th Century Model Notary Documents that Relate to Issues in the Built Environment

The following is a citation of four model notary documents that relate to issues in the built environment. They relate to those that the author encountered in Cordoba. Page numbers refer to those in the edition by (Chalmeta and Corriente, 1983). Ibn al-Attar's method of communicating and presenting his model notary documents is by first giving it a title, followed by the language for the document, then the rational and/or argument is discussed under the title of *Fiqh*, i.e. the legal basis and justification for the document.

117–118 – Servitude, or abutting, to a wall between two neighbors.

192–193 – On renting a house to Muhammad bin Ahmed.

369–370 – Two neighbors, one is powerful and the other is weak. The former created a condition that overlooks his weak neighbor who is reluctant or afraid to object. [A powerful neighbor means somebody who is socially connected, and/or rich].

371–373 – On somebody who recently built a gargoyle that directs rainwater onto his neighbor's house.

The following is a translation of the model document on pages 117–118, to provide an idea of its style and content:

Document on Abutting a Wall

So and so (name of party) abuts his neighbor's, so and so (name of party), wall that separates their two houses that are located in so and so neighborhood (name), that is close to the mosque (name of mosque),

B.S. Hakim, *Mediterranean Urbanism: Historic Urban / Building Rules and Processes*, DOI 10.1007/978-94-017-9140-3,
© Springer Science+Business Media Dordrecht 2014

their orientation to the *Qibla* is so and so (orientation), and the street (name) to which their doors open. This wall is located east of so and so's (name) house, and west of the house that has the wall. The abutter can build on the wall with a thickness and height so and so (measurements) with adobe or adobe bricks. He can add so many (number) of *iklib* (technical term) towards his house, and *raf* (technical term) with tiles or tiles and mud. He can build a *skifa* (gallery) onto the wall with this or that (names of materials used) and the use of wooden planks or reeds, and its tiles to be held together with mud mortar. The abutting agreement is in perpetuity. The owner of the wall granted his neighbor the right to abut his wall as a good neighborly gesture and to please God. The abutter agreed to the conditions, thanked his neighbor and commenced work on the project. The owner of the wall was informed of the cost involved, without imposing any conditions on the abutter. Both parties witnessed each other on the agreement and its date was recorded on it.

Legal Considerations

If the abutting agreement is for a limited time period, I would indicate that. In this situation the wall's owner may remove the abutter's additions when the time period ends. If the time period is not mentioned, or unknown, and the wall's owner wanted to remove the abutter's additions, he cannot do that, unless he needs to demolish the wall and rebuild it. He can do so with consideration that the abutter has benefited from his additions with adequate passage of time. If the agreement is in perpetuity, then the owner of the wall cannot remove the additions the abutter made onto the wall, regardless if the owner needs the wall or not.

If the wall collapses during the period of the agreement and the owner of the wall rebuilds it, the abutter can rebuild what he previously added to the wall. If the owner of the wall refuses, the abutter can nevertheless rebuild what he had before. If however the owner of the wall wants to benefit from it with changes or additions that would possibly damage the abutter's additions, the latter can prevent the owner from doing so, unless the owner of the wall pays the abutter all of the cost that was incurred for his additions.

Reference

Chalmeta, P., & Corriente, F. (Eds.). (1983). *Formulario Notarial Hispano-Arabe por el alfaqui y notario Cordobes Ibn al-Attar (s. X)*, Madrid (Arabic and Spanish).

Appendix 9
Ordenanzas de Toledo – A Collection of Rules from the 14th Century that Is Associated with the Institution of *Alarife*

The articles are listed sequentially as they are in the original manuscript. Arabic numbers replace the original Roman numbers.

1. Who assigns *alarife* and who shall be the *alarife* and what virtues they should have.
2. What work does the *alarife* do.
3. On streets, town squares (plazas) and areas formed by converging streets or corner of houses. These areas belong to the King and cannot be built on.
4. Space between two houses that allows rainwater to pass through is shared if the rainwater is collected from the roofs of the two houses. If from one house then it belongs to that owner.
5. Who is responsible for constructing and maintaining the drain for the village. See Ibn al-Rami case on pp. 52–53 of (Hakim, 1986).
6. On mills and norias (no description are translated for articles 6 through 14).
7. On how to repair the *Azudes*.
8. How jointly owned mills are repaired.
9. How water is shared when a mill owner wants to repair it.
10. What is the punishment for someone who builds a dam or similar structure that causes damage to a mill or any other property?
11. On the punishment for someone who damages a dam or a mill of any kind.
12. How mills are rented if they are jointly owned.
13. How to appraise a mill to be rented.

B.S. Hakim, *Mediterranean Urbanism: Historic Urban / Building Rules and Processes*, DOI 10.1007/978-94-017-9140-3,
© Springer Science+Business Media Dordrecht 2014

14. On the punishment for someone that fishes in a river (or spot on a river bank?) that belongs to another man.

15. How the *heras* (threshing floor for wheat or grain) shall be divided among heirs without dividing it by walls that would obstruct the wind. A wall may be built to a maximum height of half a man.

16. How to establish a servitude, for access and egress, to a property surrounded by other properties.

17. Establishing a servitude for access of water from one property that owns the source of the water, to another. The lapse of time of one year is also indicated in this case.

18. On public and private baths. Who owns them and how their pipes and chimneys must avoid damage to neighbors.

19. On ovens and *hornos*. Whether public or private, they must not damage the neighbors. An old vs. a new ovens are subject to different rules.

20. On dove houses. Their location and the damages they create.

21. Damage caused by dove houses to towers and upper levels of roofs.

22. Of house(s) that exceed in height adjacent house(s). Avoiding damage from rainwater. Desire of upper level to build higher and his need to build a wall.

23. Ownership and benefits of shared walls. How the lapse of time affects ownership and usage of the wall.

24. Conduits or channels that may cause damage to the neighbor(s).

25. Roof projections toward the street must not project more than one third the width of the street.

26. *Sobrados* (Sabat) over streets. The clearance height must allow a knight in full armor to pass through. Will the knight be carrying his spear vertically?

27. Fear of a leaning wall that would collapse, and how to avoid potential damage.

28. Walls must be rebuilt over their original foundations.

29. On building on top of somebody else's construction, and who is responsible for repair and maintenance of the walls, foundations and gutters.

30. On shared walls and related agreements.

31. On avoiding damage due to chimneys and overlooking the neighbor from a spot or via a window. What size should the window be? And issues related to an adjacent empty lot that has a channel

in it and its owner wants to build on it. Or when this empty plot is used to deposit dung on it.

32. Digging a basement and/or a well near a neighbor's wall and getting permission for it.
33. How a neighbor deals with noise from his adjacent neighbor due to the pounding of nails or hammers, or due to the commotion caused by animals.
34. Opening a door opposite the neighbor's door across the street is not allowed without the agreement of the neighbor, including doors of shops or baths.
35. Built-in benches against the wall are not allowed in narrow streets.
36. How to divide a building among heirs, that is, constructed of masonry, that can or cannot by divided. How does the *alarife* resolve it?
37. On the purchase and sale of a building that has flaws in it and the role of *alarife*.
38. On pawing of houses or other constructions such as a room, hotel, bath or store. It deteriorates while being pawned, who is responsible.
39. Responsibilities of the tenant (renter) for any kind of damage (s) while he is a tenant.
40. On master-masons that, through their shoddy work, create damage to a building project due to their lack of skills or due to negligence.
41. On master-masons not being paid for their work by the owner of the project and how to resolve such problems.

References

Hakim, B. S. (1986). *Arabic-Islamic cities: Building and planning principles.* London.

Izquierdo Benito, R. (1986). Normas sobre edificaciones en Toledo en el siglo XV. *Anuario de Estudios Medievales, 16,* 519–532.

Appendix 10
Alarife Ordinances of Cordoba, 1786

Part 1 – Index of Articles as Published in the 1786 Manuscript. Translation of Those Articles with Bold Numbers Is Included in Part 2 of This Appendix

Note: each article is followed by the number(s) of the framework [ ] that was used in documenting the *alarife* Toledo rules that are a century earlier and are included in chapter 3. Here are the headings for that framework:

1) Who are the *alarifes*?; 2) Assignment and work of the *alarifes*; 3) Avoiding and negating damage; 4) Servitudes; 5) Rights of earlier usage; 6) Privacy of neighbor must be respected; 7) Maintenance of streets and keeping them clean; 8) Streets and houses; 9) Rules related to houses; 10) Relationship between upper and lower construction; 11) Purchase / sale, pawing, tenants, and heirs.

1. Who may appoint *alarifes*, and what qualities they should possess [1].
2. First thing the *alarife* has to do after being sworn in.
3. Land use issues – where to build. King owns all streets and access.
4. On city sewers and who should construct and repair them when it becomes necessary [8].
5. On *añoras* and wells [3, 10].
6. How irrigation wheels should be made and repaired.
7. How mills should be prepared by the owners of crop lands.
8. How water should be fetched when one wishes to repair his mill.

B.S. Hakim, *Mediterranean Urbanism: Historic Urban / Building Rules and Processes*, DOI 10.1007/978-94-017-9140-3,
© Springer Science+Business Media Dordrecht 2014

9. On the penalty deserved by whoever constructs a dam or other edifice to divert water from a mill on another property.
10. What the penalty is for whoever destroys a mill dam or any other type of dam.
11. How food mills should be rented.
12. How improvements should be calculated when mills and water mills are rented.
13. On the penalty deserved by he who fishes in another's river location.
14. On how crop fields should be divided between brothers without erecting a wall that damages one or the other.
15. Servitude – On the entrances to houses and other properties contained within properties [4].
16. Servitude – On water that comes to one property by traversing another [4].
17. Damage from privy on neighbor [3].
18. Ovens: damage from, and do not build near existing oven [3].
19. Dovecotes: do not create near neighbor, unless it was there before [3].
20. Towers and attics damaged by pigeon coops [3].
21. Building on top of a lower floor [10].
22. Possession of party wall and the lapse of time [9].
23. Overhang from a roof onto another's roof [3, 8].
24. Width of balcony towards street [8].
25. *Sobrado* (room) over street must allow Knight in full armor to pass under [8].
26. Wall feared to collapse [3, 9].
27. Rebuilding within one's property boundaries. Avoid extending onto street [5, 9].
28. Claiming one's water even if it was watering another's trees [4].
29. Shared walls, and if one party wants it higher [9].
30. Damage from smoke, and damage to empty plot [3].
31. Digging a basement without damage to neighbor [3, 10].
32. Noise through neighbor's wall, and method to determine nuisance [3].
33. New door must not be opposite neighbor's door [6].
34. Constructing bench within street width is not allowed [8].

35. Partition of a house, shop or other building – if it can or cannot be partitioned [11].

36. On the buying and sale of houses, plots, or other properties that have defects [11].

37. On houses and other buildings used as collateral.

38. On renting items.

39. On builders who do their work poorly or deceitfully.

40. What works builders should promise to do for hire for the property owners.

41. On how construction work should be divided up.

42. Irrigation channel must not be built next to someone else's wall [3, 9].

43. On what can and cannot be built onto streets and sidewalks by owners of adjoining properties [8].

44. Drains cannot be located on streets, but must be within one's property [8].

45. Digging in streets is not allowed [3, 8].

46. Rainwater that falls from one roof onto another [3, 9].

47. Avoid building fireplace onto a party wall [3, 9].

48. On those who know their wall needs repair and do nothing, then it falls down and damages their neighbor's house [3].

49. Avoid building a new well or *Anora* next to an existing one [3, 5].

50. Solar access to neighbor must be respected when changes are made [Issue not in Toledo].

51. Flow of sewage water between houses [8].

52. Roof that collapsed ten years earlier [9].

53. Weeds that creep onto streets from adjacent property must be removed [7, 8].

54. On potters.

55. On masons who take from one property to give to another.

56. On roofers attempting to sell their bad work.

57. On roofers who make roof tiles and brick from good clay.

58. Digging out street for rocks is not allowed [7, 8].

59. Blocking water flow [5, 9].

60. Changes to a party wall within one's house must be carefully considered [9].

61. Rebuilding next to a narrow street – must widen the street by one foot [8].

62. Throwing waste onto streets and cul-de-sacs and adjacent walls is not allowed [8].

63. No one to take measurements without the supervision of *alarife*.

64. On those who move landmarks and break boundary stones [6].

65. On those who rent another's house by the year.

66. On millstones bought for use by water mills.

67. On millstones that beat flour.

68. On mills with ill-prepared grain receptacles.

69. On mills that have their joints out of place or the eye of their millstone worn.

70. Designating street access for more than two parties [4].

71. & 72. Blank. No information provided.

73. Whenever *alarifes* are commissioned, they must take an oath [2].

74. Blank. No information provided.

75. *Alarifes* must provide measurements for any plot given by the city [2].

76. When rebuilding a wall the Master Mason must not take any space from the adjoining street [8, 9].

77. Who pays for a party wall between neighbors whose floors are at different levels [9].

78. Thickness of a party wall that would prevent sound transmission [3, 9].

79. What can and cannot be changed to a shared party wall [9].

80. When rebuilding a Master Mason must not invade the street's width [8].

81. Poor work by a Master Mason must be re-done at his expense [9].

82. Master Mason who builds a wall on poor foundations must rebuild it at his expense.

83. City grants usage of space on a street to a person, the adjoining neighbor cannot prevent its use [8].

84. Party wall between two neighbors – one wants to lower it for solar access and other refuses. This article relates to #50. Toledo rules do not include issues related to solar access.

85. On streets that residents request to be paved.

86. Digging a drain close to a neighbor's well [9].

87. Trees within 3 feet of a neighbor's wall, block the sun & create other damages [3, 9].

88 & 89. To prevent damage, trees and vegetable gardens must be at a distance of 3 feet or more from a neighbor's wall [3, 9].

90. Wash basin must be 3 feet or more from a neighbor's wall [3, 9].

91. Water pipes inside a house must be covered by lime and sand and 3 feet away from a neighbor's wall [3, 9].

92. Toilet (privy) must not be built against a neighbor's wall, nor located in a place where its odour bothers the neighbor [3, 9].

93. On builders who leave uneven areas in structures near other houses or royal roads.

94. On houses that are sold with building material.

95. On houses sold with troughs.

96. Party walls/ no opening allowed from either side [9].

97. Directing water from one well to another is not allowed if the aquifer of one dries out [3].

98. Shared wall issue / damage to wall [3, 9].

99. The builder who wishes to hold a hearing or settle a dispute without a license.

100. On the dregs left in olive presses.

101. Land use issue: Inn or tavern not allowed in a neighborhood due to damage caused [3 –land use issue].

102. On pumice stones used by barbers.

103. Technique and building material for constructing wall (related to articles 80, 81, 82 above).

104. Building a projection towards or over street; the street width is used for determining dimensions [8].

105. Allowing a person to sell merchandise outside, if his house is on a street that leads to a square [8].

106. On money changers and others who open their coffers.

107. It is not allowed to dump trash, dirt, or manure on someone else's wall [3].

108. On rubbish that obstructs a stream [10].

109. Using a narrow street for repair work [8].

110. On he who builds a large building on royal lands.

111. On he who takes stone from a new quarry.

112. On estates that grant houses for life.

113. On public quarries, used for all buildings, mills, water mills, and kilns.

114. On water mills and mills that are in disrepair or under no ownership on the riverbank.

115. Clear street of debris of a fallen wall. Debris to be removed within nine days [3, 7, 8].

116. On instruments of wood and stone used for household chores.

117. On those who build new wells or clean old ones.

118. On plaster brought to town to be sold by weight.

119. Two neighbors own a well jointly. Giving water by one owner to a third party must get consent of other owner.

120. Exposing interior of adjoining house while working on roof must be fixed [3, 9].

121. Problems due to division of one house into two or three units [9].

122. Entry / Exit used by many cannot be partitioned. Repair by all who use it [4].

123. Rebuilding and its effects on neighbor. Technical specifications indicated that would prevent damage [3, 9].

124. Methods of permanently shutting windows, doors, or fireplaces that are in dispute [3, 6, 9].

125. How to determine if overlooking occurs. Techniques for checking visual corridors [6].

126. Mitigating damage that would result from the wrong location of a stable [3, 9].

127. Opening a window for embellishment and that would not over-look a neighbor [6].

128. It is allowed to rebuild a flat roof if the result does not overlook and blocks the sun from the neighbor [6, 9].

129. Let no one throw water on someone else's house.

130. Laundries must not be on streets, preferably indoors or on a river bed [land use issue].

131 & 132. Any building activity must first be endorsed with a license from the City.

133. Master Mason's bad work must be redone at his expense [link to articles 80, 81, 82].

134. Demolish in front of their main gate [3, 8].

135 & 136. Damage to streets due to activities of a festival [7, 8].

137. Damage to waste water pipes due to activities mentioned in articles 135, 136 [3, 8].

In the manuscript of 1786 – after the above article 137 – there is a reference to a book, dated from 1503, titled *Peso de los Alarifes, y balanar de los Maestros, y Officiales*. Fifteen of its 143 articles are included. They are:

1. Somebody who has been a tenant for a year or longer is responsible to clear the privy before leaving [11].
2. Building a door that faces a public building is allowed [6].
3. Dispute regarding a window in a house that is two years or older [3, 6].
4. Drain of wastewater onto street must be enclosed [3, 7, 8].
5. Repair of a house towards street or alleyway and the damage that results must be repaired [8].
6. On houses rented for a determined period.
7. On those who take houses on two or three estates.
8. Making changes to shared/party walls and related technical problems [9].
9. On builders who accept pay for bridges or sewers.
10. On certain repairs to houses.
11. Fixing external wall from street side requires a license. Time allowed is nine days [8].
12. No selling of merchandise outside of house in winter due to rain and streets are muddy [8].
13. When selling outdoors it must be within the width of four feet or the width of a balcony [8].
14. Glassware that is exhibited without protection. A person who damages it is not liable [7, 8].
15. The general rule is not to allow selling of merchandise on the street, at any location [7, 8].

Index of Carpentry Regulations

1. On the knowledge and expertise of someone who wishes to be certified as a master carpenter.
2. On the same subject as Article 1.
3. On the same thing, as mentioned above.
4. Let no one be paid for work without being certified.
5. On apprentices of this trade.

6. Alarife must not judge any work done by carpenters unless there is someone present from the mayor's office or the carpenter's guild.
7. Master masons must not do woodwork or anything else pertaining to carpenter's trade.
8. If a carpenter closes his business shop, he may not establish it again without being recertified.
9. No practitioner of this trade, unless a mayor or overseer, may appraise anything.
10. On how a mayor and overseers should be chosen.
11. On the rights due to those who are certified and their obligations.
12. On those who have carpentry shops.

More Carpentry Regulations

1. On how master carpenters should be appointed.
2. Let no table-maker buy wood, brought to this city, and resell it.
3. Let no other peddler buy such wood.
4. Let no master practitioner of this trade buy wood in bulk that arrives in this city without following the regulations outlined in this Article.
5. Let no practitioner or master of this trade go beyond five leagues from the city to buy wood, under the penalties established.
6. Let no one buy in bulk, in order to resell them, any dough kneaders that come into this city.
7. Let no one buy pine in bulk to resell or peddle it.

Part 2 – Translation of Selected Articles from the 1786 Manuscript

<u>Front Cover:</u>
Ordinances of Alarifes
Of this Very Noble and Very Loyal
City of Cordoba
Taken literally from the original manuscripts that
the aforementioned city has in its files for the use of the City's
Master Masons and Carpenters
Cordoba. MDCCLXXXVI
In the office of Don Juan Rodríguez de la Torre
In compliance with the established legislation
(For the image of the cover, see Fig. 3.6)
* * *
<u>Starting from Folio 3 of the manuscript:</u>
Comienzan Las Ordenanzas de Los Alarife
(The ordinances of the *Alarife* start here)
[Footnotes provided by the translator]

We the Consejo[42] and the *Corregidor* of the noble and loyal city of Cordoba inform the Mayors, *Alguaciles*[43] and of other authorities of this City and its land, the Mayors of the *dehesas* and the Board of *Alarifes*, and to any person, and to whom it may concern of the following: That we in the Council talk in the debates and the trials that constantly take place about the buildings of the aforementioned city and its land. And the reason for this is the lack of ordinances by which it is possible to judge. We have talked about this matter with Pero Lopez, our Alarife, so that he, and other Masons, could find whether such ordinances concerning the profession of Alarife and constructions existed in this City. And if these were found, they had to be brought to the Town Hall of this City. And in the event that such ordinances did not exist, that they must be made according to

---

Due to technical reasons footnote numbers continue from last footnote in Appendix 3.

[42] This is a general term for council: It can mean all the authorities in a Town Hall or a board of professionals: architects, etc.

[43] Constable

established customs, that is the customary way of doing things.[44] These customs are old in the aforementioned city, and Pero Lopez looked for these old ordinances, and he wrote Chapters (Articles) of ordinances concerning the mentioned profession, taking from those old ordinances, which he understood as relevant for the maintenance and embellishment of the buildings. And finally the regulations that these ordinances contain must be abided by.[45] He then brought these ordinances to the Town Hall, and we requested Licenciado Juan Ortiz from Garate, Mayor of the City, to see them, and we also requested the lawyers of our Town Hall to look at them, which they did, and they confirmed that they were good and accurate, and in agreement with the Law designed to judge the mentioned buildings, the list of which we heard, so in consequence we agreed in confirming that those ordinances are fitting to regulate this City and its estate, and the contents of these ordinances follows:

Article 1. In order to be accredited to perform their duties, the Alarifes—which means expert men—have to be commissioned by the City. The Alarifes that perform their profession must, in order to be accredited as Alarifes—which *per se* means experts—be commissioned by the City, which enables them to enforce the law, with great skill, and those eligible to be Alarifes must meet the following criteria: to be law-abiding,[46] and of good reputation, and devoid of harmful greed, and they be wise, and well-versed in the Art and other nuances, so that they are capable of judging the trials[47] in a straightforward manner according to their expert knowledge, and because they have been doing so for a long time, and that they be even-tempered. And they must be honest, and make peace among the parties. And they must judge on behalf of the Mayor, with prudence, always placing God above all else, and always looking for the good and the honor of the City which has commissioned them to this task.

---

[44] The Spanish term is *uso,* which translates as 'the way it is always done'.

[45] The original text is unclear here. It says, *por dende se obiesen de juzgar los debates que obiesen en ellas,* suggesting that the ordinances provide a reliable text by which one can judge the controversies that arise between different parties.

[46] Meaning that they have never been convicted of a crime.

[47] It possibly includes disputes and conflicts, an idea that is expressed very often in the rest of the text.

And if they fear God, they must prevent themselves from judging wrongfully, and may they feel mercy, and Justice, and must give each party what it deserves according to the law, and if they fear the law of the city, they must prevent themselves from judging wrongfully.

Article 2. After the Alarifes have been commissioned, the first thing that they must do is to be sworn in at the Town Hall of the City. They also have to report which walls, and Towers and fences of the city (and anything else) are in faulty condition, and they must report this to the city Regidores,[48] so they command that everything that needs to be repaired must be repaired, and they have fixed anything that is damaged in the mentioned walls and *adarbes*,[49] as the *borujo* (olive waste), and manure, and accumulations of *alpechin*,[50] and they must not allow any man to build anything (house, dovecot or mill) next to *adarbes* and in addition no resident should be allowed to dig a ditch in said *adarbes*, without a license from the City, and if the city grants him a license, he must dig it in such a manner that nobody can enter or exit through it.

Article 3. All men in the village (*pueblo*) who would like to farm, must build their houses outside the city boundaries (*muros de la Ciudad*), and if they wish to build houses, oil mills, bakeries, copper-smith facilities, looms, taverns, chapels, or anything within the city walls, it must be in the Town's estate.[51] All licenses must be granted by the King, as well as by the Town. Proceeding in such manner, any construction that is to be sold, bought, traded or transferred and the owner's inheritors may therefore inherit them as their own property. All Squares, and streets and corners, all of it is for the King, and all is the King's property, and no man can claim it as his.

---

[48] *Corregidor*: Alderman:, a) judge of a region or b) mayor of a town, appointed by the King. This typically happened in extraordinary circumstances.

[49] *Adarve* (also found written as *Adarbe*): Also the sort of inward sidewalk of the wall of a town or fortress designed so that the defenders may repel the attacks. (*DRAE*: *Diccionario de la Real Academia Espanol de la Lengua*).

[50] A liquid residue produced in the olive oil extraction process. The text suggests that these materials cause damage.

[51] *Realengo* in the original. This term refers to land owned by the township, and as such it could not be sold to individuals (*DRAE*).

Article 5. No man is allowed to dig a well or *añora*[52] underneath, or close to *lobor*[53] or to someone else's walls, or close to an old well in a way that might damage it or that water might seep through. Nor is he allowed to dig it so close that water from the old well transfers to this new one, or if a new *añora* is built, and in the event they build it nearby, but had no place to dig it, it must be built according to the capacity and depth of the old well, in a such a way that neither of them remains without water.

Article 15. If a man has a house, or vineyard or vegetable garden or other properties and the owners of neighboring properties prohibit him from passing through their properties, and this man says that there must be an entrance and an exit, the Mayor must order the Alarifes to go, and if they find that there is in fact an entrance and an exit, he must be allowed to enter and exit. However, in the event that they could not find an exit, they must check which is the shortest and least obstructive way, and they must command the construction of an entrance and an exit, since every property must have an entrance and an exit.

Article 16. Any man that brings water to irrigate his vegetable garden, and has another estate, and this water that he obtained is flowing through another man' estate creating a *Madre*,[54] he must say: that he does not want to allow this, that this customarily has never gone through that place, or around that place. If the owners reached an agreement, or there was in fact a previous arrangement that may have happened, and if this is allowed for a year and a day,[55] or longer, to be on the land and in that place, leaving and entering, and not taking him to trial, this agreement is valid due to the water's worth. And if the former inheritors permit the water to go through and in fact it goes through a pre-existing course, and they want to do otherwise, they cannot do that anymore, since they allowed him to do it in the first place.

Article 17. Every privy, whether it is a resident's or the King's, must be built without harming any other resident. It must not bother anyone because of a water pipe, or manure, or hay, fire, smoke or ash. And whoever builds one may not use the excuse that he is a powerful

---

[52] Word not found in *DRAE*.

[53] Word not found in *DRAE*.

[54] Natural channel.

[55] This is a formulaic expression often used in legal language.

man, and if he builds one it must not bother the neighbors, unless it was built prior to his neighbors' houses being built.

Article 18. Any man that wants to build a *horno*[56] for the Council, must build it if he gets a license from the City, and in that case, the smoke coming out of the oven shall not bother the neighboring houses, nor should fire be placed adjacent to the neighboring house's wall. And in the event he built it on a street where there is already an existing bakery, it must be declared what location would best serve the Town and the neighborhood, so that one does not force the other one out of business.

Article 19. Dovecots cannot be made, nor shall they be made, within the City limits, since Pigeons cause great harm to the houses' roofs. And in the event a man has a license to build one, and eventually builds one, he must not make the perch of the Pigeons adjacent to peoples' roofs, since Pigeons cause noise and they provoke conflicts among men; this applies if the Dovecot is not older than the neighbors' roofs.

Article 20. Any man whose Pigeons have damaged any other man's roof or lofts or his poultry yard, must pay the man any damages his Pigeons have caused, and apologize to his neighbors for the damage.

Article 22. Any man that takes, or has already taken, possession of someone else's wall,[57] and a year goes by, and there are no claims against it, and then the owner of the wall says and swears that he did not know or see the other man take possession of his wall, and the Mayor orders that he relinquish the wall, and in the event two years went by, or longer, the owner must never lose his property, as long as nobody demonstrates that the owner of the wall was not in the city.

Article 23. No man may build the overhang of his house's roof against any one else's house, and hanging further than it used to be, and if he must rebuild it, it must be built in such manner that the part that hangs out the furthest must measure one and a half bricks, which equals two spans.[58]

---

[56] Meaning either an oven or a bakery. The text seems to suggest the latter.

[57] The text is ambiguous in this respect; however, it does not provide any information on how someone can take possession of a wall.

[58] This refers to the distance of a spread hand from thumb to little finger.

Article 24. Any man that builds an *ajimez*[59] or balcony hanging over the street, must not make it so it extends out more than a quarter of the street's width, so that if the neighbor opposite of his house might wish to build a balcony himself, half of the street's width will remain uncovered. And if either of those two balconies extends further, the Alarife must command its demolition, by order of the Mayor.

Article 25. Any man that builds a loft which crosses the street, and covers it, must do it of a height that would allow an armed Knight to pass underneath it without difficulty, so that this construction does not get in his way, nor prevents him from passing through the street. And if this loft is built lower, so that it interferes with the passers-by, the Alarife must command its demolition, by order of the Mayor.

Article 26. If any man has a damaged wall that presents danger, and fears that it may harm anyone in any manner, the Alarife must command its demolition, as stipulated by the Mayor. And this must be done before the wall harms or kills anyone, and in the event that the owner would not want to repair it or rebuild it, and the wall fell and killed a man, or harmed anyone in any way, the Mayor must urge the owner to compensate for the harm, or to reimburse for the loss from this event, and must avoid letting other people be blamed for this event. And in case the owner of the faulty wall or responsible for the poor construction work is not on Earth any longer, the Alarife must inform the Mayor and the Mayor must command its demolition, and the Alarife and two Master Masons must assess the cost, and the owner of the wall must pay for the costs of the repair.[60]

Article 27. No one should extend building beyond the old foundation lines of a house, nor extend them so that they reach someone else's house, nor must he build beyond his property, and in addition we also decree that they must not extend into the streets, or dig holes, or interfere with people's paths on the street.

---

[59] A type of balcony, very popular in Al-Andalus

[60] The original text is unclear here: It seems to entail that there may be two owners of the faulty wall, or the owner who inherits the building with the wall, particularly since it assumes the original owner already dead.

Article 28. Any man who transfers water from one estate to another, and he does so through the ground by *azequia de tierra*[61] or *almatriche*[62] and comes to realize that some water is being lost due to this system, he can, at any point, gather and protect this water with a construction or by any other means. And this can be done even in the event that the owner of the estate into which water is being lost claims that he was growing trees with that water. Not even that case prevents the former man from protecting and gathering his water however and whenever he wants.

Article 29. If the walls are made at two people's expenses, and on two people's ground, or if it were witnessed by two men, or had wood inserted on both sides or arches attached to them, or had wood (beams ?) loaded on both sides,[63] or arches attached to them, or door frames on both sides, or if the house is split in two, or if it has *padrón*[64] of overhangings, on both sides, or if these walls are adjacent to other walls, and if they have been built for some time already, and if the Alarifes have considered all these matters, they can say that they are shared. And we say that if two men build a wall at both their expenses, and they raise it a little, and one of them says that he does not want to raise it any higher since it is not necessary for his house, and the other man says that he needs to raise it higher for his house, we say that the latter can indeed raise it higher, and build it for his home and load, as long as it does not affect the stability of the wall. And if the other man whose wall is shorter wants eventually to build his house higher, he can also do it, without keeping the wall he built previously, and without asking his neighbor for funding.

Article 30. No man is allowed to start a smokehouse in such a place that smoke harms his neighbors, or allow the smoke to leave his house in such a way that it upsets his neighbors, or that this annoys them, and he must not excuse himself from preventing this, even in the

---

[61] Irrigation ditch.

[62] According to *DRAE*, *almatriche* also means 'irrigation ditch'. There does not seem to be a difference between these two terms.

[63] This is the literal meaning of this expression.

[64] In architectural terminology, a padrón is a column which has an engraved inscription to commemorate some event. It is unclear how it relates to *alas* (overhangings).

event that the smokehouse is in fact older than his neighbor's house, and the smoke is light, and if it could be reduced so that it does not harm the neighborhood.

If anyone has a canal on a empty[65] estate for a year and a day[66] without the owner of the lot presenting a complaint, knowing this fact, then the former is allowed to have as many canals as he wants until they start to build on the lot. And in addition, the empty lot does not lose its rights, and in the event that a *gotera*[67] fell on the lot and when the owner of the estate builds his house, the other man who is the owner of the house with the *gotera* must pick it up and remove his water. And in the event that anyone threw manure in the empty lot, and the owner was approving of this for a year and day, the other man is then allowed to throw manure until the owner of the lot decides to build houses or profit from the land in any way he wishes.

Article 32. If a man complains to his neighbor because he does not let him sleep because he is noisy, or because when he's sleeping the latter makes noise or is damaging the foundations of his house, or walls, with a forge, and hammers, or with a drop hammer to flatten *esparto*,[68] or with a loom or with any other tool, the Alarife, by order of the Mayor, must come to assess the damage of the walls (caused by the noise), or foundations, and must bring a bowl, filled to the brim with fine sand, and put it by the wall where the alleged noise comes from. And in the event that the sand spills or falls onto the ground, overflowing the brim, the Alarife must command that noise to stop, because it damages the walls and the foundations of the house. And in addition we say that, if the noise is produced at night near the sleeping room, the Alarifes must command it to cease, so that they leave every man to be the master of his own time.

Article 33. No one is allowed to make a door in his house directly opposite of his neighbor's (door), if his neighbor does not like it. And we add that neither the privy nor the *Alfondigas*[69] should be made

---

[65] The adjective *yermo* can mean barren, fallow, or empty.

[66] See footnote no. 55.

[67] The original meaning of *gotera* is leaking, or any construction designed to gather water (i.e. from a roof).

[68] *Esparto:* grass.

[69] Word not found.

with their doors opposite each other, which is great distribution,[70] but if they are to be made it must be *contra pasada*,[71] on the part where it is more covered, that is in the gap of the door that must be made brand new, towards the part that has more area covered in the neighbor's house.

Article 34. No man is allowed to build a stone bench on the street, or in an alley, because they interfere with the horse traffic and people's paths, and if anyone builds one, the Alarifes must command its demolition, by order of the Mayor.

Article 35. When someone requests a partition, whether it is of a house, or shop, or forge or anything else, the Alarifes must go to the site, by order of the Mayor, to partition it, and if it is something that may be partitioned, it must be done by the Alarifes to the best of their God-given abilities, and they have to draw lots, and each one should take what corresponds to each. In case the Alarifes see it cannot be partitioned, and that if it had to be partitioned it would ruin the value, it then must not be partitioned, and the Alarifes must attest that it cannot be partitioned without losing its value, and it must be ordered to be auctioned and sold, and this way the inheritors of the sale proceeds will have no reason to complain, since we have seen many times that parties will not sell their possessions out of jealousy.

Article 36. Any man who buys a house, lot, or any other property, and afterwards discovers a problem with it (something that the buyer did not know, or did not see, such as the seeping of water into the house) or that by law he must provide water from his well to another house, or that by law there must be another entrance and an exit in it, or for any of those things that the new owner has to take care of, but that he did not know about and swears that in fact he did not know, if this is not taken to trial, then the Alarifes should judge it, and he/they[72] must know the price of the property, or house or lot, and be aware of the quality of the offense that was discovered, and command the seller to refund the buyer the full cost of the property, plus compensation for the

---

[70] The meaning of this is unclear.

[71] Word not found in *DRAE*.

[72] The text suggests a third person singular, but the context suggests the Alarifes must know the price of the property.

damage, and if it is found that the buyer knows about all these things, or any other things, the transaction may be considered valid.

Article 42. No man should build a main irrigation channel if the water runs by someone else's wall, not even if it is a partitioning wall, because irrigation channels, even those which are well built, are always dangerous, since a great deal of water runs through them so they rot the walls. And in the event someone builds one along someone else's wall, or along a partitioning wall, and then someone complains that it is damaging his property, the Alarifes must go and visit, by order of the Mayor, and they must command its demolition, unless he has made it along his own wall or by his roof,[73] by agreement of both parties.

Article 44. No man is allowed to build a drain on King's Road, to pour the water of his house onto it, or build a gutter that leaves his house above the ground for draining rain water, or any type of pipe for his sewage. This drain must be made indoors, and if he does otherwise, the Alarifes must order its demolition, and shut it down, and *sacar a pison*[74] at his expense.

Article 45. No man is allowed to dig in the streets, or Squares, or markets, to get soil, or rocks, or to look for pipes, or to uncover[75] the main irrigation channel,[76] without a license by the City, and if this was granted by the City, the digging must be done under supervision of the Alarifes, who act by order of the Mayor, because it is true that until now many people, and all of them without a license, have dug on their own and thrown soil onto the streets, and afterwards they fill the holes with manure and rubbish, and consequently streets are damaged and obstacles consisting of dirt and mud are created.

Article 46. Any man whose house's roof is as high as his neighbor's, or slightly higher, and water from this roof falls on the

---

[73] The text does not specify how the channel would be positioned in relation to a roof.

[74] This is unclear in the original. *Pison* is defined as 'a heavy instrument to flatten the soil' or 'a construction officer, specialized in building walls'. The expression *sacar a pison* is obscure. It might mean to get dirt out so it can be flattened.

[75] *Descubrir* in the original text. *Descubrir* means to 'discover', 'uncover' or 'expose'.

[76] *Madre Vieja* in the original text

neighbor's, and at a later time this neighbor wants to raise the roof or the main room a little higher, and the owner of the roof which is now lower complains, and says that because now the (other man's) roof is a little higher than before, water falls onto his roof, and damages it, in this case the Alarifes must visit the place, by order of the Mayor, and if it is true that this is happening, this man (whose roof is now higher) must be excused, because it is true he was being harmed before, and if he *estruye*[77] the lower roof, unless if it was not by condition[78] or agreement on both parts, then (he,) the owner of the higher building(,) must build a solid *sobrecinta*[79] over his neighbor's roof, until this man matches the height of the taller roof, whenever he wishes to do so.

Article 48. Any man that sees that one of the walls of his house is damaged, or dangerous, and does not fix it or demolish it or repair it by adding adobe bricks, and it falls and harms someone else's wall, or roof, or any other part of his neighbor's house, he must pay a fine and pay the whole cost of the repair. However, in the event that the owner of the damaged wall or roof claims he did not see the potential harm, the former is not obligated to pay any damages his faulty wall may have caused.

Article 49. If a man wants to build a Well or *Añora*, he cannot build it close to a neighboring wall, or close to another Well or *Añora*, where it could be harmful. And in the event that he builds it close to a neighboring wall and it harms his neighbor, the Alarifes must be called, by order of the Mayor. And if the wall is in danger of falling, or is damaged, the man who ordered the construction of the Well, or *Añora*, must pay the full cost of rebuilding it. And we add, that it must not be built close to the old Well or an old *Añora*, to avoid, due to the proximity, water flowing from the old to the new well. And in the event that he builds it close to his neighbor's Well or *Añora*, he is not allowed to dig deeper than his neighbor's, to ensure that both have enough water. And in the event that he digs the well deeper than his

---

[77] This word does not exist in Spanish, it is probably a confusion with *destruye*, which means destroys.

[78] Probably the meaning is unless he damages it on purpose.

[79] Word not found. The context suggests, nevertheless, that this must be some sort of containment wall.

neighbor's, and water flows from the old well to the new one, and the owner complains, the Alarifes must be called, by order of the Mayor, and he must level it out with the old well, or dig the old well deeper to level them out, all at his own expense.

Article 50. We add that the Alarifes must watch and take into account the position of the Sun in relation to the houses in the month which has the greatest number of short days, which is December. And in December, they must do so on Santa Lucia's Day,[80] at noon, which is the day when the Sun is lowest during the whole year. And doing this, the Alarifes can judge the height of the buildings. Moreover, the Alarifes must also, in order to judge the houses, get inside of them and assess how they are built, and see in which quadrant the Sun enters at noon, so that this is in agreement with the main gate, and the position of the Sun, to be fair to all parties.

Article 51. If any house receives water from another house, by way of an open water pipe, above the ground, there is no reason why this house should receive any water other than rainwater, because the sewage water runs dirty from the house, and in case these waters have to go through the house, the sewage must be channeled through a covered water pipe underneath the surface, since the foul odors are a constant source of dispute between neighbors.

Article 53. The Alarifes must announce from the day of Carnival until the day of Palm Sunday that anyone who possesses Vineyards, Olive groves, Vegetable Gardens or Rose Bushes, or any other estates they may have, if these properties have fenced boundaries along the Royal roads, they must weed out the undergrowth, so that the roads are clear and people can make good use of them, by being able to pass without obstacle, under penalty to those who did not weed out their property for a year.

Article 58. In addition we say that no man is allowed to move rocks from his property onto the road, or dig a *gavia*[81] through it, or dig a *sangredera de agua*,[82] or dig to get stone, under the penalty of six hundred *maravedis* every time he does any of the above mentioned things.

---

[80] The 13th of December.

[81] Drainage ditch.

[82] Irrigation channel.

Article 59. Any man that blocks the Creek or the place where the water flows, or where it normally flows, and harms a house, or property, he must pay the Alarifes for each time he does this twelve *maravedis*, and he must unblock any *cerradura*,[83] and demolish the pipe, so that water runs through where it used to previously, and he must pay the damage to the owner of the property, or the house, of everything he had damaged.

Article 61. If any Master Mason builds the house of some man on public property (literally: that belongs to the streets, or the *ejidos*,[84] or the Squares), if he demolishes a house which is much older and that faces a *calle de trato*,[85] and the street is narrow, and if he has to rebuild it, the street has to be a foot wider, to widen the Royal Street, and he must proceed in the same fashion on the Squares. And any Mason that does not comply with this regulation must pay a penalty of six hundred *maravedis* to the Alarifes.

Article 70. If the Alarifes are called to solve a dispute between several parties, and those parties exceed two, and this dispute is over where to assign a road where it is more convenient to the vineyards or any other place, the Alarife must designate the closer road, so it is more convenient. And if it is in the vineyards, he must cut two rows of trees, one on one side and one on the other, and the Alarife must put there the boundaries, and the signs, where he has designated the way, and anyone who removes the signs has to pay a fine to the Council and the Alarifes of six hundred *maravedis*.

Article 76. Any Master Mason must call the Alarifes whenever he demolishes a wall and it falls downs, when he is about to build it again he must call the Alarifes, if both are in the City at the same time, and if they are not, he must call one prior to demolishing the wall. And if it falls before he rebuilds it, he must take the measurements of the width the Street as it used to be, so that the wall can be rebuilt again, and any Master Mason that does not abide by these rules must pay the Alarifes.

---

[83] This is a general term for any device used to close or contain something. In this case it would mean levee.

[84] Common land (estate).

[85] Expression could not be found, assumed to mean a commercial street or a street with merchants.

Article 77. Any inhabitant of the city whose house is lower in the ground that his neighbor's, and there was a dispute, and the Alarifes have to go to see it, by order of the Mayor, and they have to measure the height from one floor to other, and the upper half will be paid by both parties, and the lower half will be at the expense of the owner of the house which is lower in the ground.

Article 80. No Master Mason is allowed to take anything from the street or from anyone else's house when building or repairing or digging the foundations of a construction that leads into the Royal streets. We also add that no man that digs, repairs, or fixes a wall is allowed to take anything from the street or someone else's house, and if he did otherwise he must restore everything to the way it was, and demolish any of the constructions he has built, and the Alarifes must command this demolition, at the expense of the Master Mason that built it, and pay penalty of six hundred *maravedis*.

Article 81. We also say that the Master Mason who uses flawed, thin wood to cover the roof of a house, or lays poor tiles, even when this has been ordered by the Owner of the house, or leaves holes in the roof, and there is dispute about this, the Alarifes must go to this house, by command of the Mayor, and they must command its demolition, and redo it at the expense of the Master Masons or Master Mason who had done it, and they must this time employ good wood and tiles, and it must be well built.

Article 82. No Master Mason should build a wall over an ill-built excavation, or bad foundation, or with poor instruments, or in a place where the final construction does not sit well, and is dangerous, even if the owner commands it, and if the Master Mason complies with this, the Alarifes must go and have the whole damage corrected at the Master Mason's expense.

Article 84. We say that any walls that are between two neighbors, and are unused, and the owners are neighbors and one of them would like to shorten one of these walls so he gets more sunlight, and the other neighbor declares he wants it as it is. If a dispute arises from this lack of agreement, the Alarifes must visit this site, by order of the Mayor, and they must order that the walls remain as they used to be.

Article 86. We say that no one should dig a drain in his house close to someone else's Well, and in case he still has to build one, it must be diverted the distance corresponding to a Toledo rope,[86] and if there was a dispute, even after proceeding in such manner, the Alarifes must visit this site, by order of the Mayor, and if they attest that in fact this neighbor is affected by the drain, they must command its closure and *sacar a pison.*[87]

Article 87. We command, and say, that it often happens that neighbors plant orange trees, and fig trees, or peach trees, or pomegranate trees, or Grapevines, or any other sort of tree, close to other neighbors' walls, within a range of three feet from the wall, which equals the length of a measuring stick. And when these trees are planted, within a year they are still small and growing, and they grow little by little every year, and they grow up, pushing towards the walls, and this bothers the neighbors, blocking the sunlight, and by growing they uncover the neighbors' houses (privacy), and they harm roofs with their leaves, and if there is a dispute on this matter, the Alarifes must go, by order of the Judge, and they must command that any branches that block the sun be hacked off, or anything that bothers the neighbors, if one can see a neighbor's house by climbing the tree. So we say that if any of the aforementioned trees are growing within three feet of the walls and harm the irrigation channels with their roots, and rot with the irrigation water, this causing a dispute, the Alarifes must go to that site, by order of the Mayor, and they must cut those trees at ground level.

Article 88. Nobody can build a vegetable garden at his house next to someone else's house walls, not even if it is a partition wall, because it is true that walls are harmed by the plants' roots and with the constant flow of water for the plants. In the event of this causing controversy, the Alarifes must be sent there, by order of the Mayor, and must command the garden to be moved, or trees from the wall, at a distance of three feet.

Article 89. We say that any man that wishes to plant Trees at his *Casa de Parras,*[88] or in any other manner, he must plant them three feet away from his neighbor's wall, and if he proceeds otherwise and his neighbor sees it, and a dispute arises for this cause, the Alarifes

---

[86] This must have been a type of standard measurement.

[87] Expression not found. It refers to some type of institution, or board of officers.

[88] Literally grapevine house, possibly referring to a vineyard property.

must visit this site, by order of the Mayor, and they will mandate that the trees be planted further away, or cut them, so that the neighbor's wall does not receive any damage.

Article 90. We say that no man is allowed to build a washing sink or place a wash basin (near a neighbor's house), since the splashing of the water harms the walls, and in case there is a dispute over this matter, the Alarifes must visit this site, by order of the Mayor, and if they found a washing sink, or wash basin, they must command that they be located somewhere else, and place them at least three feet away from the neighbor's wall so it does not harm it.

Article 91. The waterpipes built inside a house must not be built next to another house's wall, or if they must be built this way, they have to be at least three feet away from the neighboring house's wall, and well built, and covered by lime and sand, to avoid the rotting which is expected, and if there is conflict, the Alarifes must visit the work, by order of the Mayor, and they must have those pipes demolished, and rebuilt the proper way, so that there is no harm to the neighbors.

Article 92. No man is allowed to install a privy against someone else's wall, nor in a place where the odor bothers his neighbor, or harms the wall or his neighbor's well, and if he acts otherwise, the Alarifes must be sent to inspect the site, by order of the Mayor, and they must shut it down and remove it, so it does not harm anyone.

Article 97. We say that not all the places[89] underground are the same, and that it is natural that some of them, from which old wells are made, have little water whereas others have plenty of it. And it also happens that some of them lose all their water after a storm, and the well makers sometimes, either to please their Masters or for the money they receive, find some else's well and steal the water from it. And we say that this is not a good deed and in case there is a dispute, the Alarifes must come to visit the site, by order of the Mayor, and he who committed this fault must pay, under command of the Alarifes and the Council.

Article 101. We say that no Country Inn or Tavern may be built on private estates' land, because they cause harm to the neighborhoods, and if anyone did otherwise, and a dispute arises, the Alarifes must

---

[89] It obviously refers to aquifers.

visit the site, by order of the Mayor, and have it demolished, and if he has to build it, it must be on *calmo*[90] ground, away from properties, and harm's way, and with a licence from the City.

Article 104. No one is allowed to build without license from the City, and if a man has to build, it must be tall/high, so that it is not in the Knights' way when they are riding on a horse, and walls must not be made wider, especially in a narrow alley, than one quarter of the width, and the distance between the roofs must be half,[91] and anyone who proceeds otherwise, the Alarifes must come to visit him and have him demolish the wall [Related to Articles 24 & 25].

Article 107. No man should dump trash, manure, dirt or stones, by someone else's walls, because bad neighbors always harm walls, and in the event there is a conflict, the Alarifes should be sent, by order of the Mayor, and they must have those things removed, at the expense of whoever dumped it in the first place.

Article 115. It happens many times that a wall falls down, or a house on a Royal Street, and it blocks the street and prevents people from going through it, and its owner does not care about it and leaves it like that for a long time. We hereby say that the Alarifes must find out who owns the house and have him rebuild whatever needs to be rebuilt, or remove anything that blocks the street. And they must also give him a time line for the things he needs to do, and in the event he does not meet the deadline, he must pay according to the regulations of the Alarifes, and they must have him remove anything on the street, at his own expense.

Article 117. Those who do such things, tend to throw a lot of dirt or mud onto the street when they have finished the construction, and the remains of the construction and the mud stays there for a long time, and they must be required by the Alarifes to remove this soil or mud within nine days, or they have to put it in their properties, and if they failed to meet this deadline, they have to pay the Alarifes.

---

[90] The literal meaning of *calmo* is 'calm, relaxed'. The particular meaning of this word in context is unclear. It could refer to a site that is isolated from a neighborhood.

[91] The text explains this measurement in relation to the width of the street. It divides it into four quarters.

Article 119. We say that if two neighbors own a water well, neither of them is the sole owner of the well. And this is whether the well is in a house, or an estate, neither of these two may give water to other neighbors without a license, or without agreement of the other owner, and if a dispute arose from this matter, the Alarifes must go there and judge according to the ordinances.

Article 122. And we say that the area where people enter and exit cannot be partitioned, because what belongs to all does not belong to just one man, and if those areas need to be repaired, it must be paid for by all the owners, and if a dispute arises over this matter, the Alarifes must visit the site by order of the Mayor, and give to each one what is right according to the ordinances.

Article 124. If there is any dispute over windows, doors or fireplaces, the Alarifes must command that the frames of the windows be removed, and their thresholds, and they must be blocked. The frames of the doors have to be removed so no one can claim they are doors, and they must block the chimney of the fireplace, because it often happens that it is blocked only lightly and afterwards it is being unblocked little by little.

Article 125. That from there[92] (if?) the houses are exposed, and *agraviar*,[93] they cannot complain about that, until (he/ they) build(s) a stairway to climb to the window, or arches, or make pavement to climb onto it, and look from there, and if they saw that it is exposed, or bothering his neighbors, and a dispute arose, the Alarifes must go, by order of the Mayor, and give to each one what is right according to the ordinances.

Article 126. Against them we say, that any man who builds a stable with its back against a sleeping room does not have the right to do so, because of the noise that animals make at night. And furthermore, this annoys and bothers his neighbor, and if he builds a stable not next to the living room, but makes it where somebody else's walls are, he must make the manger beside this other person's wall, so that he can avoid damaging his neighbor's wall. And in the event someone acts

---

[92] The text says *desde allí* which can be interpreted as 'from that point (in time or space).

[93] *Agraviar*: to offend, to worsen a situation, or to tax something (*DRAE*). The meaning of this verb, given the context, is unclear.

otherwise, and there is a conflict between these two men, the Alarifes must visit the place, by order of the Mayor, according to the ordinances, and each must be given his own right.

Article 127. Anyone who is able, willing, and makes a window without exposing anyone else's house, and wants to do so for the embellishment of the City, and it is not opposite another house, may do so, and if there was a conflict about this, the Alarifes must visit, by order of the Mayor, and must give each one his own rights, according to the ordinances.

Article 128. Any man who wishes to rebuild a flat roof, can do so as long as he does not expose his neighbor's house, or block the sun to another house, and abiding by all other conditions he may do so, since such buildings embellish the City.

Article 130. We hereby say that the laundries[94] must not be on streets where there is trade and many neighbors. This is because laundries are businesses that use a great deal of water, and produce strong odors, and heat, and smoke. And if they have to be built, it must be done in a spacious area. All this could be solved if those businesses were indoors, without bothering the neighbors, and even better if it were not this way, so that they were moved to the riverbed.

Article 131. No man is allowed to lay adobe bricks, or repair or demolish anything, without license from the City, under penalty of paying six hundred *maravedis*.

Article 132. That no man can lay adobe bricks, or disrupt any bridges, or sewers, or remove any of their bricks even if they are on his land,[95] under penalty of six hundred *maravedis*.

Article 133. That any construction Master Mason who does piece-work,[96] and damages someone else's wall, is obligated to rebuild it, and restore it to the condition it was in before the damage.

---

[94] In addition to washing clothes, these shops also dyed fabrics.

[95] 'They' refers to bridges and sewers.

[96] *Destajo* in the original. This refers to masons getting paid according to what they have accomplished, rather than at a daily rate.

Appendix 11
Definitions of Terms Related to the Phenomenon of *Emergence*

The phenomenon of self-regulating and adaptive systems has been the focus of many disciplines for at least the last 50 years, such as in physics, biology, economics, and geography. It has been scrutinized by mathematics and has captured the imagination of social scientists whose interpretations brought the findings of these various disciplines, especially the life sciences, closer to urban planning and design. The following are brief definitions of the primary terms used to explain the phenomenon of *Emergence*:

Emergent Form: The outcome that results from a bottom up organization, which follows its own set of rules that are often fairly simple.

Complex adaptive system: A form of system containing many autonomous agents who self-organize in a co-evolutionary way to optimize there separate values.

Self-regulation: When a complex adaptive system self-organizes itself it would need rules to follow during processes of change and growth. It thus forms such rules to follow, and they are generally few and simple.

Negative Feedback: Negative feedback tends to return the system to a balanced tranquil state where equity is maintained between adjacent neighbors.

Generative Program vs. Descriptive Program: A generative program is based on bottom up rules that are understood and followed by various actors in a system. Their aggregate decisions create a

B.S. Hakim, *Mediterranean Urbanism: Historic Urban / Building Rules and Processes*, DOI 10.1007/978-94-017-9140-3,
© Springer Science+Business Media Dordrecht 2014

unique emergent form. Whereas a descriptive program is one that is usually top down directed and instructed where all actors follow the same rules regardless of their particular micro condition, resulting in a predictable outcome.

Non-linearity: Linear is a property of straight lines, of simple proportions, of predictability. Nonlinear on the other hand applies to systems that do unpredictable things, that cannot be exactly predicted and need to be approximated.

Agents and Aggregate Agents: The basic elements of a Complex Adaptive System are agents. Agents are semi-autonomous units that seek to maximize their fitness by evolving over time. Agents scan their environment and develop schema. Schema are mental templates that define how reality is interpreted and what are appropriate response for a given stimuli. The term Aggregate Agents is used to refer to the aggregate result of decisions and acts by a number of agents.

Index

Note: Bold page numbers denote figures.

B.S. Hakim, *Mediterranean Urbanism: Historic Urban / Building Rules and Processes*, DOI 10.1007/978-94-017-9140-3,
© Springer Science+Business Media Dordrecht 2014